Pokémon

BLACK VERSION   WHITE VERSION

The Official Pokémon Strategy Guide

Staff

PUBLISHED BY
The Pokémon Company
International
333 108th Ave NE, Suite 1900
Bellevue, WA 98004

TM, ®, and © The Pokémon
Company International.
All rights reserved.

EDITOR-IN-CHIEF
Michael G. Ryan

TRANSLATORS
Hisato Yamamori
Tim Hove
Sayuri Munday

EDITORS
Kellyn Ballard
Blaise Selby
Hollie Beg
Wolfgang Baur

COVER DESIGN
Eric Medalle
Bridget O'Neill

ACKNOWLEDGEMENTS
Heather Dalgleish
Yasuhiro Usui
Mikiko Ryu
David Numrich
Rey Perez
Antoin Johnson

Naoya Sugie
Hank Woon
Eoin Sanders

DESIGN & PRODUCTION
Prima Games
Mario De Govia
Shaida Boroumand
Fernando Bueno
Stephanie Sanchez
Melissa Smith
Jamie Bryson
99 Lives Design, LLC
Adam Crowell
Emily Crowell
Oliver Crowell
Sonja Morris

ISBN: 978-0-307-89060-3

10 11 12 13 LL 10 9 8 7 6 5 4 3 2 1

Published in the United States using materials from the
Pokémon Black and Pokémon White Official Complete
Adventure Clear Guide. Published in Japan by Media Factory,
Inc.

SPECIAL THANKS TO:
Editor: Shusuke Motomiya and ONEUP, Inc.
Design & Layout: RAGTIME CO., LTD., and SUZUKIKOUBOU, Inc.

Everything is new in the world of Pokémon!

With *Pokémon Black Version* and *Pokémon White Version*, Pokémon enters a whole new chapter. Whether you're a longtime fan or a Pokémon beginner, these games are for you!

Tips for Beginners

Pokémon opens a new chapter

Become a Pokémon Trainer and set out on a new adventure with your Pokémon.

The world of Pokémon is full of exciting adventures, just waiting to be discovered, and you get to be the hero of this epic story.

At the beginning of your adventure, choose one Pokémon as your partner.

One of these three Pokémon—Snivy, Tepig, or Oshawott— will become your first partner. It's up to you to choose!

Snivy

Tepig

Oshawott

Lilligant

Whimsicott

Accelgor

Escavalier

Your adventure takes place in the brand-new Unova region, full of Pokémon you've never seen before!

Pokémon Black Version and *White Version* take place in the recently discovered Unova region.
Unova is filled with Pokémon you've never seen before, and exciting new places like the bustling metropolis called Castelia City!

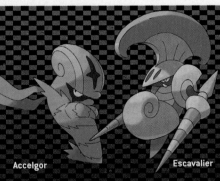

Goal #1

Become the Champion!

Every Pokémon Trainer has two major goals in mind. The first, to battle other Trainers and Gym Leaders to claim victory and become the Pokémon League Champion! You'll need to train a strong Pokémon team to defeat these tough opponents.

Goal #2

Complete the Pokédex!

And, catch every kind of Pokémon in the Unova region to complete your Pokédex!
You have a long road ahead of you, but the challenge is sure to make you—and your Pokémon team—even stronger!

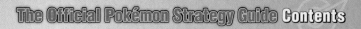

Special Sections

Town and Route
Quick Index

Route 8

Route 9

Shopping Mall Nine

Dragonspiral Tower

Moor of Icirrus

Anville Town

Icirrus City

Icirrus City Gym
Pokémon Fan Club
Aha's House

Celestial Tower

Tubeline Bridge

Twist Mountain

Challenger's Cave

Route 7

Mistralton City

Mistralton City Gym
Move Family's House
Cargo Service

Route 6

The Season Research Lab

Mistralton Cave

Guidance Chamber

Chargestone Cave

Driftveil Drawbridge

Route 5

Driftveil City

Driftveil City Gym
Driftveil Market
Move Tutor's House

Nimbasa City

Nimbasa City Gym
Musical Theater
Battle Subway
Big Stadium
Small Court
Battle Institute

Relic Castle

Cold Storage

Desert Resort

This is the map of the Unova region, where your adventure awaits. All of the cities, towns, routes, caves, and other important places are listed.

Victory Road

...al Chamber

Route 10

...dge Check Gates

Route 11

Route 12

Pokémon League

N's Castle

(You cannot go there after you've completed the main story.)

Giant Chasm

Lacunosa Town

Village Bridge

Village Sandwiches

Opelucid City

...pelucid City Gym
...attle House
...rayden's House

Route 13

Move Tutor's House

Undella Town

Big Villa
Cynthia's Villa

Entralink

Lostlorn Forest

Abundant Shrine

Poké Transfer Lab

Route 14

Undella Bay

Abyssal Ruins

Black City	Pokémon Black Version
Market	
White Forest	Pokémon White Version
Mayor's House	

Marvelous Bridge

Route 16

Route 15

Wellspring Cave

Dreamyard

Striaton City

Striaton City Gym
Trainers' School
Fennel's Lab

Skyarrow Bridge

Route 4

Pinwheel Forest

Challenge Rock
Rumination Field

Route 2

Route 3

Pokémon Day Care
Preschool

Accumula Town

Nacrene City

Nacrene City Gym
Café Warehouse
Nacrene Museum
Loblolly's House

P2 Laboratory

Route 18

Route 1

Castelia City

Castelia City Gym
Royal Unova
Passerby Analytics HQ
Pokémon Massage
Name Rater
Casteliacone
GAME FREAK
Battle Company
Café Sonata
Studio Castelia

Route 17

Nuvema Town

Your House
Cheren's House
Bianca's House
Juniper Pokémon Lab

Weekly Event Calendar

	Monday	Tuesday	Wednesday
Events	—	**Castelia City** **Time** Anytime In the spring, summer, and autumn, you can buy a Casteliacone at the stand on Mode Street.	**Nacrene City** **Time** Anytime Visit Café Warehouse, and the Waitress will give you a Soda Pop.
	—	—	—
	—	—	—
Nimbasa City **Big Stadium** **Time** Anytime	**Baseball** Except for 2 P.M. through 5 P.M., you can battle Trainers at the stadium.	**Soccer** Except for 2 P.M. through 4 P.M., you can battle Trainers at the stadium.	**Football** Except for 2 P.M. through 4 P.M., you can battle Trainers at the stadium.
Nimbasa City **Small Court** **Time** Anytime	**Tennis** Except for 10 A.M. through 11 A.M., you can battle Trainers at the court.	**Basketball** Except for 10 A.M. through noon, you can battle Trainers at the court.	**Tennis** Except for 10 A.M. through 11 A.M., you can battle Trainers at the court.
Castelia City *Royal Unova* **Time** Evening (After finishing the main story)	**Battle Challenge** When you defeat four Trainers, you will receive a Lava Cookie.	**Battle Challenge** When you defeat three Trainers, you will receive a Berry Juice.	**Battle Challenge** When you defeat four Trainers, you will receive a Lava Cookie.

In the Unova region, some items are sold only on certain days of the week, and some Trainers will battle you only on specific days. Check this calendar for all the events.

Thursday	Friday	Saturday	Sunday
—	**Tubeline Bridge** **Time** Evening, Night When you defeat the boss of the Bikers, he will rename his team after your lead Pokémon.	**Anville Town** **Time** Anytime Traders gather when there is a train on the turntable. Three people will exchange items with you.	**Anville Town** **Time** Anytime Traders gather when there is a train on the turntable. Three people will exchange items with you.
—	**Dreamyard** **Time** Anytime Go to the tall grass in the basement and Musharna will appear (after finishing the main story).	**Nuvema Town** **Time** Anytime At Juniper Pokémon Lab, you can have a Pokémon battle against Bianca (after finishing the main story).	**Lacunosa Town** **Time** Night, Late Night Talk to him and he'll give you one of the following Berries: Pecha Berry, Bluk Berry, Lum Berry, Leppa Berry.
—	—	—	**Nuvema Town** **Time** Anytime At Juniper Pokémon Lab, you can have a Pokémon battle against Bianca (after the Hall of Fame.)
Baseball Except for 2 P.M. through 5 P.M., you can battle Trainers at the stadium.	**Soccer** Except for 2 P.M. through 4 P.M., you can battle Trainers at the stadium.	**Football** Except for 2 P.M. through 4 P.M., you can battle Trainers at the stadium.	**Baseball** Except for 2 P.M. through 5 P.M., you can battle Trainers at the stadium.
Basketball Except for 10 A.M. through noon, you can battle Trainers at the court.	**Tennis** Except for 10 A.M. through 11 A.M., you can battle Trainers at the court.	**Basketball** Except for 10 A.M. through noon, you can battle Trainers at the court.	**Tennis** Except for 10 A.M. through 11 A.M., you can battle Trainers at the court.
Battle Challenge When you defeat five Trainers, you will receive an Old Gateau.	**Battle Challenge** When you defeat four Trainers, you will receive a Lava Cookie.	**Battle Challenge** When you defeat six Trainers, you will receive a RageCandyBar.	**Battle Challenge** When you defeat seven Trainers, you will receive a Rare Candy.

Check P. 49 for more on times of day.

At the challenge rock, you can obtain a Star Piece

 Where **Pinwheel Forest Entrance**

Bring a Fighting-type Pokémon with your party and try to smash the challenge rock. You'll obtain one Star Piece a day.

 p. 89

 Show the right Pokémon and receive a Berry

 Where **Castelia City Studio Castelia**

Show a Pokémon of the requested type to the Harlequin and receive one of the following Berries a day: Aspear Berry, Cheri Berry, Chesto Berry, Pecha Berry, Rawst Berry.

 p. 95

 Ride the Ferris wheel after a Pokémon battle

 Where **Nimbasa City in front of the Ferris wheel**

After you defeat the Nimbasa City Gym Leader, defeat the Trainer in front of the Ferris wheel to ride it. The Trainer changes depending on the season and your gender.

 p. 108

 Show the right Pokémon and receive a Heart Scale

 Where **A house in Driftveil City**

In the house to the west of the Pokémon Center is a lady who'll give you a Heart Scale if you show her a Pokémon with the move she wants to see.

 p. 117

 The Parasol Lady will give you a Rock

 Where **Route 8**

One of the Parasol Ladies gives you a Damp Rock in the morning, a Heat Rock during the afternoon, a Smooth Rock in the evening, and an Icy Rock at night.

 p. 155

 Pick up Props from this Pokémon Musical fan

Where **A house in Opelucid City**

In the house west of the Pokémon Center is an old man who gives you a Prop a day until you've received all four of them.

 p. 161/165

 Have fun with new Rotation Battles or Triple Battles

Where **Opelucid City Battle House**

In the Battle House, you can challenge a Trainer to a Rotation Battle in *Pokémon Black Version* or a Triple Battle in *Pokémon White Version*.

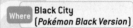 p. 161/165

 Battle with Morimoto

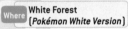 Where **Castelia City GAME FREAK**

You can battle Morimoto on floor 22F of the GAME FREAK building. Morimoto's Pokémon are at high levels, so they're pretty tough!

 p. 94

 Receive Fossils to restore Pokémon

Where **Twist Mountain Lower Level 1**

Talk to the Worker on the Lower Level 1 of Twist Mountain and receive one Fossil a day to restore Pokémon from other regions.

 p. 194

 Visit Cheren for a daily dose of battling

Where **Victory Road 7F**

Talk to Cheren on Route 5 and go to Victory Road 7F to battle him once a day.

 p. 196

 Battle Trainers in the city

Where **Black City (*Pokémon Black Version*)**

Talk to the people in the city and you can have a Pokémon battle once a day. You'll receive a reward from the city's boss based on the number of wins.

 p. 209

 Show the right Pokémon and receive a Berry

Where **White Forest (*Pokémon White Version*)**

Show the mayor the Pokémon he wants to see and receive one of the following Berries a day: Leppa Berry, Pecha Berry, Bluk Berry, Lum Berry, Chesto Berry.

 p. 211

Visit Cynthia in the spring to challenge her to a battle

Where **Undella Town Cynthia's Villa**

Talk to Cynthia in the Villa in the spring and you can battle her once a day. You cannot battle her in the summer, and she's not there in the autumn or winter.

 p. 216

Challenge the entire Riches family to battle

Where **Undella Town Big Villa**

Battle Draco outside first, then more and more of his family members will challenge you. Defeat Miles, the sixth family member, to end the event.

 p. 217

Visit Route 13 to pick up some hard-to-find items

Where **Route 13**

This man with sunglasses gives you an item every day. He has 27 different items to give away, and most of them cannot be obtained by any other method.

 p. 222

Do a good job waiting tables and you'll receive a Lum Berry

Where **Village Bridge Restaurant**

Defeat Baker Chris and talk to her for a job offer! Take orders and serve the customers correctly, and you'll receive a Lum Berry.

 p. 230

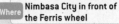

In the Unova region, you can revisit certain places or people every day to receive an item or have a Pokémon battle. Check this list and visit them every day! Events colored ● are available after finishing the main story.

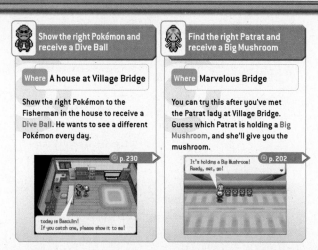

Show the right Pokémon and receive a Dive Ball

Where A house at Village Bridge

Show the right Pokémon to the Fisherman in the house to receive a Dive Ball. He wants to see a different Pokémon every day.

p. 230

today is Basculin! If you catch one, please show it to me!

Find the right Patrat and receive a Big Mushroom

Where Marvelous Bridge

You can try this after you've met the Patrat lady at Village Bridge. Guess which Patrat is holding a Big Mushroom, and she'll give you the mushroom.

p. 202

It's holding a Big Mushroom! Ready, set, go!

Unova Region / Recommended Route

Below is a recommended route for your adventure. Use this guide to check your progress or figure out where to go next.

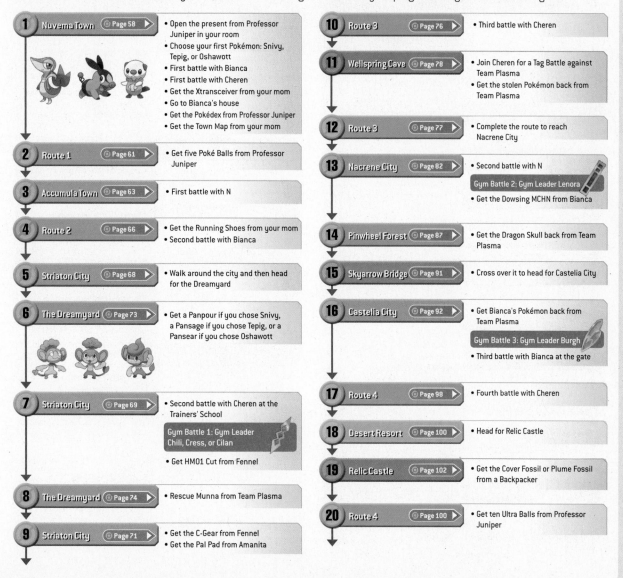

1 Nuvema Town Page 58
- Open the present from Professor Juniper in your room
- Choose your first Pokémon: Snivy, Tepig, or Oshawott
- First battle with Bianca
- First battle with Cheren
- Get the Xtransceiver from your mom
- Go to Bianca's house
- Get the Pokédex from Professor Juniper
- Get the Town Map from your mom

2 Route 1 Page 61
- Get five Poké Balls from Professor Juniper

3 Accumula Town Page 63
- First battle with N

4 Route 2 Page 66
- Get the Running Shoes from your mom
- Second battle with Bianca

5 Striaton City Page 68
- Walk around the city and then head for the Dreamyard

6 The Dreamyard Page 73
- Get a Panpour if you chose Snivy, a Pansage if you chose Tepig, or a Pansear if you chose Oshawott

7 Striaton City Page 69
- Second battle with Cheren at the Trainers' School

Gym Battle 1: Gym Leader Chili, Cress, or Cilan
- Get HM01 Cut from Fennel

8 The Dreamyard Page 74
- Rescue Munna from Team Plasma

9 Striaton City Page 71
- Get the C-Gear from Fennel
- Get the Pal Pad from Amanita

10 Route 3 Page 76
- Third battle with Cheren

11 Wellspring Cave Page 78
- Join Cheren for a Tag Battle against Team Plasma
- Get the stolen Pokémon back from Team Plasma

12 Route 3 Page 77
- Complete the route to reach Nacrene City

13 Nacrene City Page 82
- Second battle with N

Gym Battle 2: Gym Leader Lenora
- Get the Dowsing MCHN from Bianca

14 Pinwheel Forest Page 87
- Get the Dragon Skull back from Team Plasma

15 Skyarrow Bridge Page 91
- Cross over it to head for Castelia City

16 Castelia City Page 92
- Get Bianca's Pokémon back from Team Plasma

Gym Battle 3: Gym Leader Burgh
- Third battle with Bianca at the gate

17 Route 4 Page 98
- Fourth battle with Cheren

18 Desert Resort Page 100
- Head for Relic Castle

19 Relic Castle Page 102
- Get the Cover Fossil or Plume Fossil from a Backpacker

20 Route 4 Page 100
- Get ten Ultra Balls from Professor Juniper

21 Nimbasa City (Page 105)
- Defeat Team Plasma and get the Bicycle from the Day-Care Man
- Get the Vs. Recorder from a woman
- Get HM04 Strength from a man
- Get the Prop Case from the owner of the Musical Theater
- Third battle with N

22 Anville Town (Page 109)
- Walk around the town

23 Route 16 Lostlorn Forest (Page 110)
- Walk around Route 16 and Lostlorn Forest

24 Nimbasa City (Page 108)
Gym Battle 4: Gym Leader Elesa

25 Route 5 (Page 112)
- Fifth battle with Cheren
- Meet Champion Alder

26 Driftveil Drawbridge (Page 114)
- Cross over it to head for Driftveil City

27 Driftveil City (Page 116)
- Clay asks you to find Team Plasma

28 Cold Storage (Page 121)
- Catch Team Plasma

29 Driftveil City (Page 118)
Gym Battle 5: Gym Leader Clay
- Fourth battle with Bianca
- Get HM02 Fly from Bianca

30 Route 6 (Page 124)
- Go through it to head for Chargestone Cave

31 Chargestone Cave (Page 126)
- Clay opens the entrance for you
- Fourth battle with N

32 Mistralton City (Page 129)
- Cedric Juniper upgrades your Pokédex

33 Route 7 (Page 132)
- Go through it to head for the Celestial Tower

34 Celestial Tower (Page 135)
- Talk to Skyla on 5F

35 Mistralton City (Page 130)
Gym Battle 6: Gym Leader Skyla

36 Route 7 (Page 133)
- Go through it to head for Twist Mountain

37 Twist Mountain (Page 136)
- Sixth battle with Cheren
- Get HM03 Surf from Alder

38 Route 17 (Page 140)
- Head for Route 18 from Route 1

39 Route 18 P2 Laboratory (Page 142)
- Get a Pokémon Egg from the Treasure Hunter
- Get HM05 Waterfall

40 Mistralton Cave (Page 143)
- Catch Cobalion in the Guidance Chamber

41 Pinwheel Forest (Page 90)
- Catch Virizion in the Rumination Field

42 Icirrus City (Page 146)
Gym Battle 7: Gym Leader Brycen

43 Dragonspiral Tower (Page 151)
- Meet N and Zekrom (Reshiram) on 7F

44 Desert Resort (Page 101)
- Go through it to head for Relic Castle

45 Relic Castle (Page 104)
- Battle Team Plasma and go to B5F

46 Nacrene City (Page 86)
- Get the Light Stone (Dark Stone) from Lenora

47 Route 8 (Page 154)
- Head for the Moor of Icirrus

48 Moor of Icirrus (Page 154)
- Walk around the Moor of Icirrus

49 Route 8 (Page 156)
- Fifth battle with Bianca

50 Tubeline Bridge (Page 156)
- Cross over it to head for Route 9

51 Route 9 (Page 157)
- Go through it to head for Opelucid City

52 Opelucid City (Pokémon White Version Page 164) (Pokémon Black Version Page 160)
- Hear about the Legendary Dragon-type Pokémon at Drayden's house

Gym Battle 8: Gym Leader Drayden (Iris)
- Get the Master Ball from Professor Juniper
- Hear about the storm at the gate

53 Route 7 (Page 134)
- Encounter Tornadus (Thundurus)
- Tornadus (Thundurus) will fly around the Unova region and you can now catch it

54 Route 10 (Page 168)
- Seventh battle with Cheren
- Go through the Badge Check Gates

55 Victory Road (Page 171)
- Catch Terrakion in the Trial Chamber

56 Pokémon League (Page 174)
- Battle the Elite Four: Shauntal, Grimsley, Caitlin, and Marshal
- N's Castle appears

57 N's Castle (Page 180)
- Catch Reshiram (Zekrom)
- Fifth battle with N
- Final battle with Ghetsis

Ending — *Your adventure continues!*

After finishing the main story

1 Nuvema Town Page 186
- Looker asks you to find the Seven Sages
- Looker gives you the Super Rod
- Cedric upgrades your Pokédex to the National Pokédex

2 Marvelous Bridge Page 201
- The Shadow Triad gives you the Adamant Orb, Lustrous Orb, and Griseous Orb

3 Route 15 Page 204
- You'll be able to use Poké Transfer at Poké Transfer Lab

4 Black City Pokémon Black Version Page 208
- Explore and talk to people

4 White Forest Pokémon White Version Page 210
- Explore and talk to people

5 Route 14 Page 212
- Find Giallo of the Seven Sages

6 Abundant Shrine Page 214
- Have both Tornadus and Thundurus in your party and go to the shrine
- Catch Landorus

7 Undella Town Page 216
- Get HM06 Dive from a woman
- Battle Cynthia (Rematches are available only in the spring)

8 Undella Bay Page 218
- Use Dive to go to the Abyssal Ruins

9 Abyssal Ruins Page 218
- Explore the ruins

10 Route 13 Page 221
- Go through it to head for Lacunosa Town

11 Lacunosa Town Page 224
- Restore your Pokémon to full health and head for Giant Chasm

12 Giant Chasm Page 225
- Catch Kyurem

13 Route 12 Page 228
- Go through it to head for Village Bridge

14 Village Bridge Page 229
- Cross over it to head for Route 11

15 Route 11 Page 231
- Go through it if you want to go back to Opelucid City

16 Route 18 Page 187
- Find Rood of the Seven Sages

17 The Dreamyard Page 188
- Find Gorm of the Seven Sages

18 Relic Castle Page 191
- Find Ryoku of the Seven Sages
- Catch Volcarona

19 Route 5 Page 192
- Talk to Cheren

20 Cold Storage Page 193
- Find Zinzolin of the Seven Sages

21 Chargestone Cave Page 193
- Find Bronius of the Seven Sages

22 Challenger's Cave Page 195
- Explore Challenger's Cave

23 Victory Road Page 196
- Eighth battle with Cheren (You'll be able to battle him daily after that)

24 Pokémon League Page 196
- Battle the Elite Four
- Battle Champion Alder

Hall of Fame — Set out to complete your Pokedex!

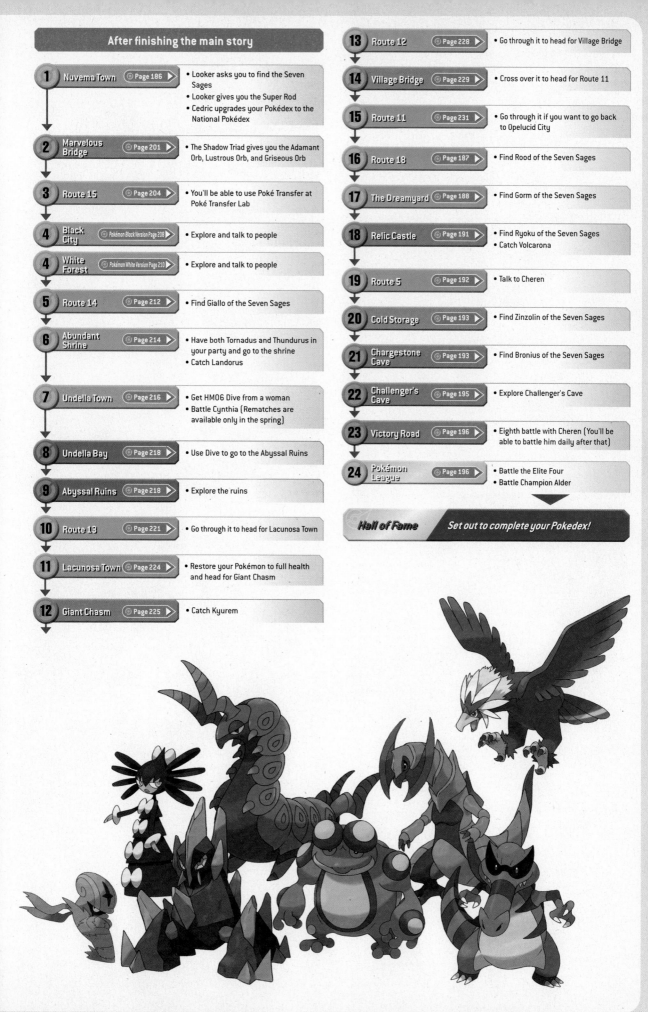

HERO
■Hero

Boy

HEROINE
■Heroine

Girl

FRIEND
■Your childhood friend

I'm the professor's bodyguard! Well, that's probably not necessary, but you have to protect important things!

Bianca

FRIEND
■Your childhood friend

Taking people's Pokémon by force is not right. That is not real strength!

Cheren

■Key Characters

PROFESSOR

■ Professor ── Aurea Juniper

My name is Professor Juniper, and I am researching when and how the creatures called Pokémon came into existence.

PROFESSOR

■ Professor ── Cedric Juniper

Heh! The professor who gave you the Pokédex is my daughter!

SUPPORTER

■ Scientist ── Fennel

I'm Fennel, and as you can see, I'm a scientist. In fact, the subject I'm researching is Trainers!

POKÉMON TRAINER

■ A mysterious boy ── N

I think my friends and I should test you to see if you can see this future, too.

We're Pokémon Trainers too, but we're fighting for a different reason. Unlike you two, we're fighting for the freedom of Pokémon!

That's right! We must liberate the Pokémon! Then, and only then, will humans and Pokémon truly be equals.

TEAM PLASMA
■ Grunt ——— Female

If their Pokémon are liberated, Trainers will no longer be Trainers! We are in the right!

TEAM PLASMA
■ Grunt ——— Male

TEAM PLASMA
■ One of the Seven Sages ——— Ghetsis

GYM LEADERS

■ Striaton City ——— Cilan/Cress/Chili
Triple Trouble

The fundamentals of Pokémon battling are type matchups! They're important!

Cilan

Cress

Chili

GYM LEADER

■ Castelia City ——— Burgh
Premier Insect Artist

Umm... That's right. You! Use Bug-type Pokémon!

GYM LEADER

■ Nacrene City ——— Lenora
An Archeologist with Backbone

Curiosity is the spice of life! Without it, life is bland!

GYM LEADER

■ Driftveil City —— Clay
The Underground Boss

Ya always want to live honestly fer yerself and yer Pokémon.

GYM LEADER

■ Nimbasa City —— Elesa
The Shining Beauty

May you always continue to be a person who brightens your surroundings.

GYM LEADER

■ Icirrus City —— Brycen
Ice Mask

Don't limit yourself to hot or cold, but use them both to your best advantage.

GYM LEADER

■ Mistralton City —— Skyla
The High-Flying Girl

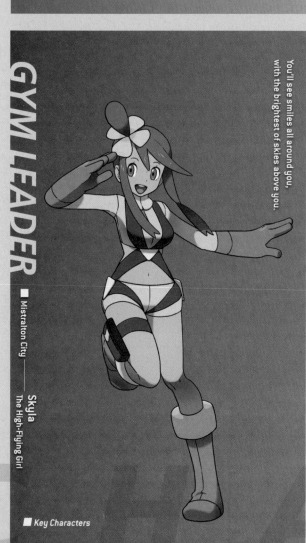

You'll see smiles all around you, with the brightest of skies above you.

■ Key Characters

GYM LEADER

■ Opelucid City ——

Drayden
The Spartan Mayor

Sincere Trainer, keep growing stronger!

GYM LEADER

Know what? You were very strong! I'll never forget you, ever!

■ Opelucid City ——

Iris
The Girl Who Knows the Hearts of Dragons

ELITE FOUR

■ Elite Four ——

Shauntal

Beginnings are important, whether in a good novel or a good battle!

ELITE FOUR

I never thought you would use that move.... Not a bad choice at all.

■ Elite Four ——

Grimsley

■ Key Characters

17

Oh, so strong.
That makes my heart dance!

ELITE FOUR

■ Elite Four —— Marshal

I get the feeling a wonderful time
is about to start. I'm excited!

ELITE FOUR

■ Elite Four —— Caitlin

I won't lose! I'll fight for all Trainers who love their Pokémon,
and for all Pokémon who believe in their Trainers!

CHAMPION

■ Champion —— Alder

■ Key Characters

How to Use This Book

‹‹‹‹ Choose the section you want to learn more about ››››

Primer for Pokémon Training

This primer has basic information on the games and the world of Pokémon. It also explains the features new to *Pokémon Black* and *Pokémon White*.

Page 20

Unova Adventure Walkthrough

From Nuvema Town all the way to defeating Champion Alder, this walkthrough will guide you through your adventure.

Page 56

List of Trainers to Battle

The complete list of Pokémon Trainers you meet throughout your adventure. It also covers people who give you items.

Page 235

Pokémon Form Changes and Special Evolutions

Pokémon that change their Forme, such as Giratina and Shaymin, as well as Pokémon that evolve under special conditions, such as Magnezone and Leafeon.

Page 247

Index

The index lists page references for important people and items, including TMs and HMs. It's a quick way to find the information you're looking for.

Page 253

Primer for Pokémon Training

There are many different kinds of Pokémon

Pokémon are strange and wondrous creatures whose lives are still largely shrouded in mystery. Though many Pokémon live out in fields or under the waves, there are still others who live together in partnership with humans. Nobody knows how many Pokémon there are in all, and new kinds are being discovered all the time.

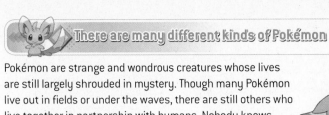

Become Friends with Pokémon

How to obtain Pokémon

To succeed in your adventure, you'll have to partner up with Pokémon and use their powers to help you. So get acquainted with the various ways to obtain Pokémon.

How to obtain Pokémon

Catch wild Pokémon

Most Pokémon inhabit places like fields, caves, and bodies of water. Go discover and catch them.

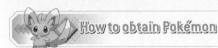
A wild Patrat appeared!

Get them through story events

You can get Pokémon, Pokémon Eggs, and Pokémon Fossils as the story unfolds, so be sure to talk to townspeople.

Trainer obtained the Egg!

Evolve them through battle

As Pokémon build up their strength by battling, some of them will evolve. After evolution, the Pokémon's name and appearance will change.

Congratulations! Your Vanillite evolved into Vanillish.

Link Trade with friends

Some Pokémon are especially hard to obtain. The easiest way to get them is by trading with a friend.

Where to find wild Pokémon

Wild Pokémon love nature, and their habitats include tall grass, caves, desert, wetlands, lakes, rivers, etc. Be sure to walk around when you come across such areas, and see what kinds of Pokémon you can find!

These are major areas where you find Pokémon

Tall Grass

Wetlands

Cave

Desert

Water Surface

Fishing (After finishing the main story)

Landed a Pokémon!

How to catch wild Pokémon

You can't catch wild Pokémon without a Poké Ball. Even if you have one, Pokémon won't just hop into a Poké Ball. They can be hard to catch unless you tire them out first. Try these three tips!

Wild Double Battles in the dark grass

Starting with Route 3, you'll notice some dark grass here and there. In these areas, two wild Pokémon can attack you at once. If you want to catch one of them, you have to defeat the other first.

Tips for catching Pokémon

1   Reduce HP

A Pokémon's HP is a measure of how tired it is. Once HP reaches zero, that Pokémon faints. When you try to catch a Pokémon, use moves to attack and lower HP as much as possible without making it faint. When the HP bar is red, it means that Pokémon is weak. Try throwing a Poké Ball!

2   Inflict status conditions

Some Pokémon moves inflict status conditions on their targets (p. 32). A Pokémon saddled with a status condition, such as Poison or Paralysis, is easier to catch. Of the six status conditions, Sleep and Frozen are the most effective. Lower the target's HP and use status conditions to maximize your chances of success.

3   Use the right Poké Ball

From the basic model to the Luxury Ball and Master Ball, there are 14 different kinds of Poké Balls, each specialized for a certain use. Always use a Poké Ball that's effective for the kind of Pokémon you want to catch—it's a basic Pokémon-catching principle.

Adventure Info

Teach your party useful Pokémon-catching moves

Lowering a wild Pokémon's HP and using status conditions make it easier to catch Pokémon. A Watchog that knows Super Fang or Hypnosis can come in handy!

Watchog

Catch a Patrat on Route 1 and raise it to Lv. 20 to evolve into Watchog. Watchog will learn Mean Look at Lv. 36.

Examples of moves good for catching Pokémon

Super Fang	Normal	It cuts the target's HP to half.
Hypnosis	Psychic	It makes the target fall into a deep sleep.
Mean Look	Normal	The target becomes unable to flee.

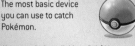 **Use the right Poké Ball for each Pokémon**

Pokémon Black and *Pokémon White* have a total of 14 different Poké Ball types. Each Poké Ball's special effects depend on factors such as Pokémon type or the location of the battle. Learn the best uses for each Poké Ball and use the right one for the Pokémon you're aiming to catch.

Poké Balls available in the Unova region

Poké Ball
The most basic device you can use to catch Pokémon.

How to make it available at Poké Mart:
| Sold from the beginning |

Great Ball
Better at catching Pokémon than the Poké Ball.

How to make it available at Poké Mart:
| Obtain a Gym Badge |

Ultra Ball
Better at catching Pokémon than the Great Ball.

How to make it available at Poké Mart:
| Obtain five Gym Badges |

Master Ball
It is the ultimate ball that will surely catch any Pokémon.

How to get one:
| Opelucid City (Professor Juniper) |

Premier Ball
Same as a regular Poké Ball. Given as a bonus at Poké Marts.

How to get one:
| Buy 10 Poké Balls at once |

Heal Ball
Restores a captured Pokémon's HP and status.

Poké Mart that carries this ball:
| Striaton City, Nacrene City, etc. |

Net Ball
Good for catching Bug- and Water-type Pokémon.

Poké Mart that carries this ball:
| Nacrene City, Castelia City, etc. |

Nest Ball
The lower the Pokémon's level, the more effective it is.

Poké Mart that carries this ball:
| Castelia City, Driftveil City, etc. |

Quick Ball
Most effective when thrown right at the start of battle.

Poké Mart that carries this ball:
| Opelucid City, Pokémon League, etc. |

Timer Ball
The more turns that have gone by in battle, the more effective it is.

Poké Mart that carries this ball:
| Opelucid City, Pokémon League, etc. |

Repeat Ball
Good for catching Pokémon of a species you've caught before.

Poké Mart that carries this ball:
| Pokémon League |

Dive Ball
Good for catching Pokémon that live underwater.

Poké Mart that carries this ball:
| Undella Town |

Dusk Ball
Good for catching Pokémon at night or in caves.

Poké Mart that carries this ball:
| Driftveil City, Opelucid City, etc. |

Luxury Ball
Your friendship with the captured Pokémon will grow faster.

Poké Mart that carries this ball:
| Pokémon League, Undella Town |

Adventure Info — Obtain a second Master Ball!

The Master Ball is the ultimate ball that can catch any Pokémon. Normally, you can only obtain one throughout your adventure. But you can obtain a second Master Ball on the second floor in the Pokémon Center at Castelia City when you've traded Pokémon with 50 different people.

 Pokémon grow stronger as they battle

Pokémon grow strong as they battle. Winning a battle gives them Experience Points. When they gain enough points, they'll level up and their stats—Attack, HP, etc.—will increase. Let them battle to help them grow stronger.

How Experience Points work
- ▶ Your Pokémon will gain more Experience Points if it defeats a Pokémon whose level is higher than its level.
- ▶ Your Pokémon will gain less Experience Points if it defeats a Pokémon whose level is lower than its level.

What will Klink do?

As it gains Experience Points, it'll level up.

Pokémon evolve by leveling up

Some Pokémon can evolve into new Pokémon with different names. There are several ways to evolve Pokémon, but the most basic method is through battling and earning Experience Points to level up.

Evolution Example: Tympole

First Evolution

Second Evolution

Tympole   Palpitoad   Seismitoad

Other key evolution methods

Use special stones

Special stones, such as the Thunderstone or Leaf Stone, have the power to trigger Pokémon evolution instantly.

Link Trade

Some Pokémon evolve when they're traded through Link Trade.

Strengthen your friendship

Take good care of a Pokémon, and it will reward you by growing. Some Pokémon evolve if they level up while they're on friendly terms with you.

Fulfill certain conditions

Some Pokémon can be evolved under special conditions, such as trading two specific Pokémon, or leveling a Pokémon up at a certain place.

Pokémon can learn various moves

Pokémon can learn all kinds of moves, which are useful both in battle and on your adventure in general. There are more than 500 different moves, each with its own unique effects. If you put some thought into developing move sets, your Pokémon will stand out as an individual.

Axew wants to learn the move Dragon Dance.

Three fundamental kinds of moves

Attack Moves

These moves do damage by attacking the enemy. There are many variations on the basic attack move. Some moves also inflict status conditions.

Defense Moves

When your opponent has you in a tight spot, defense moves are a good idea. These moves can restore HP or cure status conditions. Some defense moves even leech an opponent's HP.

Status Moves

These moves strengthen the user or weaken an opponent. They can do anything from raising a Pokémon's stats to inflicting status conditions that gradually drain an opponent's HP.

How to teach new moves to Pokémon

◇ Level them up

Pokémon can learn various moves at predetermined levels. Once they reach a certain level, they can learn the appropriate move.

◇ Use a TM

A TM (Technical Machine) can teach a certain move to an unlimited number of Pokémon. You can use the same TM again and again on different Pokémon.

◇ Use an HM

Each HM (Hidden Machine) is programmed with a special move (p. 27). An HM can teach that move to an unlimited number of Pokémon.

◇ Have an expert teach them

During your travels, you'll meet people who can teach moves to Pokémon. There are seven moves that can be learned this way.

Pokémon have different Abilities

Each Pokémon species has various Abilities. For instance, Patrat can have the Run Away or Keen Eye Ability. Some Abilities take effect during battle, while other Abilities come in handy as you explore the region.

> **Triggered Abilities are visible**
>
> When a Pokémon's Ability is triggered in battle, messages appear for both your Pokémon and your opponent's Pokémon.

Examples of Abilities and their effects

Pickup

May pick up an item while it's in your party. The Pokémon's level determines what items you're likely to find.

Pokémon with this Ability
Lillipup

Sturdy

When its HP is full, it'll retain 1 HP if hit by a move that would knock it out.

Pokémon with this Ability
Dwebble, Roggenrola, etc.

Sheer Force

Moves will have no additional effects (such as stat changes), but the power of those moves will increase by 30%.

Pokémon with this Ability
Timburr, Druddigon, etc.

Items obtained with the Pickup Ability

Item	Low →									High
Potion	◎									
Antidote	○	◎								
Super Potion	○	○	◎							
Great Ball	○	○	○	◎						
Repel	○	○	○	○	◎					
Escape Rope	○	○	○	○	○	◎				
Full Heal	○	○	○	○	○	○	◎			
Hyper Potion	○	○	○	○	○	○	○	◎		
Ultra Ball	△	△	○	○	○	○	○	○	◎	
Revive		△	△	○	○	○	○	○	○	◎
Rare Candy			△	△	○	○	○	○	○	○
Sun Stone				△	△	○	○	○	○	○
Moon Stone					△	△	○	○	○	○
Heart Scale						△	△	○	○	○
Full Restore		▲	▲				△	△	○	○
Max Revive								△	△	○
PP Up									△	△
Max Elixir										△
Nugget	▲	▲								
King's Rock		▲	▲							
Ether				▲	▲					
Iron Ball					▲	▲				
Prism Scale						▲	▲	▲	▲	▲
Elixir							▲	▲		
Leftovers									▲	▲

◎ Often found ○ Sometimes found △ Rarely found ▲ Almost never found

 **Pokémon and Trainers become friends**

Friendship is the bond of affection and trust that can grow between a Pokémon and its Trainer. Keep a Pokémon happy and it will grow to like you, but a mistreated Pokémon will take a real dislike to you.

How to improve your friendship with your Pokémon

⚙ Give it the Soothe Bell

A Pokémon who holds the Soothe Bell can be befriended more quickly than usual.

⚙ Let it join your party and walk around

Putting a Pokémon in your party and walking around will strengthen the friendship between you.

⚙ Level it up

When a Pokémon battles to level up, it becomes friendlier.

⚙ Battle Gym Leaders with it

When a Pokémon participates in important battles such as the ones against Gym Leaders, it becomes friendlier.

⚙ Participate in the Pokémon Musical

Take your Pokémon to Nimbasa City, home of the Pokémon Musical, and let it show off up on stage!

⚙ Teach a new move with TM

Teach a new move with a TM and your Pokémon will become friendly.

⚙ Use stat-boosting items on it

If you use items to boost base stats on a Pokémon, such as Protein and Iron, your friendship will go up.

⚙ Use items on it during battles

If you use items during battles such as X Attack and X Accuracy, your friendship will go up.

⚙ Feed Berries to Pokémon

If you feed Berries such as Pomeg Berry or Grepa Berry to your Pokémon, your friendship will go up.

⚙ Give Sweet Hearts to your Pokémon

Another effective way to increase friendship is to do a Feeling Check to receive Sweet Hearts and give them to your Pokémon.

Things that annoy your Pokémon

⚙ Fainting

When it is defeated and faints in a battle, your friendship will go down.

⚙ Medicinal herbs

When you use bitter medicinal herbs such as EnergyPowder and Heal Powder, your friendship will go down.

 Pokémon have a Nature and a Characteristic

Each individual Pokémon has its own Nature and Characteristic. Depending on the Pokémon, these qualities will affect how its stats increase. Before you start training a Pokémon, check its Nature and Characteristic so that you can make the most of its strongest stats.

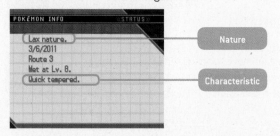

POKÉMON INFO	STATUS
Lax nature.	→ Nature
3/6/2011	
Route 3	
Met at Lv. 8.	
Quick tempered.	→ Characteristic

How Pokémon Natures affect stat growth

Nature	Attack	Defense	Speed	Sp. Attack	Sp. Defense
Hardy					
Lonely	◎	▲			
Brave	◎		▲		
Adamant	◎			▲	
Naughty	◎				▲
Bold	▲	◎			
Docile					
Relaxed		◎	▲		
Impish		◎		▲	
Lax		◎			▲
Timid	▲		◎		
Hasty		▲	◎		
Serious					
Jolly			◎	▲	
Naive			◎		▲
Modest	▲			◎	
Mild		▲		◎	
Quiet			▲	◎	
Bashful					
Rash				◎	▲
Calm	▲				◎
Gentle		▲			◎
Sassy			▲		◎
Careful				▲	◎
Quirky					

◎ Gains more upon leveling up ▲ Gains less upon leveling up

How Pokémon Characteristics affect stat growth

HP grows most	Attack grows most	Defense grows most	Speed grows most	Sp. Attack grows most	Sp. Defense grows most
Loves to eat.	Proud of its power.	Sturdy body.	Likes to run.	Highly curious.	Strong willed.
Often dozes off.	Likes to thrash about.	Capable of taking hits.	Alert to sounds.	Mischievous.	Somewhat vain.
Often scatters things.	A little quick tempered.	Highly persistent.	Impetuous and silly.	Thoroughly cunning.	Strongly defiant.
Scatters things often.	Likes to fight.	Good endurance.	Somewhat of a clown.	Often lost in thought.	Hates to lose.
Likes to relax.	Quick tempered.	Good perseverance.	Quick to flee.	Very finicky.	Somewhat stubborn.

© See page 32 for Pokémon stats ▷

 Some moves can be used as field moves

Some Pokémon moves can be used in the field to open up areas you couldn't reach before.

Field move examples

HM 01 Cut

Cuts down thin trees that are blocking your path, opening up room for you to pass.

How to get it: Given to you by Fennel in Striaton City

HM 02 Fly

Whisks you through the air and back to any town you've already visited. You'll land in front of the town's Pokémon Center.

How to get it: Given to you by Bianca in Driftveil City

HM 03 Surf

Lets you move freely on bodies of water, such as oceans and lakes, just like you would on land.

How to get it: Given to you by Alder at Twist Mountain

HM 04 Strength

Unleashes enormous strength, pushing aside stones that you normally couldn't budge. Sometimes you can push these stones into holes to open new paths.

How to get it: Given to you by a boy in a house in Nimbasa City

HM 05 Waterfall

Lets you climb waterfalls so you can see what's at the top.

How to get it: Found on Route 18

HM 06 Dive

Lets you dive into the deep ocean from dark patches in the water to explore the ocean bed.

How to get it: Given to you by a girl in front of a house in Undella Town

TM70 Flash

Illuminates dark caves and lets you explore them easily.

How to get it: Given to you by a man by the waste bin in Castelia City

TM28 Dig

Pulls you out of caves, dungeons, etc., returning you to the last entrance you went through.

How to get it: Given to you by a Worker in the prefab house on Route 4

Sweet Scent

Raises your chance of encountering wild Pokémon in areas where they live, such as tall grass or caves.

How to get it: Pokémon such as Foongus and Maractus learn it by leveling up

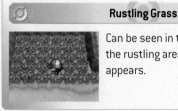

Adventure Info Track Pokémon by following the phenomena

Some of the Unova region Pokémon can be found by noticing certain phenomena in the field. There are four such special phenomena: rustling grass, dust cloud, flying Pokémon's shadow, and rippling water. Many of these Pokémon can only be caught when these phenomena appear. If you notice one of these, hurry to investigate—and catch those Pokémon!

Special places where certain Pokémon appear

● Phenomena start to appear after you obtain the first Gym Badge.

Rustling Grass

Can be seen in tall grass. Walk into the rustling area and a Pokémon appears.

Dust Cloud

Can be seen in caves. Walk into the dust cloud and you will either find an item or face a Pokémon.

Flying Pokémon's Shadow

Can be seen on Driftveil Drawbridge and Marvelous Bridge. Step on the shadow and you will either find an item or face a Pokémon.

Rippling Water

Can be seen on the water's surface. A Pokémon will appear if you surf over the rippling water or cast into it with the Super Rod.

The Unova region Pokémon that appear only at special places

Rustling Grass

Stoutland	Pansage	Pansear	Panpour	Musharna	Unfezant	Audino	Throh *Pokémon White Version only*
Sawk *Pokémon Black Version only*	Leavanny	Whimsicott *Pokémon Black Version only*	Lilligant *Pokémon White Version only*	Cinccino	Gothitelle *Pokémon Black Version only*	Reuniclus *Pokémon White Version only*	Emolga

Dust Cloud

Drilbur	Excadrill

Flying Pokémon's Shadow

Ducklett	Swanna

Rippling Water (Water Surface)

Basculin [Red-Striped Form]	Basculin [Blue-Striped Form]	Jellicent	Alomomola	Seismitoad			
Pokémon White Version only	*Pokémon Black Version only*						

Rippling Water (Fishing/After finishing the main story)

Basculin [Red-Striped Form]	Basculin [Blue-Striped Form]	Stunfisk					
Pokémon White Version only	*Pokémon Black Version only*						

Defeat Audino and gain lots of Experience Points

Audino found in rustling grass is a very good choice to help raise your Pokémon's level, because Audino gives much more Experience Points than many other Pokémon. Watch for rustling grass along routes such as 1 and 2 to find Audino—and if you beat an Audino of a higher level than your Pokémon, you can gain even more Experience Points!

Audino
Normal
ABILITIES
● Healer
● Regenerator

Adventure Info — **Some signs may give you items instead**

Two of the four special phenomena (dust cloud and flying Pokémon's shadow) may give you items instead. Each Gem will boost the power of a corresponding move just once in a battle when held by a Pokémon. Wings raise Pokémon's base stats. These items are hard to find, so be sure to investigate the dust clouds and shadows whenever you see them!

Items found in caves

Item	Chance of discovery	Poison Gem	Chance of discovery
Bug Gem	△	Psychic Gem	△
Dark Gem	△	Rock Gem	△
Dragon Gem	△	Steel Gem	△
Electric Gem	△	Water Gem	△
Everstone	△	Dawn Stone	▲
Fighting Gem	△	Dusk Stone	▲
Fire Gem	△	Fire Stone	▲
Flying Gem	△	Leaf Stone	▲
Ghost Gem	△	Moon Stone	▲
Grass Gem	△	Oval Stone	▲
Ground Gem	△	Shiny Stone	▲
Ice Gem	△	Sun Stone	▲
Item	△	Thunderstone	▲
Normal Gem	△	Water Stone	▲

△ Rarely found ▲ Almost never found

Items found on bridges

Item	Chance of discovery
Clever Wing	○
Genius Wing	○
Health Wing	○
Muscle Wing	○
Resist Wing	○
Swift Wing	○
Pretty Wing	△

○ Sometimes found △ Rarely found

Pokémon from other regions appear

After finishing the main story, you can visit areas that were inaccessible before in places such as Route 13 and Undella Town. You'll find Pokémon from other regions in those new areas. You can even catch Dragonite, Tyranitar, and Milotic, which were not available in the wild in previous titles—the only way to obtain them was through evolution!

Winning Strategies

 Learn the different types

Pokémon can be classified into 17 types, such as Normal, Fire, Water, or Grass. The matchups between these types are a key factor in determining a battle's outcome.

Examples of the 17 Pokémon types

Normal	Fire	Water	Grass
Patrat and others	Tepig and others	Oshawott and others	Snivy and others

Electric	Ice	Fighting	Poison
Blitzle and others	Cubchoo and others	Timburr and others	Trubbish and others

Ground	Flying	Psychic	Bug
Sandile and others	Pidove and others	Munna and others	Shelmet and others

Rock	Ghost	Dragon	Dark
Roggenrola and others	Yamask and others	Axew and others	Purrloin and others

Steel
Klink and others

 Pokémon moves also have types

Both Pokémon and their moves have types. This Tepig is typical of most Pokémon. Although it belongs to the Fire type, it learns moves from other types as well.

Example: Tepig

Pokémon type
Fire

Type of the move Head Smash
Rock

● **The move's type is used when attacking**

When Tepig attacks Pidove with Head Smash, look at Head Smash's type—the Rock type.

● **The Pokémon's type is used when defending**

When Pidove attacks Tepig, look at Tepig's type—the Fire type.

Turn the tables by targeting a Pokémon's weakness

Types interact like a big game of rock-paper-scissors. For instance, Water is strong against Fire, but weak against Grass. If the attacking Pokémon's move type is strong against the defending Pokémon's type, the move does increased damage.

Types have good and bad matchups

Snivy
Grass

Oshawott
Water

Tepig
Fire

Good type matchups mean increased damage!

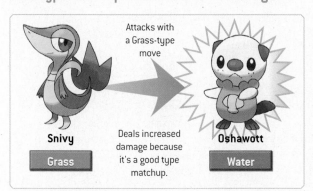

Snivy
Grass

Attacks with a Grass-type move

Deals increased damage because it's a good type matchup.

Oshawott
Water

Bad type matchups mean reduced damage...

Snivy
Grass

Attacks with a Grass-type move

Deals reduced damage because it's a bad type matchup.

Tepig
Fire

Use types to increase attack damage

Under the right conditions, your moves will do at least 50% more damage than usual. If you can keep dishing out that kind of damage, victory is sure to be within your reach. Several factors determine these increases in attack damage, but the three major ones are listed below.

How to increase damage

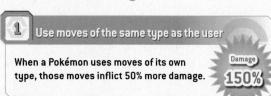

1 Use moves of the same type as the user

When a Pokémon uses moves of its own type, those moves inflict 50% more damage.

Damage
150%

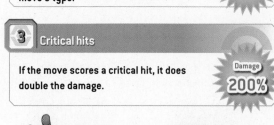

2 Use moves that the target is weak against

A move does double damage when used on a Pokémon who's weak against that move's type.

Damage
200%

3 Critical hits

If the move scores a critical hit, it does double the damage.

Damage
200%

Battle messages describe damage range

Message	Matchup	Damage
It's super effective!	Good	2–4 times damage
It's not very effective...	Fair	Half damage or less
(No message)	Normal	Regular damage
It doesn't affect...	Bad	No damage
A critical hit!	—	2 times damage

It's super effective!

Each Pokémon's overall strength depends on individual statistics, such as Attack or Defense. Six different stats indicate a Pokémon's proficiency in different areas. To raise a strong Pokémon, you'll need to understand how each stat works.

The six stats

HP

The Pokémon's health. If attacks reduce its HP to 0, the Pokémon faints.

Speed

The Pokémon's attack speed. The higher the number, the more likely the Pokémon will strike first.

Stats affecting physical moves

Attack

The higher this stat is, the more damage the Pokémon does with physical moves.

Defense

The higher this stat is, the less damage the Pokémon takes from physical moves.

Stats affecting special moves

Sp. Attack

The higher this stat is, the more damage the Pokémon does with special moves.

Sp. Defense

The higher this stat is, the less damage the Pokémon takes from special moves.

 Stats also affect the three kinds of moves

Moves belong to one of three kinds—physical, special, or status. There's an important connection between these kinds of moves and a Pokémon's stats. For instance, a Pokémon with high Attack will do the most damage if it uses physical moves.

The three kinds of moves

Physical

Physical moves are ones like Retaliate and Low Sweep. Most of these moves make direct contact with the opponent.

Special

Special moves are ones like Scald and Incinerate. Most of these moves don't bring the user into direct contact with the target.

Status

Moves like the weather-changing Rain Dance or moves that alter a user's or target's stats are considered status moves.

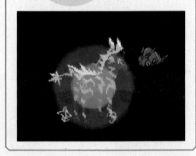

 Use status conditions to gain an advantage

Pokémon can be affected by status conditions such as Sleep, Poison, or Paralysis. These conditions can immobilize a Pokémon or eat away at its HP. Hit the other Pokémon with moves that inflict status conditions, and you'll turn the tide of battle.

Status conditions cause physical changes

The wild Throh was hurt by poison!

PRIMER FOR POKÉMON TRAINING

WINNING STRATEGIES

Status condition examples

Poison

Target's HP decreases each turn. This condition does not wear off on its own.

Effect Lowers the opponent's HP

Paralysis

Lowers Speed, and each turn there's a 25% chance that the Pokémon can't attack. This condition does not wear off on its own.

Effect Prevents the opponent from attacking, lets you strike first

Burned

Lowers Attack, and HP decreases each turn. This condition does not wear off on its own.

Effect Lowers the opponent's HP, slightly weakens the opponent's attacks

Sleep

Target is unable to attack*. This condition wears off after several turns.

Effect Prevents the opponent from attacking*, lets you attack with impunity

Frozen

Target is unable to attack. This condition may wear off when the affected Pokémon tries to attack.

Effect Prevents the opponent from attacking, lets you attack with impunity

Confused

Target will sometimes attack itself. This condition wears off after several turns.

Effect Prevents the opponent from attacking, lowers the opponent's HP

*Moves like Sleep Talk and Snore are exceptions to this rule.

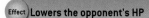 ## Make good use of your Pokémon's Abilities

Abilities are special qualities that all Pokémon possess, and each Pokémon species has its own special Abilities. Some Abilities' effects are used in the field, but most Abilities grant you an advantage in battle. Some are triggered by the opponent's attack. Learn their effects and how to effectively combine them with moves.

Abilities can tip the odds in your favor

Examples of Abilities that are helpful in battle

Unnerve

Prevents the opponent from eating Berries.

• Pokémon with Unnerve
Joltik and Galvantula

Levitate

Gives full immunity to all Ground-type moves.

• Pokémon with Levitate
Tynamo, Cryogonal, and others

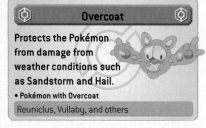

Overcoat

Protects the Pokémon from damage from weather conditions such as Sandstorm and Hail.

• Pokémon with Overcoat
Reuniclus, Vullaby, and others

Give Pokémon items to hold

Each Pokémon can hold a single item. Some held items have an effect in battle, and you can make them a key part of your strategy. The Scope Lens, for instance, boosts the holder's critical-hit ratio so the chance of dealing double damage is increased.

Examples of useful held items

 Quick Claw
Allows user to strike first sometimes

 BrightPowder
Raises evasion

 Scope Lens
Boosts the holder's critical-hit ratio

 Amulet Coin
Doubles the prize money if the holding Pokémon is brought into battle

Eviolite
Raises the Defense and Sp. Defense by 50% for a Pokémon that can still evolve

Rocky Helmet
The attacker will also be damaged on contact

Weather affects how battles go

You'll experience different weather conditions in some areas of the Unova region. The weather conditions not only change the appearance of areas but also affect Pokémon battles.

You can check the current weather condition on the Touch Screen.

The four weather conditions

Rain
When the weather condition is Rain, the power of Water-type moves goes up and the power of Fire-type moves goes down.

Sandstorm
When the weather condition is Sandstorm, each Pokémon takes damage every turn except Ground-, Rock-, and Steel-type Pokémon.

Hail
When the weather condition is Hail, each Pokémon takes damage every turn except Ice-type Pokémon.

Sunny
When the weather is Sunny, the power of Fire-type moves goes up and the power of Water-type moves goes down.

Build a strong team that covers its weak points

Every Pokémon type has its weaknesses. If you fill your team with just one type, then it only takes one supereffective move type to put your entire party at risk. Instead, try building a team with Pokémon whose strengths and weaknesses cover for each other, allowing you to take on any Pokémon you encounter.

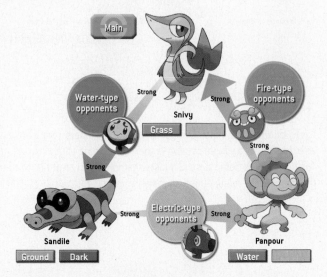

Example: Building a team around Snivy

Snivy is weak against Fire-type moves. That's why you want Panpour, a Pokémon who's strong against Fire-type Pokémon. However, Panpour is weak against Electric-type Pokémon, so add Sandile for its advantage over Electric types. Water types that have the upper hand against Sandile are at a disadvantage against Snivy.

Example: Building a team around Tepig

Tepig is weak against Water-type moves. That's why you want Pansage, a Pokémon who's strong against Water-type Pokémon. However, Pansage is weak against Flying-type Pokémon, so add Roggenrola for its advantage over Flying types. Grass types that have the upper hand against Roggenrola are at a disadvantage against Tepig.

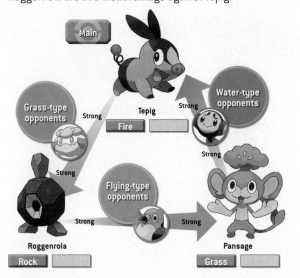

Main

Tepig — Fire

Grass-type opponents — Strong

Water-type opponents — Strong

Strong

Flying-type opponents

Roggenrola — Rock

Pansage — Grass

Strong

Strong

Strong

Example: Building a team around Oshawott

Oshawott is weak against Grass-type moves. That's why you want Pansear, a Pokémon who's strong against Grass-type Pokémon. However, Pansear is weak against Ground-type Pokémon, so add Sewaddle for its advantage over Ground types. Fire types that have the upper hand against Sewaddle are at a disadvantage against Oshawott.

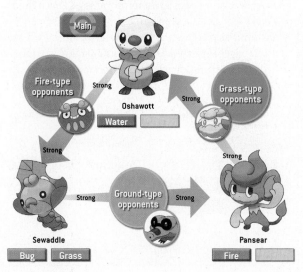

Main

Oshawott — Water

Fire-type opponents — Strong

Grass-type opponents — Strong

Strong

Ground-type opponents

Sewaddle — Bug Grass

Pansear — Fire

Strong

Strong

Strong

Adventure Info Raise Pokémon of other types to prepare for the tougher battles that lie ahead

Effective Pokémon against the Elite Four

Tough battles—such as the ones against the Elite Four and N—await you at the end of your adventure. You'll want to take advantage of the weakness of their Pokémon, but the Elite Four's Pokémon are of various types. You'll have a tough time challenging them if you raise only a few Pokémon. Here are some Pokémon that have effective moves against the Elite Four's Pokémon.

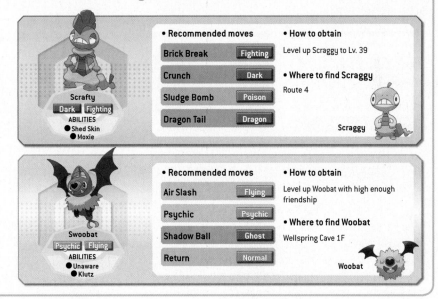

Scrafty
Dark Fighting
ABILITIES
● Shed Skin
● Moxie

• **Recommended moves**

Brick Break	Fighting
Crunch	Dark
Sludge Bomb	Poison
Dragon Tail	Dragon

• **How to obtain**
Level up Scraggy to Lv. 39

• **Where to find Scraggy**
Route 4

Scraggy

Swoobat
Psychic Flying
ABILITIES
● Unaware
● Klutz

• **Recommended moves**

Air Slash	Flying
Psychic	Psychic
Shadow Ball	Ghost
Return	Normal

• **How to obtain**
Level up Woobat with high enough friendship

• **Where to find Woobat**
Wellspring Cave 1F

Woobat

Adventure Info Pansage, Pansear, and Panpour can be quite helpful

The Pansage, Pansear, or Panpour you receive in the Dreamyard can be quite a helpful addition to your party. It would be a waste to stop training them after your Striaton City Gym battle. These three evolve with special stones, but they won't learn moves by leveling up once they are evolved. You should let them learn useful moves before they evolve.

A good way to raise Pansage

These moves are especially useful for Pansage. Leech Seed is a move that plants a seed on the target to steal some HP every turn. SolarBeam is another move to turn to, as it is one of the strongest Grass-type moves. Its power is as high as 120. Usually, SolarBeam requires an extra turn to charge up, but if the weather is Sunny, it can be used immediately.

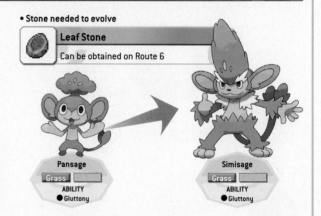

• **Stone needed to evolve**

Leaf Stone
Can be obtained on Route 6

Pansage — Grass — ABILITY ● Gluttony

Simisage — Grass — ABILITY ● Gluttony

• Recommended moves to learn by leveling up			• Recommended moves to learn with TM	
Leech Seed	Grass	Lv. 16	Sunny Day	Fire
Seed Bomb	Grass	Lv. 22	SolarBeam	Grass
Torment	Dark	Lv. 25	Rock Tomb	Rock
Crunch	Dark	Lv. 43		

A good way to raise Pansear

A move that stands out among the moves Pansear can learn is Flame Burst. It can damage adjacent Pokémon in Double and Triple Battles. Another good move is Incinerate. It burns up any Berry held by the target, so you can spoil your opponent's strategy.

• **Stone needed to evolve**

Fire Stone
Can be obtained in the Desert Resort

Pansear — Fire — ABILITY ● Gluttony

Simisear — Fire — ABILITY ● Gluttony

• Recommended moves to learn by leveling up			• Recommended moves to learn with TM	
Yawn	Normal	Lv. 16	Will-O-Wisp	Fire
Flame Burst	Fire	Lv. 22	Grass Knot	Grass
Amnesia	Psychic	Lv. 25	Fire Blast	Fire
Crunch	Dark	Lv. 43		

A good way to raise Panpour

Here are some moves that are especially useful for Panpour. Scald, unlike other typical Water-type moves, can cause a Burn. Your opponents will surely be caught off guard when you use this move. The move Blizzard can turn the tables. When Panpour faces Grass-type Pokémon that have the upper hand against it, you can use this advantageous move to double the damage.

• **Stone needed to evolve**

Water Stone
Can be obtained in Driftveil City

Panpour — Water — ABILITY ● Gluttony

Simipour — Water — ABILITY ● Gluttony

• Recommended moves to learn by leveling up			• Recommended moves to learn with TM	
Scald	Water	Lv. 22	Dig	Ground
Taunt	Dark	Lv. 25	Double Team	Normal
Brine	Water	Lv. 34	Blizzard	Ice
Crunch	Dark	Lv. 43		

Catch Pansage, Pansear, and Panpour

You will receive a Pansage, Pansear, or Panpour in the Dreamyard, but you can also catch wild ones in Pinwheel Forest and Lostlorn Forest. Look for them in the rustling grass (page 28). Catch all three for their great support and to complete the Unova Pokédex.

● **Appears in Pinwheel Forest and Lostlorn Forest rustling grass**

A wild Pansage appeared!   wild Pansear appeared!   A wild Panpour appeared!

Adventure Info   ## Raise Pokémon using the Lucky Egg or Exp. Share in the new region

It is important to raise not only your primary Pokémon, but also the support Pokémon in *Pokémon Black* and *Pokémon White*. But it is hard to raise other Pokémon when you are busy raising the main Pokémon. Here is a way to raise your team effectively with useful items such as Lucky Egg and Exp. Share.

Lucky Egg   Gain more Experience Points than usual

Lucky Egg is an item that gives 50% more Experience Points than usual. It is most effective if you let the lead Pokémon hold it.

Snivy gained a boosted 265 Exp. Points!

Lucky Egg

• **How to obtain Lucky Egg**

1. Professor Juniper gives you one at the Chargestone Cave
2. The sunglasses-wearing man on Route 13 gives you one

Exp. Share   Raise multiple Pokémon at once.

When you have a Pokémon hold Exp. Share, it can gain Experience Points without battling as long as it's in your party.

Pansage gained 193 Exp. Points!

Exp. Share

• **How to obtain Exp. Share**

1. Defeat a Janitor at the Battle Company in Castelia City
2. Show a Pokémon from Lv. 25 through Lv. 49 to the Pokémon Fan Club chairman in Icirrus City

Combining both items

1 When one Exp. Share is held (and the levels of the Pokémon are the same)

The Experience Point distribution is shown when the lead Pokémon holds a Lucky Egg and a Pokémon in your party holds an Exp. Share.

The Experience Points gained through battles

Battle $\frac{1}{2}$ x 1.5!   In your party $\frac{1}{2}$

2 When two Exp. Shares are held (and the levels of the Pokémon are the same)

The distribution is shown when the lead Pokémon holds a Lucky Egg and two Pokémon in your party each hold an Exp. Share.

The Experience Points gained through battles

Battle $\frac{1}{2}$ x 1.5!   In your party $\frac{1}{4}$ In your party $\frac{1}{4}$

Using the Game Functions

 How to use the game menus

Throughout your journey, you can press the X Button to show the main menu on the Touch Screen. Once you learn what the different options are and what information they contain, you'll have no problem finding your way.

Menu screen

Communication Features
Communication features currently being used or available are shown.

Current time
Shows the current time, according to the clock feature of the Nintendo DS.

Nintendo DS battery level
The mini-scale graph of the Nintendo DS battery status is shown.

1	POKÉMON	POKÉDEX	2
3	BAG	Trainer	4
5	SAVE	OPTIONS	6

Using the game functions

1 Pokémon
Displays the Pokémon currently in your party. You can also access detailed info on each.

2 Pokédex
A device that records Pokémon data, including how many you've seen and caught.

3 Bag
Stores the items you've collected. Open it to use the items inside.

4 Trainer Info
Shows how far you've come as a Trainer. You can check which Gym Badges have been obtained and other data.

5 Save
Tap here to save your game. Be sure to save often.

6 Options
Adjust the gameplay options to your liking.

 Pokémon

Tap "POKÉMON" on the menu to see a list of your current party Pokémon. You can also view more info about your Pokémon or use field moves, such as Fly or Flash. To use these field moves, just select a Pokémon, then the move.

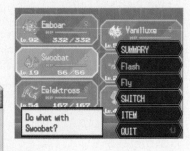

What you can do with the party Pokémon screen

SUMMARY	SWITCH	ITEM	FIELD MOVE
Shows where you caught the Pokémon, its moves, its stats, and more.	Move a Pokémon around in your lineup. The top-left is the first Pokémon and the top-right is the second Pokémon to join a battle.	Lets you give a Pokémon an item to hold or take away its held item.	Lets your Pokémon use a field move, such as Fly or Flash.

Check Pokémon data under Summary

Three screens of Pokémon data

From the party Pokémon screen, choose "SUMMARY" to view a Pokémon's info. There are three separate pages of info.

● Trainer Memo and Info on the Pokémon

The top screen shows the Pokémon's Nature, Characteristic, and more. General information is on the lower screen.

● Stats and Battle Moves

The top screen shows the Pokémon's stats and its Ability. The lower screen shows the moves it knows.

● Ribbons

Only for the Pokémon transferred with Poké Transfer (p. 205). The lower screen shows any Ribbons it has earned.

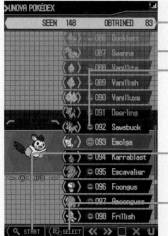

Pokédex

The Pokédex is the device that automatically records Pokémon data. Whenever you encounter a Pokémon in the field or in a Trainer battle, it's added to your list of Pokémon seen. Once you catch it, it's added to your list of Pokémon obtained.

Pokédex screen

The number of Pokémon seen and Pokémon obtained

Pokémon List

Icon to show it has been obtained
When you've caught or obtained a Pokémon through trade, it'll be registered in your Pokédex and the Poké Ball icon is shown.

Search
You can narrow down the Pokémon you are looking for by Pokédex number, name, type, and more.

Switches between the Unova Pokédex and National Pokédex
(after you've obtained the National Pokédex)

Boy's Pokédex

Girl's Pokédex

How Pokédex entries are registered

① No Pokédex data

Before you encounter a certain Pokémon species, there's nothing but a blank space reserved for it and its Pokédex number.

② Name and habitat recorded

When you see a Pokémon, its name and appearance are added to the Pokédex. Tap "AREA" and its habitat is also displayed.

③ Detailed information added

Once you catch a Pokémon, the Pokédex records its type, size, description, and more. The Pokédex entry is now complete.

You can also check gender and color differences

Tap "FORMS" to check gender and form differences. You can also check Shiny Pokémon you've obtained.

 Bag

Your Bag is where you store the items you collect on your journey. You'll have it from the beginning of your adventure. For your convenience, items are automatically sorted into one of five Cases inside it.

Boy's Bag

Girl's Bag

Items in your Bag are sorted into one of five Cases

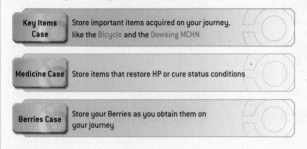

Key Items Case Store important items acquired on your journey, like the Bicycle and the Dowsing MCHN

Medicine Case Store items that restore HP or cure status conditions

Berries Case Store your Berries as you obtain them on your journey

Items Case Store items for Pokémon to hold, evolution stones, and more

TMs & HMs Case Store your TMs and HMs

The Ready function of the Y Button

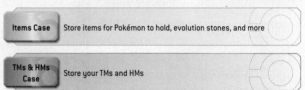
Register frequently used items

Some of the Key Items can be assigned to the Y Button, also known as the Ready button, for quick access. This is a very useful feature. Six Key Items can be assigned, including the Bicycle and the Dowsing MCHN.

Tap "REGISTER" — Press the Y Button

You can also register frequently used screens

There is more to the Y Button than registering Key Items. You can also register screens for quick access, as long as they have a box to check in the bottom-right corner, such as the Pokédex and individual Cases of your Bag.

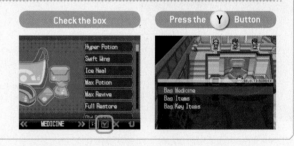
Check the box — Press the Y Button

Trainer Info covers your Trainer Card and Gym Badges. Tap the icon labeled with your name to access it at any time. Your Trainer Card records lots of information, so don't forget to check it out!

Trainer Info screen

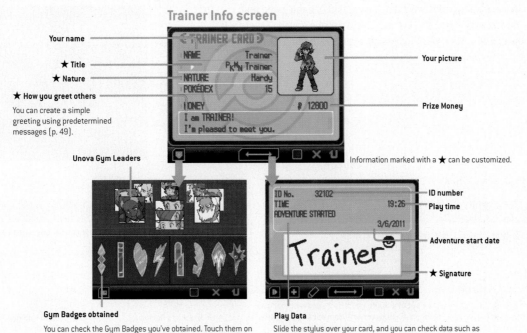

Your name

★ Title

★ Nature

★ How you greet others

You can create a simple greeting using predetermined messages (p. 49).

Your picture

Prize Money

Information marked with a ★ can be customized.

Unova Gym Leaders

ID number

Play time

Adventure start date

★ Signature

Gym Badges obtained
You can check the Gym Badges you've obtained. Touch them on the screen to shine them if they don't gleam like they used to.

Play Data
Slide the stylus over your card, and you can check data such as the first Hall of Fame, Link Battles and Trades, and more.

Trainer Card Features

Tap to customize

You can personalize the information on your Trainer Card by tapping it. Remember that the information is viewed through Tag Mode and the Union Room.

Your Trainer Card gets upgrades

After you've finished the main story or meet a certain condition, your Trainer Card is upgraded from the Normal Rank, Green, to the Bronze Rank, Purple. There are a total of five Ranks, and your Trainer Card gets upgraded every time you meet certain conditions.

Options

The Options menu lets you adjust game settings to suit your own preferences, making it easier to play. For instance, if the game text scrolls by too slowly, you can increase the message speed. If there's a gameplay feature you want to change, open the Options menu and change it to your liking.

The Options menu

What you can do with the Options menu

1 Text Speed

Choose from slow, mid (middle), or fast text speeds.

2 Battle Scene

Choose whether you want to see battle animations when Pokémon enter battle and use their moves.

3 Battle Style

When you defeat one Pokémon out of a team, you'll be asked whether you want to switch your own Pokémon. If you want to automatically stay with your current Pokémon, select "SET" to turn off these messages.

● Shift

Pros

After defeating a Pokémon, you can switch to one better suited to the next opponent.

Cons

You'll be asked frequently if you want to switch Pokémon.

● Set

Pros

Lets you keep battling with a single Pokémon (to focus on leveling it up).

Cons

In Set mode, you have to use up a turn to switch your Pokémon after beating one.

4 Sound

Choose between stereo and mono sound.

5 Save Before IR

You can choose to save the game before infrared is launched.

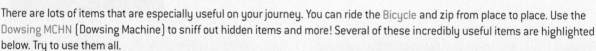

Get a handle on using these handy items

There are lots of items that are especially useful on your journey. You can ride the Bicycle and zip from place to place. Use the Dowsing MCHN (Dowsing Machine) to sniff out hidden items and more! Several of these incredibly useful items are highlighted below. Try to use them all.

Town Map

It's the map of the entire Unova region including its cities, towns, routes, caves, and bridges. Places you've visited are shown in gray, and they will turn blue as you visit them. You can also see your current position. Touch the "+" icon to magnify.

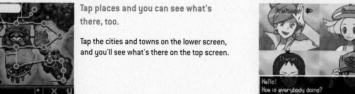

Tap places and you can see what's there, too.

Tap the cities and towns on the lower screen, and you'll see what's there on the top screen.

• **How to obtain the Town Map**

Your mom gives it to you in Nuvema Town

Xtransceiver

A high-tech transceiver with a camera function. It allows up to four-way calls. The color differs between male and female Trainers. You can communicate with various people including your friends and Professor Juniper at important moments in the game.

Your friends give you useful information

It's a useful item that enables you to talk to your friends, Professor Juniper, and your mom face to face.

• **How to obtain the Xtransceiver**

Your mom gives it to you in Nuvema Town

Dowsing MCHN

It can detect items that are hidden in forests and caves. Follow the arrow shown on the lower screen and check where it blinks for a hidden item.

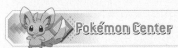

It's like a treasure hunt!

You cannot pick up an item if you are standing right on top of it. Step aside, face the spot where you were, then press the A Button.

• How to obtain the Dowsing MCHN

Bianca gives it to you in Nacrene City

Bicycle

The Bicycle lets you travel even faster than the Running Shoes allow. It's a good idea to register it to the Y Button as soon as you get it (p. 40). Zip through towns, routes, and bridges with it.

Faster than running...usually

The Bicycle is usually the faster way to get around, but it gets bogged down in sand. When you're in places like the Desert Resort, you're better off just walking.

• How to obtain the Bicycle

After you defeat Team Plasma in Nimbasa City, the Day-Care Man gives it to you

Town Shops and Services

Pokémon Center

Pokémon Centers are facilities that support Pokémon Trainers. Pokémon Centers in the Unova region are separated into two floors. The first floor has both the Poké Mart and the Pokémon Center, where you can heal your Pokémon. The second floor has three rooms where you can enjoy different types of communication features.

2F Communications Area

Geonet is a globe that lets you register where you live. At the Global Terminal, you can set up trades and battles with Trainers all over the world. Trade or battle with friends with whom you've exchanged Friend Codes at the Wi-Fi Club. Enjoy a variety of activities with the people who have entered the same room in the Union Room.

1F Pokémon Center

If you speak to the person at the Pokémon Center's reception counter, your Pokémon's HP, PP, and status conditions will be healed for free. Use the PC on the left side of the counter to deposit or withdraw Pokémon to take on your adventure, or organize your items. Also, use Help to read detailed, illustrated explanations of how to play the game.

1F Poké Mart

In *Pokémon Black* and *Pokémon White*, the Poké Mart is no longer a separate facility. You'll find it right inside the door of every Pokémon Center. Now you can heal your Pokémon and buy items in the same place!

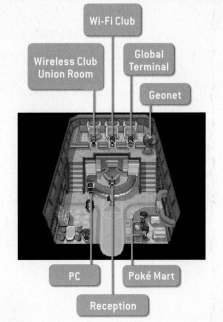

Wi-Fi Club

Wireless Club Union Room

Global Terminal

Geonet

PC

Poké Mart

Reception

Poké Mart

The Poké Mart is a shop inside the Pokémon Center that sells a variety of useful goods for adventures. As you get more Gym Badges, the selection at the Poké Mart grows even better. There are two clerks:

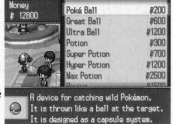

Money ₽ 12800		
	Poké Ball	₽200
	Great Ball	₽600
	Ultra Ball	₽1200
	Potion	₽300
	Super Potion	₽700
	Hyper Potion	₽1200
	Max Potion	₽2500

A device for catching wild Pokémon. It is thrown like a ball at the target. It is designed as a capsule system.

The upper clerk sells the same goods in every town, and the lower clerk sells products unique to the city you're in.

● Items sold at the Poké Mart (and conditions for sale)

Item	Price	Condition	Explanation
Antidote	100	●	Cures Poison.
Parlyz Heal	200	●	Cures Paralysis.
Poké Ball	200	—	An item for capturing wild Pokémon.
Awakening	250	●	Cures Sleep.
Burn Heal	250	●	Cures Burn.
Ice Heal	250	●	Defrosts a Pokémon that has been frozen solid.
Potion	300	—	Restores the HP of one Pokémon by 20 points.
Repel	350	●	Prevents weak wild Pokémon from appearing for 100 steps after its use.
Super Repel	500	▲	Prevents weak wild Pokémon from appearing for 200 steps after its use.
Escape Rope	550	●	Escape instantly from a cave or a dungeon.
Full Heal	600	■	Cures all status ailments.
Great Ball	600	●	A Ball that provides a higher Pokémon catch rate than a standard Poké Ball.
Max Repel	700	■	Prevents weak wild Pokémon from appearing for 250 steps after its use.
Super Potion	700	●	Restores the HP of one Pokémon by 50 points.
Hyper Potion	1,200	▲	Restores the HP of one Pokémon by 200 points.
Ultra Ball	1,200	■	A Ball that provides a higher Pokémon catch rate than a Great Ball.
Revive	1,500	▲	Revives a fainted Pokémon and restores half of its HP.
Max Potion	2,500	◆	Completely restores the HP of a single Pokémon.
Full Restore	3,000	★	Fully restores the HP and heals any status problems of a single Pokémon.

Conditions for Purchasing

No mark   Sold from the beginning
●   After earning one or two Gym Badges
▲   After earning three or four Gym Badges
■   After earning five or six Gym Badges
◆   After earning six or seven Gym Badges
★   After earning all eight Gym Badges

Amanita's (Someone's) PC

The PC is a convenient device where you can deposit Pokémon you've caught, or withdraw them to take them on your adventure. There's one on the first floor of every Pokémon Center. At the start of your adventure, it's called "Someone's PC," but after you talk to Amanita in Striaton City, the name changes to "Amanita's PC." You'll be using the PC a lot during your adventure, so here's how to do it!

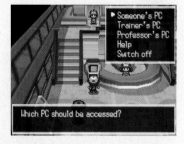

Which PC should be accessed?

● What you can do with Amanita's PC

Deposit Pokémon

Use this when you want to put Pokémon from your party into the PC Box. Also, you can see the status of the selected Pokémon, mark it, or release it.

Krokorok is selected.

Withdraw Pokémon

Use this to move Pokémon from your PC Box into your party. To use this function, you need space in your party. If you're already traveling with six Pokémon, you can't take another Pokémon with you, even if you select it.

Deerling is selected.

Move Pokémon

In addition to depositing and withdrawing Pokémon, you can also move Pokémon from one Box to another or swap Pokémon from the Boxes with the ones in your party.

Foongus is selected.

Battle Box

You can move up to six Pokémon from your PC Box that you often use in battles into your Battle Box. When you battle with your friends, you can select whether to use the Pokémon in your Battle Box or the Pokémon in your party.

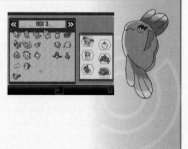

Move Items

You can organize the items held by your Pokémon. You can give an item a Pokémon is holding to a different Pokémon, or you can put the item back into your Bag.

Exp. Share is selected.

Your PC

Use the PC with your name on it to store Mail held by a Pokémon you traded. Access this PC to read your Mail whenever you want. To send Mail when trading Pokémon, you can buy Mail at the Poké Mart and have a Pokémon hold it.

● What you can do on your PC

Mailbox

Your mailbox saves up to 20 received messages. You can reread or delete saved Mail. Regardless of who sent the Mail saved in your mailbox, you can have your Pokémon hold it.

When trading, have your Pokémon hold Mail

When trading with friends and family, give your Pokémon Mail to hold. The recipient will be happy even if it's just a short message.

Professor's PC

Use the Professor's PC to check the completeness of your Pokédex. The professor will judge how many Pokémon you've seen, and if you've seen more than 150 Pokémon, she will judge the number you've obtained. Consult the Professor's PC for help in completing your Pokédex.

● Get TMs from Professor Juniper

Professor Juniper gives you TMs as presents after you've seen a certain number of Pokémon. When the "Number Seen" in your Pokédex reaches this point and you access the Professor's PC, she will tell you she has something for you and ask you to come to the Lab. Go to the Juniper Pokémon Lab in Nuvema Town to receive your gift.

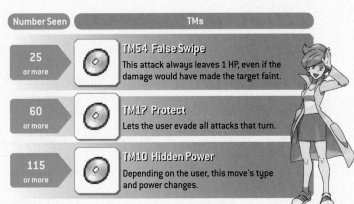

Number Seen	TMs
25 or more	**TM54 False Swipe** This attack always leaves 1 HP, even if the damage would have made the target faint.
60 or more	**TM17 Protect** Lets the user evade all attacks that turn.
115 or more	**TM10 Hidden Power** Depending on the user, this move's type and power changes.

Help

Help shows you important information and images that explain how to enjoy *Pokémon Black* and *Pokémon White*. As you proceed through the story, the content increases.

● Conditions for increasing Help content

Displayed from the beginning

After obtaining the C-Gear

After finishing the main story

 **TV shows**

You'll find TVs in houses in every city, and there's even one in your room. Stand in front of the TV and press the A Button to watch whatever's on! TV shows can be divided into three categories: shows about records, lectures, and variety shows. There are 13 different shows in all, offering all kinds of information about the world of Pokémon. Every now and again, take a break and enjoy some TV!

On today's "Your Pokémon," we will introduce an energetic little one.

● TV Programs and Content

Time and Genre	Program Name	Content
From zero to 9 minutes after the hour Records	Cartoon	A cartoon about a Pokémon Trainer who has the same name as you! Depending on your gender, the show will be slightly different.
From 10 to 34 minutes after the hour Lecture	Moves for Living	A show that explains moves.
	The Waving Weaving Walk	A show that explains Abilities.
	What's That?	A show that explains items.
From 35 to 59 minutes after the hour Variety	Personality Assessment and Horoscope	A show with personality assessments based on horoscopes for the Unova region.
	The National Gymquirer	A show where you can hear rumors about the Gym Leaders.
	KOUKAN TALK	A show that teaches helpful Japanese phrases to Pokémon Trainers.
	Eyes on Unova	A program with reports on the Unova region and Trainer interviews.
	Sparkling Musical Moves	A show where you can see Pokémon Musicals.
	PokéQuiz	A quiz show where contestants are quizzed on Japanese Pokémon names.
	Your Pokémon	A show that introduces special Pokémon from around the region.
	Today's Recommended Item	A fantastic TV shopping show.
	Unova News	A news program that brings the latest in Unova region news.

Details   Check Your Pokémon Horoscope

On the TV show "Personality Assessment and Horoscope," you can learn about the horoscope in the Unova region that corresponds to the month you were born. For example, the sign of people born in January is Sawsbuck, and it's Simipour for people born in February. All of the Pokémon star signs you see in the TV show are listed here. What's your sign?

January	Sawsbuck	May	Bouffalant	September	Gothorita
February	Simipour	June	Klink	October	Lampent
March	Alomomola	July	Crustle	November	Scolipede
April	Whimsicott	August	Braviary	December	Fraxure

 **Electric bulletin board**

Striaton City: Sunny

Every gate has an electric bulletin board. When you want to read the announcements on the board, stand in front of it and press the A Button. The announcements on the electric bulletin board can be divided into three types: weather, information, and breaking news. When you start your adventure, be sure to check out the electric bulletin boards when you enter the gates, because they are a great way to get important information about the area you are going to.

● Electric Bulletin Board Info

Genre	Program Name	Content
Weather	Date and Weather	When you go from a city with a gate to another city, information about the weather on that route will be displayed.
	Rare Weather	If there is strange weather somewhere, the place where it is happening will be displayed. Also, you can learn where Tornadus or Thundurus is appearing.
Information	Mass Outbreaks	After you finish the main story, a mass outbreak—a large group of Pokémon appearing all at once—will occur somewhere once a day. Information about the mass outbreak location will be displayed.
	Regional Information	Information about the place you are heading will be displayed, matching your progress in the story.
	Advertisements	Commercials for the Poké Mart and Shopping Mall Nine are shown.
Breaking news	News Bulletins	Defeat the Gym Leaders or the Champion through the course of the story and that information will be shown here.

Other things to keep in mind

Wonderful things happen on your birthday

Register your birthday in the Nintendo DS system and something wonderful will happen on your birthday in *Pokémon Black* and *Pokémon White*. Celebrate your birthday in the game!

The Pokémon Center's greeting changes

Get a Prop at the Musical Theater

Penalty for losing battles

If all of the Pokémon in your party faint, you will be returned to the Pokémon Center. You'll lose some money when this happens, and the stronger your party is, the more money you will lose when you lose the battle.

Time and Seasons in Unova

 ## Seasonal changes

The Unova region has four seasons: spring, summer, autumn, and winter. In Icirrus City and Dragonspiral Tower, for example, snow will accumulate during winter. A season in Unova goes by at the beginning of every month in real time. So for instance, autumn is in March and winter is in April. Also, time in the Unova region moves at the same speed as actual time, and each day has periods of morning, afternoon, evening, night, and late night. These times of day change according to the in-game season.

● Changes to the scenery in each season (Route 1)

Spring	Summer	Autumn	Winter

Pink flower petals dance through the sky. Young buds are sprouting on the green trees.	The leaves of the trees have turned a dark, summery green, and yellow flowers dance through the sky.	Autumn comes to the Routes, leaves float through the sky, and the trees show brilliant autumn colors.	The ground turns as white as if a cloud had fallen onto the ground. Dried leaves blow through the sky, so everything feels extra wintry.

● Changes in time and the seasons

Spring	Late Night	Morning	Afternoon	Evening	Night
Summer	Late Night	Morning	Afternoon	Evening	Night
Autumn	Late Night	Morning	Afternoon	Evening	Night
Winter	Late Night	Morning	Afternoon	Evening	Night

Midnight 1 A.M. 2 3 4 5 6 7 8 9 10 11 Noon 1 P.M. 2 3 4 5 6 7 8 9 10 11 12

Time

■ Late Night
■ Morning
■ Afternoon
■ Evening
■ Night

Communicate with the Easy Chat System

Write by choosing words and simple phrases

Use predefined sentences

The easy chat system is a communication tool that lets you make sentences by combining prepared words and phrases. You can write your profile introduction on your Trainer Card, and write Mail to give to Pokémon to hold. There are many opportunities to use it within the game.

Write Mail and give it to your friends

Buy Mail at the Poké Mart

The Poké Mart in each city sells Mail.

If you let a Pokémon hold Mail before trading it, you can send Mail to the person you're trading with. When you are trading Pokémon via the Union Room or the Global Terminal, send a message to the person you're trading with by giving that Pokémon a Mail message to hold. The person who gets the message will surely be pleased.

Enjoy the easy chat system in other places

There are many other situations in *Pokémon Black* and *Pokémon White* where you can use the easy chat system. Use the words listed on the following pages to make fun sentences.

● Main places where you can use the easy chat system

Trainer Card's Profile Greeting

Icirrus City Aha's House

Wireless Club Union Room Chat

POKÉMON	BLITZLE	CORPHISH	DWEBBLE	GIGALITH	HOUNDOUR	LEDYBA
ABOMASNOW	BOLDORE	CORSOLA	EELEKTRIK	GIRAFARIG	HUNTAIL	LICKILICKY
ABRA	BONSLY	COTTONEE	EELEKTROSS	GIRATINA	HYDREIGON	LICKITUNG
ABSOL	BOUFFALANT	CRADILY	EEVEE	GLACEON	HYPNO	LIEPARD
ACCELGOR	BRAVIARY	CRANIDOS	EKANS	GLALIE	IGGLYBUFF	LILEEP
AERODACTYL	BRELOOM	CRAWDAUNT	ELECTABUZZ	GLAMEOW	ILLUMISE	LILLIGANT
AGGRON	BRONZONG	CRESSELIA	ELECTIVIRE	GLIGAR	INFERNAPE	LILLIPUP
AIPOM	BRONZOR	CROAGUNK	ELECTRIKE	GLISCOR	IVYSAUR	LINOONE
ALAKAZAM	BUDEW	CROBAT	ELECTRODE	GLOOM	JELLICENT	LITWICK
ALOMOMOLA	BUIZEL	CROCONAW	ELEKID	GOLBAT	JIGGLYPUFF	LOMBRE
ALTARIA	BULBASAUR	CRUSTLE	ELGYEM	GOLDEEN	JIRACHI	LOPUNNY
AMBIPOM	BUNEARY	CRYOGONAL	EMBOAR	GOLDUCK	JOLTEON	LOTAD
AMOONGUSS	BURMY	CUBCHOO	EMOLGA	GOLEM	JOLTIK	LOUDRED
AMPHAROS	BUTTERFREE	CUBONE	EMPOLEON	GOLETT	JUMPLUFF	LUCARIO
ANORITH	CACNEA	CYNDAQUIL	ENTEI	GOLURK	JYNX	LUDICOLO
ARBOK	CACTURNE	DARKRAI	ESCAVALIER	GOREBYSS	KABUTO	LUGIA
ARCANINE	CAMERUPT	DARMANITAN	ESPEON	GOTHITA	KABUTOPS	LUMINEON
ARCEUS	CARNIVINE	DARUMAKA	EXCADRILL	GOTHITELLE	KADABRA	LUNATONE
ARCHEN	CARRACOSTA	DEERLING	EXEGGCUTE	GOTHORITA	KAKUNA	LUVDISC
ARCHEOPS	CARVANHA	DEINO	EXEGGUTOR	GRANBULL	KANGASKHAN	LUXIO
ARIADOS	CASCOON	DELCATTY	EXPLOUD	GRAVELER	KARRABLAST	LUXRAY
ARMALDO	CASTFORM	DELIBIRD	FARFETCH'D	GRIMER	KECLEON	MACHAMP
ARON	CATERPIE	DEOXYS	FEAROW	GROTLE	KELDEO	MACHOKE
ARTICUNO	CELEBI	DEWGONG	FEEBAS	GROUDON	KINGDRA	MACHOP
AUDINO	CHANDELURE	DEWOTT	FERALIGATR	GROVYLE	KINGLER	MAGBY
AXEW	CHANSEY	DIALGA	FERROSEED	GROWLITHE	KIRLIA	MAGCARGO
AZELF	CHARIZARD	DIGLETT	FERROTHORN	GRUMPIG	KLANG	MAGIKARP
AZUMARILL	CHARMANDER	DITTO	FINNEON	GULPIN	KLINK	MAGMAR
AZURILL	CHARMELEON	DODRIO	FLAAFFY	GURDURR	KLINKLANG	MAGMORTAR
BAGON	CHATOT	DODUO	FLAREON	GYARADOS	KOFFING	MAGNEMITE
BALTOY	CHERRIM	DONPHAN	FLOATZEL	HAPPINY	KRABBY	MAGNETON
BANETTE	CHERUBI	DRAGONAIR	FLYGON	HARIYAMA	KRICKETOT	MAGNEZONE
BARBOACH	CHIKORITA	DRAGONITE	FOONGUS	HAUNTER	KRICKETUNE	MAKUHITA
BASCULIN	CHIMCHAR	DRAPION	FORRETRESS	HAXORUS	KROKOROK	MAMOSWINE
BASTIODON	CHIMECHO	DRATINI	FRAXURE	HEATMOR	KROOKODILE	MANAPHY
BAYLEEF	CHINCHOU	DRIFBLIM	FRILLISH	HEATRAN	KYOGRE	MANDIBUZZ
BEARTIC	CHINGLING	DRIFLOON	FROSLASS	HERACROSS	KYUREM	MANECTRIC
BEAUTIFLY	CINCCINO	DRILBUR	FURRET	HERDIER	LAIRON	MANKEY
BEEDRILL	CLAMPERL	DROWZEE	GABITE	HIPPOPOTAS	LAMPENT	MANTINE
BEHEEYEM	CLAYDOL	DRUDDIGON	GALLADE	HIPPOWDON	LANDORUS	MANTYKE
BELDUM	CLEFABLE	DUCKLETT	GALVANTULA	HITMONCHAN	LANTURN	MARACTUS
BELLOSSOM	CLEFAIRY	DUGTRIO	GARBODOR	HITMONLEE	LAPRAS	MAREEP
BELLSPROUT	CLEFFA	DUNSPARCE	GARCHOMP	HITMONTOP	LARVESTA	MARILL
BIBAREL	CLOYSTER	DUOSION	GARDEVOIR	HONCHKROW	LARVITAR	MAROWAK
BIDOOF	COBALION	DURANT	GASTLY	HO-OH	LATIAS	MARSHTOMP
BISHARP	COFAGRIGUS	DUSCLOPS	GASTRODON	HOOTHOOT	LATIOS	MASQUERAIN
BLASTOISE	COMBEE	DUSKNOIR	GENGAR	HOPPIP	LEAFEON	MAWILE
BLAZIKEN	COMBUSKEN	DUSKULL	GEODUDE	HORSEA	LEAVANNY	MEDICHAM
BLISSEY	CONKELDURR	DUSTOX	GIBLE	HOUNDOOM	LEDIAN	MEDITITE

MELOETTA	PANPOUR	REGIGIGAS	SHUCKLE	SWALOT	VESPIQUEN
MEGANIUM	PANSAGE	REGIROCK	SHUPPET	SWAMPERT	VIBRAVA
MEOWTH	PANSEAR	REGISTEEL	SIGILYPH	SWANNA	VICTINI
MESPRIT	PARAS	RELICANTH	SILCOON	SWELLOW	VICTREEBEL
METAGROSS	PARASECT	REMORAID	SIMIPOUR	SWINUB	VIGOROTH
METANG	PATRAT	RESHIRAM	SIMISAGE	SWOOBAT	VILEPLUME
METAPOD	PAWNIARD	REUNICLUS	SIMISEAR	TAILLOW	VIRIZION
MEW	PELIPPER	RHYDON	SKARMORY	TANGELA	VOLBEAT
MEWTWO	PERSIAN	RHYHORN	SKIPLOOM	TANGROWTH	VOLCARONA
MIENFOO	PETILIL	RHYPERIOR	SKITTY	TAUROS	VOLTORB
MIENSHAO	PHANPY	RIOLU	SKORUPI	TEDDIURSA	VULLABY
MIGHTYENA	PHIONE	ROGGENROLA	SKUNTANK	TENTACOOL	VULPIX
MILOTIC	PICHU	ROSELIA	SLAKING	TENTACRUEL	WAILMER
MILTANK	PIDGEOT	ROSERADE	SLAKOTH	TEPIG	WAILORD
MIME JR.	PIDGEOTTO	ROTOM	SLOWBRO	TERRAKION	WALREIN
MINCCINO	PIDGEY	RUFFLET	SLOWKING	THROH	WARTORTLE
MINUN	PIDOVE	SABLEYE	SLOWPOKE	THUNDURUS	WATCHOG
MISDREAVUS	PIGNITE	SALAMENCE	SLUGMA	TIMBURR	WEAVILE
MISMAGIUS	PIKACHU	SAMUROTT	SMEARGLE	TIRTOUGA	WEEDLE
MOLTRES	PILOSWINE	SANDILE	SMOOCHUM	TOGEKISS	WEEPINBELL
MONFERNO	PINECO	SANDSHREW	SNEASEL	TOGEPI	WEEZING
MOTHIM	PINSIR	SANDSLASH	SNIVY	TOGETIC	WHIMSICOTT
MR. MIME	PIPLUP	SAWK	SNORLAX	TORCHIC	WHIRLIPEDE
MUDKIP	PLUSLE	SAWSBUCK	SNORUNT	TORKOAL	WHISCASH
MUK	POLITOED	SCEPTILE	SNOVER	TORNADUS	WHISMUR
MUNCHLAX	POLIWAG	SCIZOR	SNUBBULL	TORTERRA	WIGGLYTUFF
MUNNA	POLIWHIRL	SCOLIPEDE	SOLOSIS	TOTODILE	WINGULL
MURKROW	POLIWRATH	SCRAFTY	SOLROCK	TOXICROAK	WOBBUFFET
MUSHARNA	PONYTA	SCRAGGY	SPEAROW	TRANQUILL	WOOBAT
NATU	POOCHYENA	SCYTHER	SPHEAL	TRAPINCH	WOOPER
NIDOKING	PORYGON	SEADRA	SPINARAK	TREECKO	WORMADAM
NIDOQUEEN	PORYGON2	SEAKING	SPINDA	TROPIUS	WURMPLE
NIDORAN ♀	PORYGON-Z	SEALEO	SPIRITOMB	TRUBBISH	WYNAUT
NIDORAN ♂	PRIMEAPE	SEEDOT	SPOINK	TURTWIG	XATU
NIDORINA	PRINPLUP	SEEL	SQUIRTLE	TYMPOLE	YAMASK
NIDORINO	PROBOPASS	SEISMITOAD	STANTLER	TYNAMO	YANMA
NINCADA	PSYDUCK	SENTRET	STARAPTOR	TYPHLOSION	YANMEGA
NINETALES	PUPITAR	SERPERIOR	STARAVIA	TYRANITAR	ZANGOOSE
NINJASK	PURRLOIN	SERVINE	STARLY	TYROGUE	ZAPDOS
NOCTOWL	PURUGLY	SEVIPER	STARMIE	UMBREON	ZEBSTRIKA
NOSEPASS	QUAGSIRE	SEWADDLE	STARYU	UNFEZANT	ZEKROM
NUMEL	QUILAVA	SHARPEDO	STEELIX	UNOWN	ZIGZAGOON
NUZLEAF	QWILFISH	SHAYMIN	STOUTLAND	URSARING	ZOROARK
OCTILLERY	RAICHU	SHEDINJA	STUNFISK	UXIE	ZORUA
ODDISH	RAIKOU	SHELGON	STUNKY	VANILLISH	ZUBAT
OMANYTE	RALTS	SHELLDER	SUDOWOODO	VANILLITE	ZWEILOUS
OMASTAR	RAMPARDOS	SHELLOS	SUICUNE	VANILLUXE	
ONIX	RAPIDASH	SHELMET	SUNFLORA	VAPOREON	
OSHAWOTT	RATICATE	SHIELDON	SUNKERN	VENIPEDE	
PACHIRISU	RATTATA	SHIFTRY	SURSKIT	VENOMOTH	
PALKIA	RAYQUAZA	SHINX	SWABLU	VENONAT	
PALPITOAD	REGICE	SHROOMISH	SWADLOON	VENUSAUR	

ABILITIES

ADAPTABILITY	HEAVY METAL	POISON POINT	TELEPATHY	AVALANCHE	COSMIC POWER	ENCORE
AFTERMATH	HONEY GATHER	POISON TOUCH	TERAVOLT	BARRAGE	COTTON GUARD	ENDEAVOR
AIR LOCK	HUGE POWER	PRANKSTER	THICK FAT	BARRIER	COTTON SPORE	ENDURE
ANALYTIC	HUSTLE	PRESSURE	TINTED LENS	BATON PASS	COUNTER	ENERGY BALL
ANGER POINT	HYDRATION	PSYCHIC	TORRENT	BEAT UP	COVET	ENTRAINMENT
ANTICIPATION	HYPER CUTTER	PURE POWER	TOXIC BOOST	BELLY DRUM	CRABHAMMER	ERUPTION
ARENA TRAP	ICE	QUICK FEET	TRACE	BESTOW	CROSS CHOP	EXPLOSION
BAD DREAMS	ICE BODY	RAIN DISH	TRUANT	BIDE	CROSS POISON	EXTRASENSORY
BATTLE ARMOR	ILLUMINATE	RATTLED	TURBOBLAZE	BIND	CRUNCH	EXTREMESPEED
BIG PECKS	ILLUSION	RECKLESS	UNAWARE	BITE	CRUSH CLAW	FACADE
BLAZE	IMMUNITY	REGENERATOR	UNBURDEN	BLAST BURN	CRUSH GRIP	FAINT ATTACK
BUG	IMPOSTER	RIVALRY	UNNERVE	BLAZE KICK	CURSE	FAKE OUT
CHLOROPHYLL	INFILTRATOR	ROCK	VICTORY STAR	BLIZZARD	CUT	FAKE TEARS
CLEAR BODY	INNER FOCUS	ROCK HEAD	VITAL SPIRIT	BLOCK	DARK PULSE	FALSE SWIPE
CLOUD NINE	INSOMNIA	ROUGH SKIN	VOLT ABSORB	BLUE FLARE	DARK VOID	FEATHERDANCE
COLOR CHANGE	INTIMIDATE	RUN AWAY	WATER	BODY SLAM	DEFEND ORDER	FEINT
COMPOUNDEYES	IRON BARBS	SAND FORCE	WATER ABSORB	BOLT STRIKE	DEFENSE CURL	FIERY DANCE
CONTRARY	IRON FIST	SAND RUSH	WATER VEIL	BONE CLUB	DEFOG	FINAL GAMBIT
CURSED BODY	JUSTIFIED	SAND STREAM	WEAK ARMOR	BONE RUSH	DESTINY BOND	FIRE BLAST
CUTE CHARM	KEEN EYE	SAND VEIL	WHITE SMOKE	BONEMERANG	DETECT	FIRE FANG
DAMP	KLUTZ	SAP SIPPER	WONDER GUARD	BOUNCE	DIG	FIRE PLEDGE
DARK	LEAF GUARD	SCRAPPY	WONDER SKIN	BRAVE BIRD	DISABLE	FIRE PUNCH
DEFEATIST	LEVITATE	SERENE GRACE	ZEN MODE	BRICK BREAK	DISCHARGE	FIRE SPIN
DEFIANT	LIGHT METAL	SHADOW TAG		BRINE	DIVE	FISSURE
DOWNLOAD	LIGHTNINGROD	SHED SKIN	**MOVE**	BUBBLE	DIZZY PUNCH	FLAIL
DRAGON	LIMBER	SHEER FORCE	ABSORB	BUBBLEBEAM	DOOM DESIRE	FLAME BURST
DRIZZLE	LIQUID OOZE	SHELL ARMOR	ACID	BUG BITE	DOUBLE HIT	FLAME CHARGE
DROUGHT	MAGIC BOUNCE	SHIELD DUST	ACID ARMOR	BUG BUZZ	DOUBLE KICK	FLAME WHEEL
DRY SKIN	MAGIC GUARD	SIMPLE	ACID SPRAY	BULK UP	DOUBLE TEAM	FLAMETHROWER
EARLY BIRD	MAGMA ARMOR	SKILL LINK	ACROBATICS	BULLDOZE	DOUBLE-EDGE	FLARE BLITZ
EFFECT SPORE	MAGNET PULL	SLOW START	ACUPRESSURE	BULLET PUNCH	DOUBLESLAP	FLASH
ELECTRIC	MARVEL SCALE	SNIPER	AERIAL ACE	BULLET SEED	DRACO METEOR	FLASH CANNON
FIGHTING	MINUS	SNOW CLOAK	AEROBLAST	CALM MIND	DRAGON CLAW	FLATTER
FILTER	MOLD BREAKER	SNOW WARNING	AFTER YOU	CAMOUFLAGE	DRAGON DANCE	FLING
FIRE	MOODY	SOLAR POWER	AGILITY	CAPTIVATE	DRAGON PULSE	FLY
FLAME BODY	MOTOR DRIVE	SOLID ROCK	AIR CUTTER	CHARGE	DRAGON RAGE	FOCUS BLAST
FLARE BOOST	MOXIE	SOUNDPROOF	AIR SLASH	CHARGE BEAM	DRAGON RUSH	FOCUS ENERGY
FLASH FIRE	MULTISCALE	SPEED BOOST	ALLY SWITCH	CHARM	DRAGON TAIL	FOCUS PUNCH
FLOWER GIFT	MULTITYPE	STALL	AMNESIA	CHATTER	DRAGONBREATH	FOLLOW ME
FLYING	MUMMY	STATIC	ANCIENTPOWER	CHIP AWAY	DRAIN PUNCH	FORCE PALM
FORECAST	NATURAL CURE	STEADFAST	AQUA JET	CHIT-CHAT	DREAM EATER	FORESIGHT
FOREWARN	NO GUARD	STEEL	AQUA RING	CIRCLE THROW	DRILL PECK	FOUL PLAY
FRIEND GUARD	NORMAL	STENCH	AQUA TAIL	CLAMP	DRILL RUN	FRENZY PLANT
FRISK	NORMALIZE	STICKY HOLD	ARM THRUST	CLEAR SMOG	DUAL CHOP	FROST BREATH
GHOST	OBLIVIOUS	STORM DRAIN	AROMATHERAPY	CLOSE COMBAT	DYNAMICPUNCH	FRUSTRATION
GLUTTONY	OVERCOAT	STURDY	ASSIST	COIL	EARTH POWER	FURY ATTACK
GRASS	OVERGROW	SUCTION CUPS	ASSURANCE	COMET PUNCH	EARTHQUAKE	FURY CUTTER
GROUND	OWN TEMPO	SUPER LUCK	ASTONISH	CONFUSE RAY	ECHOED VOICE	FURY SWIPES
GUTS	PICKPOCKET	SWARM	ATTACK ORDER	CONFUSION	EGG BOMB	FUSION BOLT
HARVEST	PICKUP	SWIFT SWIM	ATTRACT	CONSTRICT	ELECTRO BALL	FUSION FLARE
HEALER	PLUS	SYNCHRONIZE	AURA SPHERE	CONVERSION	ELECTROWEB	FUTURE SIGHT
HEATPROOF	POISON	TANGLED FEET	AURORA BEAM	CONVERSION 2	EMBARGO	GASTRO ACID
	POISON HEAL	TECHNICIAN	AUTOTOMIZE	COPYCAT	EMBER	GEAR GRIND

GIGA DRAIN	ICE PUNCH	METEOR MASH	PRESENT	SAND-ATTACK	SPIKE CANNON	THUNDERSHOCK
GIGA IMPACT	ICE SHARD	METRONOME	PROTECT	SANDSTORM	SPIKES	TICKLE
GLACIATE	ICICLE CRASH	MILK DRINK	PSYBEAM	SCALD	SPIT UP	TORMENT
GLARE	ICICLE SPEAR	MIMIC	PSYCH UP	SCARY FACE	SPITE	TOXIC
GRASS KNOT	ICY WIND	MIND READER	PSYCHIC	SCRATCH	SPLASH	TOXIC SPIKES
GRASS PLEDGE	IMPRISON	MINIMIZE	PSYCHO BOOST	SCREECH	SPORE	TRANSFORM
GRASSWHISTLE	INCINERATE	MIRACLE EYE	PSYCHO CUT	SEARING SHOT	STEALTH ROCK	TRI ATTACK
GRAVITY	INFERNO	MIRROR COAT	PSYCHO SHIFT	SECRET POWER	STEAMROLLER	TRICK
GROWL	INGRAIN	MIRROR MOVE	PSYSHOCK	SEED BOMB	STEEL WING	TRICK ROOM
GROWTH	IRON DEFENSE	MIRROR SHOT	PSYSTRIKE	SEED FLARE	STOCKPILE	TRIPLE KICK
GRUDGE	IRON HEAD	MIST	PSYWAVE	SEISMIC TOSS	STOMP	TRUMP CARD
GUARD SPLIT	IRON TAIL	MIST BALL	PUNISHMENT	SELFDESTRUCT	STONE EDGE	TWINEEDLE
GUARD SWAP	JUDGMENT	MOONLIGHT	PURSUIT	SHADOW BALL	STORED POWER	TWISTER
GUILLOTINE	JUMP KICK	MORNING SUN	QUASH	SHADOW CLAW	STORM THROW	UPROAR
GUNK SHOT	KARATE CHOP	MUD BOMB	QUICK ATTACK	SHADOW FORCE	STRENGTH	U-TURN
GUST	KINESIS	MUD SHOT	QUICK GUARD	SHADOW PUNCH	STRING SHOT	VACUUM WAVE
GYRO BALL	KNOCK OFF	MUD SPORT	QUIVER DANCE	SHADOW SNEAK	STRUGGLE	VENOSHOCK
HAIL	LAST RESORT	MUDDY WATER	RAGE	SHARPEN	STRUGGLE BUG	VICEGRIP
HAMMER ARM	LAVA PLUME	MUD-SLAP	RAGE POWDER	SHEER COLD	STUN SPORE	VINE WHIP
HARDEN	LEAF BLADE	NASTY PLOT	RAIN DANCE	SHELL SMASH	SUBMISSION	VITAL THROW
HAZE	LEAF STORM	NATURAL GIFT	RAPID SPIN	SHIFT GEAR	SUBSTITUTE	VOLT SWITCH
HEAD CHARGE	LEAF TORNADO	NATURE POWER	RAZOR LEAF	SHOCK WAVE	SUCKER PUNCH	VOLT TACKLE
HEAD SMASH	LEECH LIFE	NEEDLE ARM	RAZOR SHELL	SIGNAL BEAM	SUNNY DAY	WAKE-UP SLAP
HEADBUTT	LEECH SEED	NIGHT DAZE	RAZOR WIND	SILVER WIND	SUPER FANG	WATER GUN
HEAL BELL	LEER	NIGHT SHADE	RECOVER	SIMPLE BEAM	SUPERPOWER	WATER PLEDGE
HEAL BLOCK	LICK	NIGHT SLASH	RECYCLE	SING	SUPERSONIC	WATER PULSE
HEAL ORDER	LIGHT SCREEN	NIGHTMARE	REFLECT	SKETCH	SURF	WATER SPORT
HEAL PULSE	LOCK-ON	OCTAZOOKA	REFLECT TYPE	SKILL SWAP	SWAGGER	WATER SPOUT
HEALING WISH	LOVELY KISS	ODOR SLEUTH	REFRESH	SKULL BASH	SWALLOW	WATERFALL
HEART STAMP	LOW KICK	OMINOUS WIND	REST	SKY ATTACK	SWEET KISS	WEATHER BALL
HEART SWAP	LOW SWEEP	OUTRAGE	RETALIATE	SKY DROP	SWEET SCENT	WHIRLPOOL
HEAT CRASH	LUCKY CHANT	OVERHEAT	RETURN	SKY UPPERCUT	SWIFT	WHIRLWIND
HEAT WAVE	LUNAR DANCE	PAIN SPLIT	REVENGE	SLACK OFF	SWITCHEROO	WIDE GUARD
HEAVY SLAM	LUSTER PURGE	PAY DAY	REVERSAL	SLAM	SWORDS DANCE	WILD CHARGE
HELPING HAND	MACH PUNCH	PAYBACK	ROAR	SLASH	SYNCHRONOISE	WILL-O-WISP
HEX	MAGIC COAT	PECK	ROAR OF TIME	SLEEP POWDER	SYNTHESIS	WING ATTACK
HI JUMP KICK	MAGIC ROOM	PERISH SONG	ROCK BLAST	SLEEP TALK	TACKLE	WISH
HIDDEN POWER	MAGICAL LEAF	PETAL DANCE	ROCK CLIMB	SLUDGE	TAIL GLOW	WITHDRAW
HONE CLAWS	MAGMA STORM	PIN MISSILE	ROCK POLISH	SLUDGE BOMB	TAIL SLAP	WONDER ROOM
HORN ATTACK	MAGNET BOMB	PLUCK	ROCK SLIDE	SLUDGE WAVE	TAIL WHIP	WOOD HAMMER
HORN DRILL	MAGNET RISE	POISON FANG	ROCK SMASH	SMACK DOWN	TAILWIND	WORK UP
HORN LEECH	MAGNITUDE	POISON GAS	ROCK THROW	SMELLINGSALT	TAKE DOWN	WORRY SEED
HOWL	ME FIRST	POISON JAB	ROCK TOMB	SMOG	TAUNT	WRAP
HURRICANE	MEAN LOOK	POISON STING	ROCK WRECKER	SMOKESCREEN	TEETER DANCE	WRING OUT
HYDRO CANNON	MEDITATE	POISON TAIL	ROLE PLAY	SNATCH	TELEKINESIS	X-SCISSOR
HYDRO PUMP	MEGA DRAIN	POISONPOWDER	ROLLING KICK	SNORE	TELEPORT	YAWN
HYPER BEAM	MEGA KICK	POUND	ROLLOUT	SOAK	THIEF	ZAP CANNON
HYPER FANG	MEGA PUNCH	POWDER SNOW	ROOST	SOFTBOILED	THRASH	ZEN HEADBUTT
HYPER VOICE	MEGAHORN	POWER GEM	ROUND	SOLARBEAM	THUNDER	
HYPNOSIS	MEMENTO	POWER SPLIT	SACRED FIRE	SONICBOOM	THUNDER FANG	
ICE BALL	METAL BURST	POWER SWAP	SACRED SWORD	SPACIAL REND	THUNDER WAVE	
ICE BEAM	METAL CLAW	POWER TRICK	SAFEGUARD	SPARK	THUNDERBOLT	
ICE FANG	METAL SOUND	POWER WHIP	SAND TOMB	SPIDER WEB	THUNDERPUNCH	

TRAINER

ACE CARD
ATTACK
BAD MATCHUP
BATTLE
CHALLENGE
CHAMPION
COME ON
COURAGE
CRITICAL HIT
EASY
EASY WIN
EMERGENCY
FIGHT
FIGHTS
FOE
GENIUS
GOOD MATCHUP
INVINCIBLE
LEGEND
LOSS
MATCH
MATCH UP
MOVE
NO. 1
NO EFFECT
NO MATCH
PARTNER
POINTS
POWER
PREPARATION
REVIVE
SENSE
SERIOUS
SPIRIT
STRATEGY
STRONG
SURRENDER
TAKE IT EASY
TALENT
TRAINER
VERSUS
VICTORY
WEAK
WINS

CONNECTION

BATTLE VIDEOS
CHAT
COLOSSEUM
CONNECTION
DOUBLE
ENTRALINK

FRIEND CODE

GAME SYNC
GEONET
GTS
INFRARED
MULTI BATTLE
MUSICAL
PGL
POKÉMON DW
POKÉ TRANSFER
ROTATION
SINGLE
SPIN
SUBWAY
TAG LOG
TRIPLE
UNION
VOICE CHAT
Wi-Fi
WIRELESS

GREETINGS

...
BYE-BYE
BYE FOR NOW
CHEERS
EXCUSE ME
FORGIVE ME
GIVE ME
GO AHEAD
GOOD-BYE
GREETINGS
HELLO?
HELLO
HERE GOES
HERE I COME
HI
HI THERE
I'M SORRY
I'VE ARRIVED
LET'S GO
MEET YOU
NO
NOPE
NO PROBLEM
NO WAY
OK THEN
PARDON ME
REGARDS
SEE YA
SORRY
SO SORRY
THANKS

THANK YOU

WELCOME
WELL DONE
WHAT'S UP?
YAHOO
YEAH, YEAH
YEP
YES
YO

VOICE

AAH
AGREE
AHAHA
AIYEEH
ANGRY
BLUSH
BOO!
BOO-HOO
CRIES
CUTE LAUGH
EEK
EH?
GIGGLE
GWAHAHAHA
HAHAHA
HEEEY
HEH
HEHEHE
HE-HE-HE
HEY!
HEY
HEY?
HIYAH
HMM
HOHOHO
HUH?
HUMPH
LALALA
LET ME THINK
LOL
MMM
MUFUFU
MUHAHAHA
OH, DEAR
OH MY
OH WELL
OH WOW!
OH, YEAH
OK
OOPS
ROOOAAR!
SIGH

SNICKER

SNORT
THERE YOU GO
TUT
UGH
UNBELIEVABLE
URGH
WAHAHA
WAIL
WEEP
WHOA
WOW
YAAAH
YAY
YEAH

PEOPLE

ADULT
ALLY
AUNT
BABY
BOY
BROTHER
EVERYONE
FAMILY
FATHER
FRIEND
GAL
GIRL
GRANDFATHER
GRANDMOTHER
HER
HIM
I
KIDS
ME
MOTHER
MR.
MS.
MYSELF
OLD MAN
OPPONENT
PARENT
PERSON
RIVAL
SIBLINGS
SISTER
UNCLE
WHO
YOU

LIFESTYLE

ADVENTURE
ANIME
ANNIVERSARY
AUTUMN
BALL
BATH
BICYCLE
BIRTHDAY
BOARD
BOOK
CAMERA
CARDS
CHANNEL
CHIT-CHAT
CLASS
COMICS
COMPUTER
CONVERSATION
CRAZE
DAILY LIFE
DANCE
DATE
DEPT. STORE
DIET
DREAM
EVENT
FAIRGROUND
FASHION
FESTIVAL
FISHING
FLOWERS
GAME
GOURMET
GYM
HABIT
HERO
HEROINE
HOBBY
HOLIDAY
HOME
IDOL
INFORMATION
ITEM
JOB
KINDERGARTEN
LESSONS
LETTER
LIFE
LOOKS
MACHINE
MAGAZINE

MONEY

MOVIE
MUSIC
NAME
NAP
NEWS
PARTY
PHONE
PLANS
PLAY HOUSE
PLAYING
POCKET MONEY
POPULARITY
PROMISE
RADIO
SCHOOL
SCIENCE
SERVICE
SHOP
SHOPPING
SOFTWARE
SONG
SONGS
SPECTATE
SPORTS
SPRING
STORE
STORY
STUDY
STUFFED TOY
SUMMER
SWEETS
TALK
TEACHER
TELEVISION
TEST
TODAY
TOMORROW
TOURNAMENT
TOYS
TRAIN
TRAINING
TRAVEL
TREASURE
VACATION
VIEWING
WALK
WINTER
WORD
WORK
WORLD
YESTERDAY

FEELINGS

ADORE
ALL RIGHT
ANGER
ANTICIPATION
BEAUTY
BORED
CLEVERNESS
COOLNESS
CUTENESS
DANGER
DELIGHT
DEPRESSED
DIFFICULT
DISAPPOINTED
DISLIKE
DROOLING
ENERGETIC
ENJOYMENT
EXCITED
HAPPINESS
HAPPY
HATE
HEALTHY
IMPORTANT
INCREDIBLE
LIKES
LOVEY-DOVEY
MESSED UP
NERVOUS
NICE
NO WAY
RARE
RECOMMEND
REGRET
ROFL
SADNESS
SATISFIED
SIMPLE
SKILLFUL
SMILE
STRANGENESS
SUBTLE
SURPRISE
TEARS
TOUGHNESS
USELESS
WANT

TERM				ANIMATED	INTERNATIONAL GREETINGS

TERM	DOWSING	MISSION
BADGE	ELEGANT	NATURE
BATTLE BOX	ENTREE	PASS ORB
BATTLE TEST	GOTCHA	PASS POWER
C-GEAR	GROUP	PKMN CENTER
COLLECTION	HALL OF FAME	POKÉMON
COMPLETE	INSTITUTE	RENTAL
COOL	LAUNCHER	SYSTEM
CUTE	LEVEL	TM
DESIGN	MAIL	TOWN MAP
DIGITAL	MESSAGE	UNIQUE

ANIMATED

GOOD DAY!
HELLO!
I LOVE IT
IT'S FUN
GOOD LUCK!
HAPPY!
THANK YOU!
SUPER!!
SORRY ...
BYE-BYE!

INTERNATIONAL GREETINGS

BONJOUR
CIAO
HALLO
HELLO
HOLA
안녕하세요
こんにちは

 Prepared Sentences

Column 1 (Mail)

Hello!
[·····]!

I am [·····]!
I'm pleased to meet you.

I love [·····]!
I love [·····], too!

My favorite [·····] is
[·····]!

What's your favorite
[·····]?

I can do anything for
[·····]!

Is [·····]
[·····]?

What do you think of
[·····]?

Do you think [·····]
can [·····]?

[·····] is so
[·····]!

[·····] bothers me.

After all, it's [·····],
isn't it?

[·····] is the real
[·····]!

Did you know that [·····]
is [·····]?

[·····] is the reason
for [·····].

Have you heard of
[·····]?

[·····] is actually
[·····].

Recently, [·····]
seems [·····].

I wonder if
[·····] is yummy...

I never miss [·····].
It's part of what I do every day.

Column 2

Please!
[·····]!

Go! [·····]!

I'll battle with
[·····]!

[·····] is
[·····], right?

[·····], I'm going
with [·····]!

In comes [·····].

Watch my [·····] power
take care of [·····]!

Now [·····]
begins!

I'll show you my
[·····] strategy!

I'll shock you with
[·····]!

[·····], I see...
Go, [·····]!

Ta-da!
Here comes [·····]!

I don't think I'll
ever lose to [·····]!

[·····]!
[·····] is here!

Good luck,
[·····]!

Behold my [·····]
[·····]!

The power of [·····]!
Let me show you!

You'll choose [·····]
if I choose [·····], right?

I beg you, [·····].
Please go with [·····]!

May [·····] safely
land on [·····]!

Column 3

I win!
[·····]!

I owe my victory
to [·····]!

[·····] is strong,
isn't it?

It's [·····]
[·····] after all!

When it comes to [·····],
my choice is always [·····]!

Victory in a
[·····] battle!

Yay, [·····]!
[·····]!

Sorry, it's [·····]
[·····].

[·····]!
Thank you!

The way I feel now is
[·····]!

[·····] sure is
[·····]!

It's all thanks to
[·····].

[·····] is the toughest!

[·····]?
Wow, I'm so glad!

[·····]?
That sounds good!

I have no trouble
dealing with [·····].

[·····] is so much fun.

Huh?
[·····]?!

The power of [·····]
is awesome!

Everyone!
[·····]!

Column 4

You win...
[·····]!

[·····] is
really impressive.

Waaah! [·····]!

I want to go home with
[·····]...

[·····]!
[·····]!

I see [·····]
right in front of me!

[·····]?
I didn't see that coming!

I was confident about
[·····], too.

You're [·····],
aren't you?

[·····]!
Can't be anything else but.

I want to be like [·····]!

It might be
[·····] already...

I think [·····]
should do.

The way I feel now is
[·····]...

[·····] won't work!

Nothing beats [·····]!

My head's filled with only
[·····] now!

Is it because [·····]
was lacking?

Isn't [·····]
[·····]?

Aww... That's really
[·····]...

Column 5 (Wireless)

Yo!
I'm [·····].

Glad to meet you!
I love [·····]!

Do you like [·····]?

Let's draw! I want to draw
[·····]!

Let's battle!
I say [·····]!

I'm a [·····] Trainer!
Please battle me!

Let's have a chat!
How about [·····]?

Please trade!
I want a [·····]!

Please trade!
I'm offering [·····]!

Want to do a [·····] trade?
Here's a hint: [·····]!

Will you join me
for [·····]?

Anyone want to
[·····]?

I want to [·····]
with [·····]!

Let's go to [·····]
by [·····]!

OK!

[·····]?
I got it!

[·····]?
Hold on!

I don't want to
[·····]...

That was fun! I hope we can
[·····] again sometime.

See ya!
[·····]!

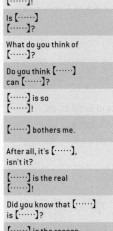

55

How to Use This Section

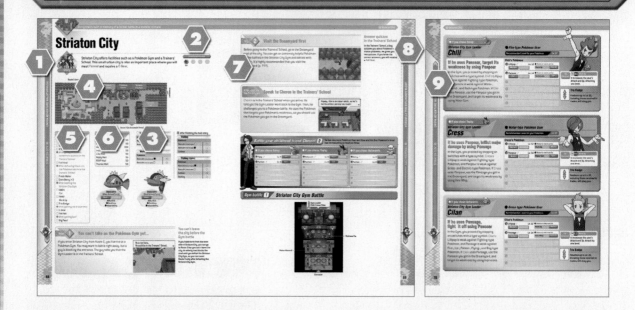

1 Story

A summary of the area's key features and story events.

2 Field Moves Needed

Check these icons to see what moves you need to access every area on the map and collect all the items.

Flash	Cut	Strength	Surf	Waterfall	Dive

3 Pokémon

These charts list the wild Pokémon appearing in the area during different seasons and so on.

Pokémon Encounter Rate

◎	Frequent	○	Average
△	Rare	▲	Almost never

Version Differences

■	Only appears in *Pokémon Black Version*
□	Only appears in *Pokémon White Version*

4 Item Locations

A Poké Ball symbol indicates where you can find an item.

5 Items

All the items found in the area, plus any special requirements for finding them.

6 Poké Mart

All the items you can buy from the lower clerk at the Poké Mart in a Pokémon Center.

7 Completion Guide

Step-by-step description of key events and what to do in order to complete all the events at that location. Use this in combination with the Recommended Route chart (p. 9).

8 Spotlight

Highlights other things you should know about the location.

9 Gym Battle

Information you'll want to know when taking on the local Gym: any special features, the Gym Leader's preferred Pokémon type, and other tips for victory.

The Unova Adventure Walkthrough is based on *Pokémon Black Version*, but all information on *Pokémon White Version* is also included.

Unova Adventure Walkthrough

Nuvema Town

Nuvema Town is the quiet town where you live. Professor Juniper, who researches Pokémon origins, also lives in the town. You will receive your first Pokémon from Professor Juniper and begin your adventurous journey.

Field Moves Needed

Items

- ● First visit
- ☐ Pokédex
- ☐ Town Map
- ☐ Xtransceiver
- ● When your Pokédex's SEEN number is 25 or more
- ☐ TM54 False Swipe
- ● When your Pokédex's SEEN number is 60 or more
- ☐ TM17 Protect
- ● When your Pokédex's SEEN number is 115 or more
- ☐ TM10 Hidden Power
- ● After finishing the main story
- ☐ Super Rod

Professor Juniper

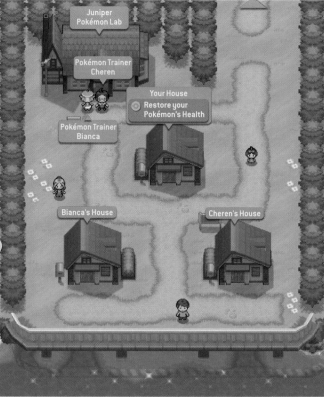

Route 1 (to Accumula Town)

- Juniper Pokémon Lab
- Pokémon Trainer Cheren
- Your House
  ● Restore your Pokémon's Health
- Pokémon Trainer Bianca
- Bianca's House
- Cheren's House

Step 1 **Open the present from Professor Juniper**

Cheren has come to your room after hearing a rumor that a present from Professor Juniper was delivered to your house. Bianca also drops by your room a moment later. Pick the starter Pokémon you want.

Pokémon type matchups

Types and moves are connected in Pokémon. Bianca will start with a Pokémon whose type is weak against your starter Pokémon, and Cheren will start with a Pokémon whose type is strong against your starter Pokémon.

● **Choose one of these Pokémon from Professor Juniper**

Snivy Lv. 5
Grass
ABILITY
● Overgrow

Tepig Lv. 5
Fire
ABILITY
● Blaze

Oshawott Lv. 5
Water
ABILITY
● Torrent

Step 2 — First battle with Bianca and Cheren

After you choose your starter Pokémon for your adventure, Bianca and Cheren will ask you to have Pokémon battles. You have to battle both of them in a row, but after you battle with Bianca, your Pokémon will be restored to full health, so battle as hard as you can.

Hey, I know!
Let's have a Pokémon battle!

Different Pokémon will fly away depending on the time

If you leave your house during the day, Pidove will fly away. If you go out after sunset, Woobat will fly away.

Battle your childhood friend Bianca! 1

Your Pokémon and Bianca's Pokémon are both Level 5. There is no difference in power, so don't worry, just fight.

● If you chose Snivy:	● If you chose Tepig:	● If you chose Oshawott:
◎ Oshawott ♂ Lv. 5 Water	◎ Snivy ♂ Lv. 5 Grass	◎ Tepig ♂ Lv. 5 Fire

Battle your childhood friend Cheren! 1

Cheren's Pokémon is also Level 5. It does not yet have moves that target your Pokémon's weakness, so go all out.

● If you chose Snivy:	● If you chose Tepig:	● If you chose Oshawott:
◎ Tepig ♂ Lv. 5 Fire	◎ Oshawott ♂ Lv. 5 Water	◎ Snivy ♂ Lv. 5 Grass

Step 3 — Your mom gives you the Xtransceiver

After your battle with Cheren, he and Bianca go downstairs to apologize to your mom about the mess the three of you made in your room. Talk to your mom, and she will give you the Xtransceiver (cross-transceiver) (p. 42).

Trainer obtained the Xtransceiver!

Xtransceiver

NUVEMA TOWN ◇ — UNOVA ADVENTURE WALKTHROUGH

Step 4 — Watch TV

There is a TV on the first floor in your house. The TV shows different, fun programs depending on the time. You can find TVs in many places, so watch TV when you have a chance (p. 46).

Host: It's time for today's "Personality Assessment and Horoscope"!

You can read Pokémon Basics on the PC in your room

You can read Pokémon Basics checking the PC in your room. If this is your first time playing a Pokémon game, make sure to read it.

Step 5 — Go pick up Bianca

The three of you decide to visit Professor Juniper to thank her for the Pokémon she gave you. Bianca goes back to her house first, so you can go there to pick her up. When you enter Bianca's house, Bianca's dad is angry and dead set against her journey.

I'm a good Trainer who got a Pokémon and everything!

Step 6 — Get a Pokédex from Professor Juniper

When you enter the Juniper Pokémon Lab, Professor Juniper will talk to you. She gives each of you a Pokédex (p. 39) and asks you to set out on a journey to register all Pokémon in the Unova region in the Pokédex.

Trainer obtained the Pokédex!

Pokédex

Step 7 — Get a Town Map from your mom

After you leave the Juniper Pokémon Lab, Bianca and Cheren catch up with you. Your mom is waiting for you in front of the Juniper Pokémon Lab. Your mom seems to know that Professor Juniper asked you three to set out on a journey. Each of you receives a Town Map (p. 42) from your mom.

Trainer obtained the Town Map!

Town Map

Step 8 — Take the first steps of your adventure on Route 1

Professor Juniper asks you to go to Route 1 so she can teach you how to catch Pokémon. Head north of the town with Cheren and Bianca and take your first steps on Route 1.

Let's all take our first step on Route 1 together!

After Pokédex's SEEN number increases — Receive a TM from Professor Juniper

Once the SEEN number of your Pokédex increases, visit Professor Juniper. She will give you a TM. You will get False Swipe if the SEEN number is 25 or more, Protect if it is 60 or more, and Hidden Power if it is 115 or more (p. 45).

Trainer obtained a TM54 False Swipe!

A small road by the shore, where you can enjoy the seascape in peace

Route 1

Story

Tall grass grows on Route 1, and you can catch wild Pokémon in the grass if you have Poké Balls. Catch wild Pokémon and add them to your party for your adventure.

 Field Moves Needed — Surf

Items
First visit
- ☐ Poké Balls ×5
- ☐ Potion

After getting Surf
- ☐ Max Ether
- ☐ Pearl

After defeating Pokémon Ranger Brenda
- ☐ Persim Berry

After defeating Pokémon Ranger Claude
- ☐ Persim Berry

Tall Grass
Pokémon	
Lillipup	◎
Patrat	◎

Tall Grass (rustling)
Pokémon	
Audino	◎

Dark Grass
Pokémon	
Herdier	◎
Scraggy	◎
Watchog	◎

Water Surface
Pokémon	
Basculin (Blue-Striped Form) ☐	◎
Basculin (Red-Striped Form) ■	◎

Water Surface (ripples)
Pokémon	
Basculin (Blue-Striped Form) ■	◎
Basculin (Red-Striped Form) ☐	◎

After finishing the main story

Fishing
Pokémon	
Basculin (Blue-Striped Form) ☐	◎
Basculin (Red-Striped Form) ■	◎
Feebas	△

Fishing (ripples)
Pokémon	
Basculin (Blue-Striped Form) ■	◎
Basculin (Red-Striped Form) ☐	◎
Feebas	◎
Milotic	△

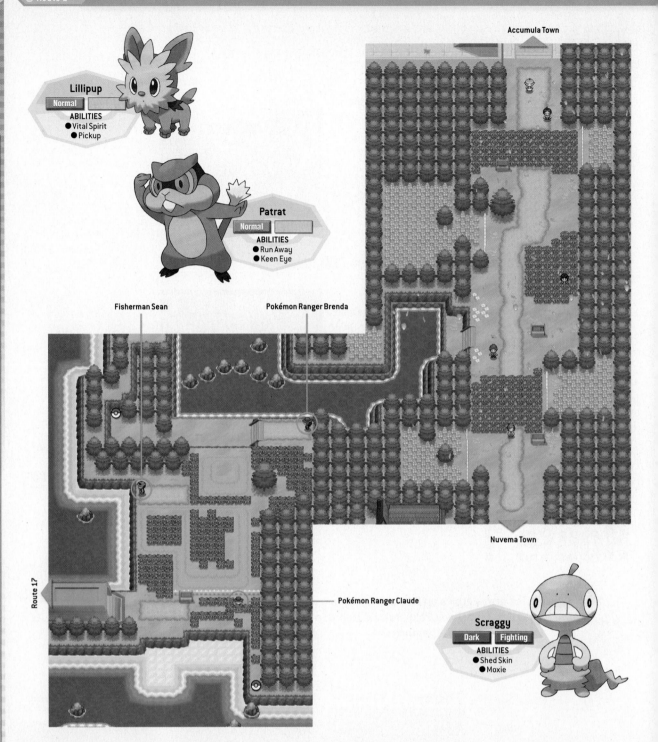

Lillipup
Normal

ABILITIES
● Vital Spirit
● Pickup

Patrat
Normal

ABILITIES
● Run Away
● Keen Eye

Accumula Town

Fisherman Sean

Pokémon Ranger Brenda

Nuvema Town

Route 17

Pokémon Ranger Claude

Scraggy
Dark Fighting

ABILITIES
● Shed Skin
● Moxie

Step **1** **Learn how to catch Pokémon**

Take Route 1 and you'll find Professor Juniper waiting for you. Professor Juniper catches a wild Patrat that was hiding in the tall grass, and she teaches you how to register it in the Pokédex (p. 22).

To make this clear, I'm going to demonstrate how to catch a Pokémon!

Home is where the healing is

When your Pokémon's HP drops from battles with wild Pokémon, go back to your house in Nuvema Town. If you talk to your mom, she restores your Pokémon's health.

Step 2 — Wild Pokémon jump out from tall grass

Bianca and Cheren ask you to compete in a Pokémon hunt using the Poké Balls you got from Professor Juniper. Use the five Poké Balls and catch as many Pokémon as you can.

A wild Patrat appeared!

Listen carefully to changes in the soundtrack

On Route 1, when you walk, the sound of a tambourine will be added to the soundtrack. The sound changes in other places, too, so listen carefully.

Step 3 — Head north to Accumula Town

Go north on Route 1, and your Xtransceiver will ring. It's a call from Professor Juniper. She is waiting in Accumula Town, and she asks you to see her soon. Head north on Route 1 to Accumula Town right away.

Right now, I'm in front of Accumula Town's Pokémon Center!

Let Pokémon hold a Berry

Some Pokémon Trainers give you Berries after Pokémon battles. If you give a Berry to a Pokémon to hold, the Pokémon will use the Berry to restore its HP or heal a status condition.

After getting Surf — Surf and head to Route 17

After receiving HM03 Surf from Alder at Twist Mountain, you can surf on the water. Use Surf at the water's edge on Route 1 and head west on the water. If you go through a gate and move further, you can reach Route 17 (p. 140).

Get Berries by defeating Trainers

After learning Surf, you can travel over the water and then battle with Pokémon Rangers Brenda and Claude. If you defeat them, each one will give you a Persim Berry.

This town offers great views due to its many hills

Accumula Town

Story

You will see Ghetsis of Team Plasma making a speech in favor of Pokémon liberation in Accumula Town. You will also meet a mysterious person, N, whom you will battle many times during your adventure.

Field Moves Needed

Items
☐ Poké Ball

Poké Mart
(Lower Clerk)

Favored Mail	50	Reply Mail	50
Greet Mail	50	RSVP Mail	50
Inquiry Mail	50	Thanks Mail	50
Like Mail	50		

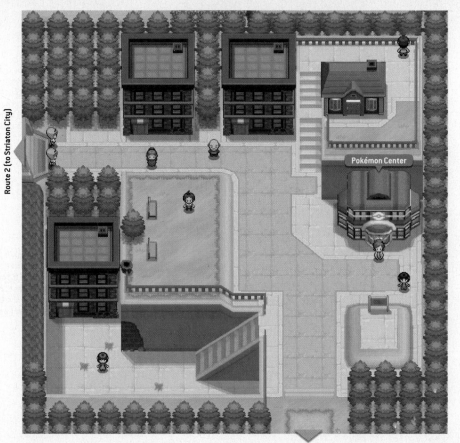

Route 2 (to Striaton City)

Pokémon Center

Route 1 (to Nuvema Town)

Step 1
Professor Juniper guides you

When you arrive in Accumula Town, Professor Juniper is waiting in front of the Pokémon Center. Talk to Professor Juniper. She will tell you how to use a Pokémon Center and a Poké Mart.

Because your Pokémon can be healed! And, what's more, it's absolutely free! ▼

Professor Juniper talks about Fennel

Professor Juniper asks you to meet an inventor named Fennel in Striaton City. Professor Juniper says Fennel is a friend of hers from long ago and will help you on your way.

Step 2
Check the PC

In every Pokémon Center, a PC is available to anyone. Check your PC. You will find Mail from Bianca (p. 45). Make sure you read it.

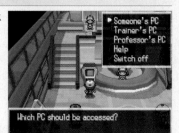

▶ Someone's PC
Trainer's PC
Professor's PC
Help
Switch off

Which PC should be accessed?

The PC has a Battle Box

Open Someone's PC in a Pokémon Center to access your Battle Box. You can keep Pokémon you want to use in battles with friends in this useful box (p. 44).

Step 3 — A speech in the plaza

When you leave the Pokémon Center, you will see a crowd of people in the plaza. Move toward the plaza. The person in the center of the crowd is Ghetsis of Team Plasma. Ghetsis gives a radical speech about liberation of Pokémon from people.

Today, ladies and gentlemen, I would like to talk to you about Pokémon liberation.

Fully prepare for a battle with N

If you head west after leaving the Pokémon Center, you will hear Ghetsis's speech and battle with N after the speech. If you need to train your Pokémon before the battle, return to Route 1 instead of heading west.

Step 4 — A mysterious person named N speaks to you

After Ghetsis, Team Plasma, and the spectators leave, a boy will speak to you. The boy identifies himself as N, and once he learns that you are traveling to complete the Pokédex, he challenges you to a Pokémon battle.

Well, Trainer, is it? Let me hear your Pokémon's voice again!

Go to Route 2 after Ghetsis's speech

Team Plasma Grunts are blocking the gate to Route 2 on the west side of Accumula Town. After Ghetsis's speech, they will disappear.

Battle the mysterious N! 1

N uses just one Purrloin, which is at Level 7. You should have leveled up the Pokémon that Professor Juniper gave you by battling wild Pokémon on Route 1. If you battle calmly, you should win this battle.

● N's Pokémon
Purrloin ♂   Lv. 7   Dark

Step 5 — Listen carefully to the soundtrack

When you enter a house on the north side of the Pokémon Center, you will find a person who plays the piano, and a person who plays drums. Talk to both of them, and the sound of piano and drums will be added to the soundtrack. If you see musicians during your adventure, talk to them to change the soundtrack.

Do you want to listen to my drum?

● Piano   ● Drums

UNOVA ADVENTURE WALKTHROUGH

Step 6 — Check the electric bulletin board in a gate

There is a gate to Route 2 on the west side of Accumula Town. Electric bulletin boards have been installed in the gates. They show important information all the time. If you see an electric bulletin board, take a good look at it (p. 47).

Step 7 — Head west to Route 2

Your next destination is Striaton City. Striaton City has a Pokémon Gym where a Leader awaits. Go through the gate on the west side of Accumula Town and head to Striaton City on Route 2.

Play Pokémon rock-paper-scissors

If you talk to a girl on the second floor in the apartment on the east side of the gate, she will ask you to play Pokémon rock-paper-scissors. You can learn Pokémon type matchups, so play with her (p. 256).

A pastoral road where novice Trainers can challenge one another

Route 2

Story

Route 2 is a short road to connect Accumula Town and Striaton City. On the way to Striaton City, Pokémon Trainers are waiting to challenge you to battles.

 Field Moves Needed — Cut, Strength

Items

- **First visit**
- ☐ Poké Ball
- ☐ Potion ×2
- ☐ Running Shoes
- **After getting Cut**
- ☐ Great Ball
- ☐ Super Potion
- **After getting Strength**
- ☐ Rare Candy

Tall Grass

Pokémon	
Lillipup	○
Patrat	○
Purrloin	○

Tall Grass (rustling)

Pokémon	
Audino	○

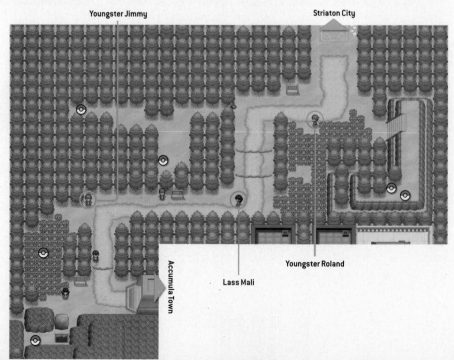

Youngster Jimmy • Striaton City • Youngster Roland • Lass Mali • Accumula Town

Audino

Normal

ABILITIES
● Healer
● Regenerator

Purrloin

Dark

ABILITIES
● Limber
● Unburden

Step 1 — Your mom gives you Running Shoes

When you step onto Route 2, your Xtransceiver will ring, and your mom will visit you. She gives you a pair of Running Shoes. Once you have the shoes, press the B Button to run. It's faster than walking!

Trainer received a pair of Running Shoes!

You can take a shortcut if you cross ledges

When your Pokémon get hurt, retrace your steps and have your Pokémon's health restored in Accumula Town. If you cross the ledges on the road, you can avoid tall grass and move safely.

Step 2 — Battle Pokémon Trainers

Pokémon Trainers who are standing on the road challenge you to battle if you make eye contact. Accept their challenges so you can level up your Pokémon. You'll receive prize money by winning battles, too.

A Trainer catches another Trainer's eye. That is the start of a Pokémon battle!

Walk around to collect items

You can find a lot of useful items for your adventure on roads, in caves, and so on. Walk around and explore those places to collect all the items.

Battle your childhood friend Bianca! 2 She has one more Pokémon than the last time and her first Pokémon's level has increased by two.

● If you chose Snivy:		● If you chose Tepig:		● If you chose Oshawott:	
● Lillipup ♀	Lv. 6 Normal	● Lillipup ♀	Lv. 6 Normal	● Lillipup ♀	Lv. 6 Normal
● Oshawott ♂	Lv. 7 Water	● Snivy ♂	Lv. 7 Grass	● Tepig ♂	Lv. 7 Fire

Step 3 — Head north to Striaton City

After you defeat Bianca in the battle, head north on Route 2. Striaton City, where you'll find the first Pokémon Gym, is very close. Battle wild Pokémon in tall grass to level up your Pokémon before visiting the Gym.

Collect items using HMs

On Route 2, you can pick up items by removing obstacles with HMs such as Cut and Strength. After your Pokémon learn HMs, visit Route 2 again.

Striaton City

Story

Striaton City offers facilities such as a Pokémon Gym and a Trainers' School. This small urban city is also an important place where you will meet Fennel and receive a C-Gear.

Field Moves Needed

Surf

Route 3 (to Nacrene City)

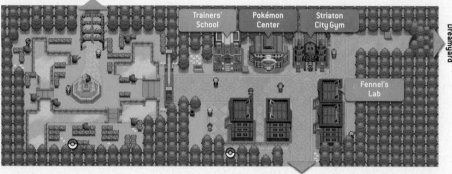

Trainers' School   Pokémon Center   Striaton City Gym   Dreamyard

Fennel's Lab

Route 2 (to Accumula Town)

Items

- ● First visit
- ☐ Dusk Ball
- ☐ Great Ball ×2
- ☐ X Speed
- ● After giving all correct answers to quizzes in the Trainers' School
- ☐ Full Heal
- ● After defeating Cheren in the Pokémon battle in the Trainers' School
- ☐ Fresh Water
- ☐ Oran Berry ×3
- ● After beating the Striaton City Gym
- ☐ HM01 Cut
- ☐ TM83 Work Up
- ☐ Trio Badge
- ● After getting the Dream Mist
- ☐ C-Gear
- ☐ Pal Pad
- ● After getting Surf
- ☐ Big Pearl

Poké Mart
(Lower Clerk)

Favored Mail	50
Greet Mail	50
Inquiry Mail	50
Like Mail	50
Reply Mail	50
RSVP Mail	50
Thanks Mail	50
Heal Ball	300

Water Surface

Pokémon	
Basculin (Blue-Striped Form) ☐	◎
Basculin (Red-Striped Form) ■	◎

Water Surface (ripples)

Pokémon	
Basculin (Blue-Striped Form) ■	◎
Basculin (Red-Striped Form) ☐	◎

Basculin
(Blue-Striped Form)

Water

ABILITIES
- ● Reckless
- ● Adaptability

Basculin
(Red-Striped Form)

Water

ABILITIES
- ● Reckless
- ● Adaptability

■ After finishing the main story

Fishing

Pokémon	
Basculin (Blue-Striped Form) ☐	○
Basculin (Red-Striped Form) ■	○
Goldeen	◎

Fishing (ripples)

Pokémon	
Basculin (Blue-Striped Form) ■	○
Basculin (Red-Striped Form) ☐	○
Goldeen	◎
Seaking	△

Step 1 — You can't take on the Pokémon Gym yet...

If you enter Striaton City from Route 2, you'll arrive at a Pokémon Gym. You may want to battle right away, but a guy is blocking the entrance. The guy tells you that the Gym Leader is in the Trainers' School.

He is not here.
He could be in the Trainers' School.

You can't leave the city before the Gym battle

If you head north from the west side of Striaton City, you can go to Route 3 but you can't leave the city. An elderly man blocks the road until you defeat the Striaton City Gym, so you can travel Route 3 only after defeating the Striaton City Gym.

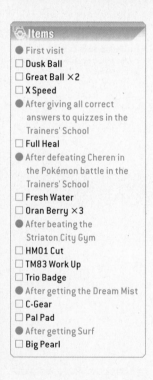

Step 2 — Visit the Dreamyard first

Before going to the Trainers' School, go to the Dreamyard east of the city. You can get an extremely helpful Pokémon for the battles in the Striaton City Gym and battles with Cheren. It's highly recommended that you visit the Dreamyard first (p. 73).

(p. 73)

Answer quizzes in the Trainers' School

In the Trainers' School, a boy quizzes you about Pokémon's status conditions. He gives you two quizzes. If you know the correct answers, you will receive a Full Heal.

After visiting the Dreamyard — Speak to Cheren in the Trainers' School

Cheren is in the Trainers' School when you arrive. He tells you the Gym Leader went back to the Gym. Then, he challenges you to a Pokémon battle. He uses the Pokémon that targets your Pokémon's weakness, so you should use the Pokémon you got in the Dreamyard.

Anyway, this is an indoor match, so let's battle without getting too rough!

Battle your childhood friend Cheren! 2

He has one more Pokémon than last time and his first Pokémon's level has increased by three.

● If you chose Snivy:

❂ Tepig ♂	Lv. 8	Fire
❂ Purrloin ♂	Lv. 8	Dark

● If you chose Tepig:

❂ Oshawott ♂	Lv. 8	Water
❂ Purrloin ♂	Lv. 8	Dark

● If you chose Oshawott:

❂ Snivy ♂	Lv. 8	Grass
❂ Purrloin ♂	Lv. 8	Dark

Gym battle 1 — Striaton City Gym Battle

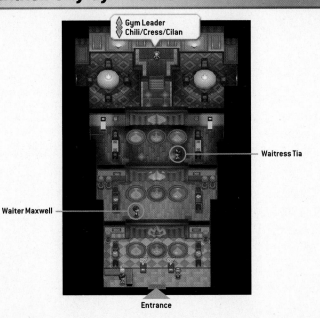

Gym Leader Chili/Cress/Cilan

Waitress Tia

Waiter Maxwell

Entrance

If you chose Snivy:
Striaton City Gym Leader
Chili

● **Fire-type Pokémon User**

| Recommended Level for your Pokémon | Lv. 17 |

If he uses Pansear, target its weakness by using Panpour

In the Gym, you proceed by stepping on switches with a type symbol. Chili's Lillipup is weak against Fighting-type Pokémon, and Pansear is weak against Water-, Ground-, and Rock-type Pokémon. If Chili uses Pansear, use the Panpour you got in the Dreamyard, and target its weakness by using Water Gun.

Chili's Pokémon

Pokémon	Lv.	Moves to watch out for:
◎ Lillipup ♂ (Normal)	Lv. 12	Work Up (Normal)
◎ Pansear ♂ (Fire)	Lv. 14	Incinerate (Fire)

TM Received — **TM 83 Work Up**
It increases the user's Attack and Sp. Attack by one level.

Trio Badge
Pokémon up to Lv. 20, including those received in trades, will obey you.

If you chose Tepig:
Striaton City Gym Leader
Cress

● **Water-type Pokémon User**

| Recommended Level for your Pokémon | Lv. 17 |

If he uses Panpour, inflict major damage by using Pansage

In the Gym, you proceed by stepping on switches with a type symbol. Cress's Lillipup is weak against Fighting-type Pokémon, and Panpour is weak against Grass- and Electric-type Pokémon. If Cress uses Panpour, use the Pansage you got in the Dreamyard, and target its weakness by using Vine Whip.

Cress's Pokémon

Pokémon	Lv.	Moves to watch out for:
◎ Lillipup ♂ (Normal)	Lv. 12	Work Up (Normal)
◎ Panpour ♂ (Water)	Lv. 14	Water Gun (Water)

TM Received — **TM 83 Work Up**
It increases the user's Attack and Sp. Attack by one level.

Trio Badge
Pokémon up to Lv. 20, including those received in trades, will obey you.

If you chose Oshawott:
Striaton City Gym Leader
Cilan

● **Grass-type Pokémon User**

| Recommended Level for your Pokémon | Lv. 17 |

If he uses Pansage, fight it off using Pansear

In the Gym, you proceed by stepping on switches with a type symbol. Cilan's Lillipup is weak against Fighting-type Pokémon, and Pansage is weak against Fire-, Ice-, Poison-, Flying-, and Bug-type Pokémon. If Cilan uses Pansage, use the Pansear you got in the Dreamyard, and target its weakness by using Incinerate.

Cilan's Pokémon

Pokémon	Lv.	Moves to watch out for:
◎ Lillipup ♂ (Normal)	Lv. 12	Work Up (Normal)
◎ Pansage ♂ (Grass)	Lv. 14	Vine Whip (Grass)

TM Received — **TM 83 Work Up**
It increases the user's Attack and Sp. Attack by one level.

Trio Badge
Pokémon up to Lv. 20, including those received in trades, will obey you.

Use TMs as much as you like

After beating the Striaton City Gym

TMs are useful items to teach moves to Pokémon just by using them. You'll get your first one when you win the Striaton City Gym battle. You can use them as often as you want, so teach moves to your Pokémon by using TMs.

Fennel gives you HM01 Cut

After beating the Striaton City Gym

When you leave the Striaton City Gym after defeating the Gym, Fennel is waiting for you. When you go to Fennel's Lab, she will give you HM01 Cut. Now you can cut trees in fields (p. 27).

Collect items by using Cut

By using HM Cut, you can go to a place on Route 2 you couldn't reach before and can get items (p. 66). Once you've received Cut, go back to Route 2 and pick up two items.

Go to the Dreamyard at Fennel's request

After beating the Striaton City Gym

Fennel asks you to bring her some Dream Mist from Munna in the Dreamyard. If she has it, she can collect saved data from Trainers. Head east and visit the Dreamyard (p. 73).

Professor Juniper's friend from college

Fennel and Professor Juniper are friends from college. When you said goodbye to Professor Juniper in Accumula Town, she told you about Fennel.

Receive a C-Gear from Fennel

After getting the Dream Mist

Speak to Fennel. She will give you a C-Gear as a token of her appreciation for helping her get the Dream Mist. A C-Gear is a device that lets you use communication features such as infrared, wireless, and online. A C-Gear is displayed on the Touch Screen on a Nintendo DS.

After getting the Dream Mist — Send your saved data through Game Sync

If you access the Pokémon Dream World in the Pokémon Global Link at www.pokemon-gl.com by using Game Sync, you can add Pokémon you can't catch in the game to your party. If you have a PC and a wireless Internet connection, give it a try.

That's right! We can collect save files of Trainers from all over the world!

Check Help on a PC

Help on a PC in a Pokémon Center is a very useful function. You can read about how to use the C-Gear. Also, you can learn about communication features using Infrared Connection and DS Wireless Communications.

After getting the Dream Mist — Amanita gives you a Pal Pad

When you are listening to Fennel, a girl named Amanita approaches you and gives you a Pal Pad. A Pal Pad can issue the Friend Codes necessary for several types of communication features. You can check Friend Codes in your Pal Pad.

Trainer obtained the Pal Pad!

Pal Pad

After getting the Dream Mist — Facilities on the second floor open in all Pokémon Centers

The second floor in the Pokémon Center is now open. On the second floor, you can find Geonet, the Global Terminal, the Pokémon Wi-Fi Club, and the Union Room. You can enjoy playing different features (p. 43).

Go to Wi-Fi Club
Info
Cancel

Would you like to use Nintendo Wi-Fi Connection?

Register in Geonet, too

If you use Geonet, you can register the place where you live on the globe. If you check the globe after a Link Trade through GTS, you can see where the Pokémon came from.

After getting the Dream Mist — Go north on Route 3

The next destination is Nacrene City (p. 82). To reach it, go west through town, head north from the fountain, and then go north on Route 3 (p. 75). Before you leave the city, stop by the Pokémon Center if your team needs healing.

Pick up a pearl after getting Surf

Once you have HM Surf, surf on the pond on the west side of the town. Speak to the man standing there, and he will give you a Big Pearl you can sell at a high price.

UNOVA ADVENTURE WALKTHROUGH

STRIATON CITY

The Dreamyard

Story

The Dreamyard is an old factory site. The plant was closed, and now the ruins are a playground for children. You will visit this place often in the story, and you can visit new sections of the Dreamyard after finishing the main story.

Field Moves Needed

Cut

Youngster Joey

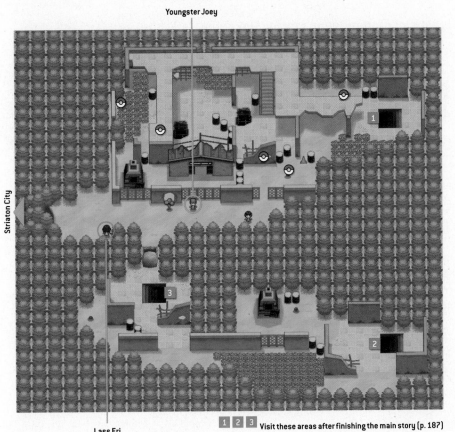

Striaton City

Lass Eri

1 2 3 Visit these areas after finishing the main story (p. 187)

Items

● First visit
□ X Defend
● After getting Cut
□ Parlyz Heal
□ Poké Ball
□ Potion
□ Repel

Tall Grass

Pokémon	
Munna	◎
Patrat	◎
Purrloin	◎

Tall Grass (rustling)

Pokémon	
Audino	◎
Musharna	△

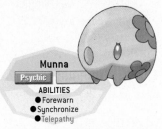

Munna

Psychic

ABILITIES
● Forewarn
● Synchronize
● Telepathy

● Munna with the Hidden Ability Telepathy don't appear in the wild.

Step 1 Battle Trainers to level up your Pokémon

After the first visit to the Dreamyard, you can challenge the Striaton City Gym. Battle the two Pokémon Trainers in the Dreamyard to level up your Pokémon.

Now let's train Pokémon together!

Step 2 — Receive a Pokémon from a girl

Talk to a girl near the factory gate. She will give you a Pokémon. The Pokémon you receive depends on which Pokémon you received from Professor Juniper at the beginning of your adventure. Let it shine in the battles with Cheren and with the Striaton City Gym Leader.

Say, do you want this Panpour of mine?

● Pokémon you can receive depending on your starter Pokémon

● If you chose Tepig:

Pansage Lv. 10

| Grass | |

ABILITY
● Gluttony

● If you chose Snivy:

Panpour Lv. 10

| Water | |

ABILITY
● Gluttony

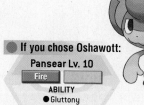

● If you chose Oshawott:

Pansear Lv. 10

| Fire | |

ABILITY
● Gluttony

Step 3 — Go back to Striaton City

There's more to the Dreamyard, though you can't reach these locations yet. Once the girl gives you the Pokémon, head back to Striaton City to battle with Cheren or challenge the Striaton City Gym (p. 69).

After getting Cut — Walk into the back with Bianca

Teach your Pokémon the move Cut using the HM01 Cut you received from Fennel in Striaton City. When you cut the tree and move forward, Bianca shows up. Walk into the back of the Dreamyard with her.

Did you hear a sound coming from the other side of that wall?

Teach your Pokémon Cut

You've just received HM01 Cut from Fennel. At this point, two of the three starter Pokémon can learn the move, as can Pansage, Patrat, and Purrloin. If you started with Tepig, try to catch one of the others.

After getting Cut — Team Plasma bully Munna

When you walk into the back of the Dreamyard, you'll find Munna. When Munna sees you and Bianca, it runs away to the north. Then some Team Plasma Grunts show up. Team Plasma seems to want the Dream Mist, too. Beat the two Team Plasma Grunts who bully Munna.

That's mean! Why? You're Trainers too, right?

After getting Cut — Ghetsis shows up, and Team Plasma Grunts run away

Even after the battles, the Team Plasma Grunts keep trying to bully Munna. Then Ghetsis shows up and scolds the Grunts, and they run away. But this Ghetsis was an illusion created by Musharna!

Ghetsis: What are you two doing goofing off?

After getting Cut — Go back to Striaton City with Fennel

After Team Plasma leaves, Musharna shows up and exits with Munna, leaving the Dream Mist behind. After Fennel shows up and gets the Dream Mist, go back to Striaton City and visit Fennel's Lab (p. 71).

Is this Dream Mist?!

Use the back stairs at the factory after finishing the main story

You can use the stairs at the back of the Dreamyard after finishing the main story. You can get items and battle many Pokémon Trainers there, so make sure to come back.

A long and winding road with lots of ponds and tall grass

Route 3

Story

On Route 3, you'll find a Pokémon Day Care to help you raise Pokémon and a lot of Pokémon Trainers, so you can train your Pokémon. The west side of the road leads to the Wellspring Cave.

Field Moves Needed — Surf

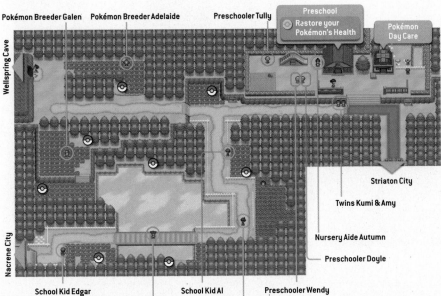

Pokémon Breeder Galen • Pokémon Breeder Adelaide • Preschooler Tully • Preschool Restore your Pokémon's Health • Pokémon Day Care • Wellspring Cave • Striaton City • Twins Kumi & Amy • Nursery Aide Autumn • Preschooler Doyle • Nacrene City • School Kid Edgar • School Kid Gina • School Kid Al • School Kid Marsha • Preschooler Wendy

Items
- ● First visit
- ☐ Repel
- ☐ Super Potion
- ● After defeating Pokémon Breeder Adelaide
- ☐ Oran Berry
- ● After visiting the Wellspring Cave
- ☐ Antidote
- ☐ Awakening
- ☐ Great Ball
- ☐ Heal Ball ×3
- ● After getting Surf
- ☐ Full Heal
- ☐ HP Up
- ☐ Max Ether
- ● After defeating Pokémon Breeder Galen
- ☐ Lum Berry

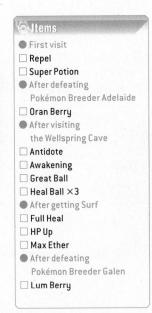

:Tall Grass

Pokémon	
Blitzle	○
Lillipup	△
Patrat	○
Pidove	◎
Purrloin	△

:Tall Grass (rustling)

Pokémon	
Audino	◎

:Dark Grass

Pokémon	
Blitzle	○
Lillipup	△
Patrat	○
Pidove	◎
Purrloin	△

:Water Surface

Pokémon		
Basculin (Blue-Striped Form) □		◎
Basculin (Red-Striped Form) ■		◎

:Water Surface (ripples)

Pokémon		
Basculin (Blue-Striped Form) ■		◎
Basculin (Red-Striped Form) □		◎

■ After finishing the main story

:Fishing

Pokémon		
Basculin (Blue-Striped Form) □		○
Basculin (Red-Striped Form) ■		○
Goldeen		◎

:Fishing (ripples)

Pokémon		
Basculin (Blue-Striped Form) ■		○
Basculin (Red-Striped Form) □		○
Goldeen		◎
Seaking		△

Blitzle
Electric
ABILITIES
● Lightningrod
● Motor Drive

Step 1 — Leave a Pokémon at the Day Care

You can leave a Pokémon (or two) at the Pokémon Day Care and have it raised for you. If you do, go visit them after you enjoy your adventure for a while. The Pokémon will have leveled up. You need money to use the Day Care, but it's convenient. Make good use of the service.

Leaving two Pokémon

At first, you can leave only one Pokémon in the Pokémon Day Care. But once you get a Bicycle in Nimbasa City, you can leave two Pokémon in the Day Care (p. 105). If you leave two Pokémon, a Pokémon Egg may be found there later.

Step 2 — Fight your first Double Battle

Twin Pokémon Trainers stand at the entrance of the Preschool. If you catch their eyes, you'll have a Double Battle with them—your first Double Battle! In a Double Battle, the Pokémon in the first and the second positions in your party participate. Have a strong Pokémon in the second position, too.

Heal your Pokémon in the Preschool

In the Preschool, you can have your Pokémon's health restored. Since you have to battle many Pokémon Trainers in a row on Route 3, if your Pokémon get hurt, have them healed in the Preschool.

Battle your childhood friend Cheren! 3

His first Pokémon's level has increased by six since you had the second battle with him. You may have a difficult battle because he targets your Pokémon's weakness.

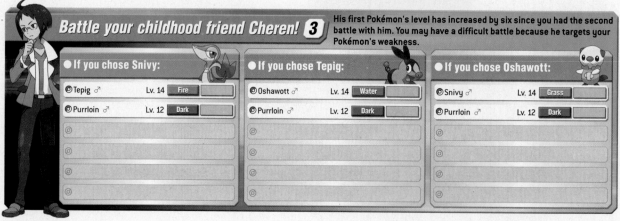

● If you chose Snivy:

◎ Tepig ♂	Lv. 14	Fire
◎ Purrloin ♂	Lv. 12	Dark

● If you chose Tepig:

◎ Oshawott ♂	Lv. 14	Water
◎ Purrloin ♂	Lv. 12	Dark

● If you chose Oshawott:

◎ Snivy ♂	Lv. 14	Grass
◎ Purrloin ♂	Lv. 12	Dark

Step 3 ▶ Chase Team Plasma and head west

After defeating Cheren in the battle, you'll see Team Plasma run away to the west. Then, Bianca and a girl come running after them. It turns out that Team Plasma stole a Pokémon from the girl, and the Grunts are running away. Chase Team Plasma with Cheren.

Step 4 ▶ A special Pokémon in the rustling grass

After you get your first Gym Badge, rustling grass appears. If you step on the rustling grass, you can meet uncommon Pokémon. If you see this special grass, rush into it and catch a Pokémon (p. 28).

A wild Audino appeared!

Step 5 ▶ Go to the Wellspring Cave where Team Plasma fled

If you go to the west side of Route 3, you'll see an entrance into the Wellspring Cave. According to Cheren, the Team Plasma Grunts who stole the girl's Pokémon fled into this cave. Go inside the cave and beat Team Plasma (p. 78).

▶ YES
NO

Trainer, your Pokémon's HP is fine, and you're ready to go, right?

You can't go south at first

If you try to go south to the gate to Nacrene City, you can't because Bianca asks you to get the Pokémon back first. Bianca disappears only after you win against Team Plasma in the Wellspring Cave.

After visiting the Wellspring Cave — Two Pokémon may pop out from darker grass

On Route 3, you will see darker-colored grass. If you encounter wild Pokémon in the dark grass, two Pokémon may appear at the same time—a Double Battle! If you want to catch one of the two Pokémon, you must make the other Pokémon faint first.

Oh! A wild Patrat and Pidove appeared!

Get Berries by defeating Trainers

If you defeat Pokémon Breeder Adelaide, she will give you an Oran Berry. If you defeat Pokémon Breeder Galen after getting Surf, he will give you a Lum Berry. Battle both of them, and collect Berries.

After visiting the Wellspring Cave — Go south to Nacrene City

When you save the girl's Pokémon from Team Plasma, Bianca will leave and you can go to the gate on the west side. Head to the next destination, Nacrene City, defeating Trainers on the way. Go through the gate (p. 82).

Wellspring Cave

Story

The Wellspring Cave is the first cave you visit. The Team Plasma Grunts who fled after stealing the Pokémon are inside the cave. You'll find Pokémon Trainers on B1F, and you can battle with them after getting HM03 Surf.

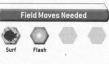

Surf   Flash

■ 1F

Team Plasma Grunt   Team Plasma Grunt   Team Plasma Grunt

Route 3 (to Striaton City)

A

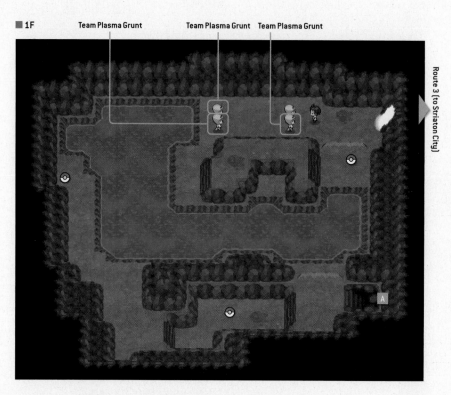

Items

● First visit
☐ TM46 Thief
● After getting Surf
☐ Dive Ball
☐ Elixir
☐ Escape Rope
☐ Mystic Water
☐ TM47 Low Sweep
☐ TM52 Focus Blast

1F • B1F

Cave

Pokémon	
Roggenrola	◎
Woobat	◎

Cave (dust cloud)

Pokémon	
Drilbur	◎

Water Surface

Pokémon	
Basculin (Blue-Striped Form) ■	◎
Basculin (Red-Striped Form) ☐	◎

Water Surface (ripples)

Pokémon	
Basculin (Blue-Striped Form) ■	◎
Basculin (Red-Striped Form) ☐	◎

■ After finishing the main story

Fishing

Pokémon	
Basculin (Blue-Striped Form) ☐	○
Basculin (Red-Striped Form) ■	○
Poliwag	◎
Poliwhirl	△

Fishing (ripples)

Pokémon	
Basculin (Blue-Striped Form) ■	○
Basculin (Red-Striped Form) ☐	○
Poliwhirl	◎
Poliwrath	△

Roggenrola
Rock
ABILITY
● Sturdy

Woobat
Psychic   Flying
ABILITIES
● Unaware
● Klutz

■ B1F

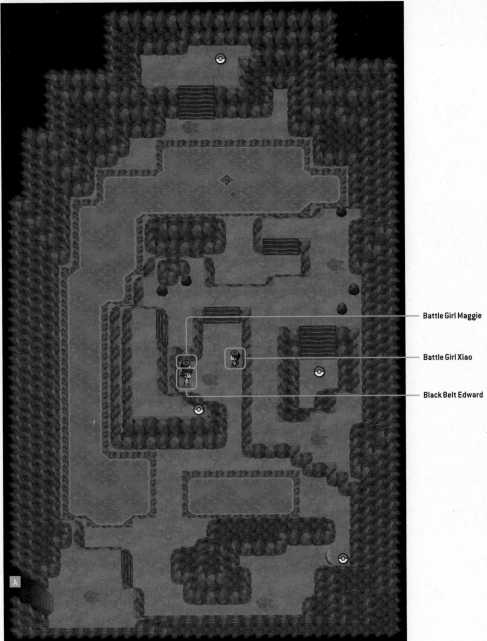

— Battle Girl Maggie

— Battle Girl Xiao

— Black Belt Edward

A

Step 1 Beat the Team Plasma Grunts

When you enter the Wellspring Cave, Cheren and Team Plasma are glaring at each other. The Team Plasma Grunts say the child cannot use a Pokémon to its full potential and challenge you to battle. It's a chance to win the girl's Pokémon back. Beat the Grunts.

Rush to dust clouds

When a dust cloud appears in the Wellspring Cave, you can meet an uncommon Pokémon or get an item. Hurry and step on the dust cloud (p. 28).

Step 2 — Challenge Team Plasma to a Tag Battle

Once a battle has started, Team Plasma Grunts join in and attack you at the same time. Challenge them to a Tag Battle with Cheren. In a Tag Battle you cooperate with an ally and battle using one Pokémon each. When you win the battle, the Grunts return the girl's Pokémon.

We've got each other's back when it counts. Let's show them how it's done!

Step 3 — Get an item and return to Route 3

Your goal in the Wellspring Cave is accomplished once you recover the Pokémon from Team Plasma, but before leaving the cave, you can collect an item. Get TM46 Thief, and go back to Route 3 (p. 77).

After getting Surf — Explore B1F by using Surf

Once you've received HM03 Surf from the Champion Alder at Twist Mountain, teach the move to a Pokémon. Then surf on the water and go to the back of the cave. Go everywhere on 1F and B1F, and collect all the items.

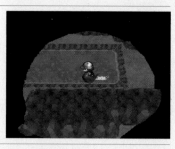

Use Flash

B1F is pitch black and you can't see anything around you. Light the way with Flash. You can get TM70 Flash in Castelia City and teach the move to a Pokémon.

Nacrene City

Story

Nacrene City is a city of artists where storehouses built 100 years ago have been restored. It's also home to Café Warehouse, a stylish café for such a rural area. You'll also visit a museum where Pokémon can be restored from Fossils.

Field Moves Needed

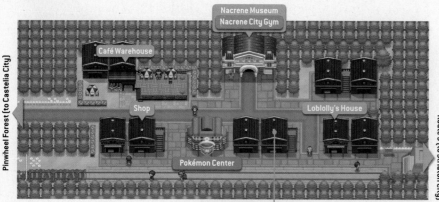

Nacrene Museum
Nacrene City Gym

Café Warehouse

Shop

Loblolly's House

Pinwheel Forest (to Castelia City)

Route 3 (to Striaton City)

Pokémon Center

Pokémon Black Version
Trade: Petilil
(Receive Petilil in exchange for Cottonee)

Pokémon White Version
Trade: Cottonee
(Receive Cottonee in exchange for Petilil)

Items

First visit
- ☐ Chesto Berry ×3
- ☐ Fresh Water
- **If you answered "Snivy" to the woman's question**
- ☐ Miracle Seed
- **If you answered "Tepig" to the woman's question**
- ☐ Charcoal
- **If you answered "Oshawott" to the woman's question**
- ☐ Mystic Water

After defeating the Nacrene City Gym
- ☐ Basic Badge
- ☐ Dowsing MCHN
- ☐ TM67 Retaliate
- **After visiting the Relic Castle**
- ☐ Dark Stone (*Pokémon White Version*)
- ☐ Light Stone (*Pokémon Black Version*)

Poké Mart
(Lower Clerk)

Favored Mail	50
Greet Mail	50
Inquiry Mail	50
Like Mail	50
Reply Mail	50
RSVP Mail	50
Thanks Mail	50
Heal Ball	300
Net Ball	1,000

Shop

X Sp. Def	350
X Special	350
X Speed	350
X Attack	500
X Defend	550
Dire Hit	650
Guard Spec.	700
X Accuracy	950

Step 1 — Cheren shows you the city

If you head west after entering the city, Cheren will talk to you. Cheren leads you to the Pokémon Center. In front of the Pokémon Center, Cheren gives you Chesto Berries and tells you about the Nacrene City Gym Leader.

If you have a Fighting-type Pokémon, it might give you a big advantage.

Meet furniture designer Loblolly

If you tuck in a Pokémon using Game Sync after choosing a piece of furniture that Loblolly talks about, the furniture will be added to a Dream Catalogue in the Pokémon Dream World of the Pokémon Global Link at www.pokemon-gl.com.

Step 2 How strong is your Pokémon friendship?

Speak to a woman in the second house to the right of the Pokémon Center. She will rate your friendship with the Pokémon at the head of your party. Friendship can influence Pokémon evolution, and some Pokémon evolve with high friendship (p. 26).

It's a little bit friendly to you...
Something like that.

Buy items useful for battles

Items for sale at the shop increase a Pokémon's stats by one level in battle, although using one takes up a turn. Use the item depending on your strategy and get an advantage in a battle.

Step 3 Trade Pokémon with a person in the city

Speak to a woman on the second floor in the second house to the right of the Pokémon Center, and she will ask you to trade Pokémon. The Pokémon you give and receive in trade differ between *Pokémon Black Version* and *Pokémon White Version* (p. 150).

▶ YES
NO

Would you like to trade your Cottonee for my Petilil?

Trade with five townspeople

You can trade Pokémon with five people in the Unova region (including places you can visit after finishing the main story). Some trade Pokémon from other regions (p. 150).

 Step 4 Give Pokémon an item

Speak to a woman in the second house to the left of the Pokémon Center. She will give you an item depending on the answer you give. If you answer Snivy, you'll get a Miracle Seed; if you answer Tepig, a Charcoal; and if you answer Oshawott, a Mystic Water.

Trainer obtained a Miracle Seed!

Rock Smash is useful in the Gym battle

Speak to a Battle Girl at the entrance of Pinwheel Forest, and she will give you TM94 Rock Smash. This will be useful in the Nacrene City Gym battle, so it's good to get it first.

 Step 5 Visit Café Warehouse on Wednesdays

Café Warehouse is a stylish café in a rural area that has a special on Wednesdays. Speak to a Waitress, and she will give you a Soda Pop. Soda Pop is an item to restore the HP of one Pokémon by 60 points.

Our café has a special on Wednesdays!
Here, have a Soda Pop!

Enjoy the sound of an accordion

You'll find a man who is playing the accordion at the terrace outside Café Warehouse. If you get closer to him, the sound of the accordion is added to the soundtrack.

● **Accordion**

Step 6 **The second encounter with the mysterious N in front of the Gym**

I think my friends and I should test you to see if you can see this future, too.

When you are about to enter the Nacrene City Gym, N comes out and speaks to you. N talks about his ideal relationship with Pokémon and the future for a while. After he finishes his story, he challenges you to a Pokémon battle.

Battle the mysterious N! 2

N uses three Pokémon, all at Level 13. Target their weaknesses. Attack his Pidove with Electric-, Ice-, and Rock-type moves, Tympole with Grass- and Electric-type moves, and Timburr with Flying- and Psychic-type moves.

● **N's Pokémon**

Pidove ♂	Lv. 13	Normal	Flying
Tympole ♂	Lv. 13	Water	
Timburr ♂	Lv. 13	Fighting	

Step 7 **The Pokémon Gym is inside the Nacrene Museum**

The Nacrene City Gym is located at the back of the Nacrene Museum. In the museum, a Pokémon Fossil can be turned back into a living Pokémon. Speak to the assistant director, Hawes. He will explain the museum exhibits in detail.

Since you were kind enough to visit, I'll give you a tour of the museum.

The assistant director Hawes is Lenora's husband

After the assistant director Hawes explains the exhibits, he tells you that the Nacrene City Gym Leader Lenora is his wife.

Gym battle 2 — *Nacrene City Gym Battle*

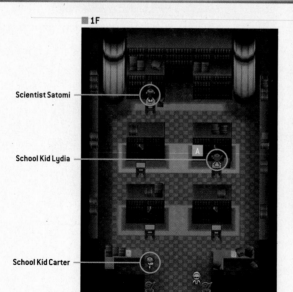

■ 1F

Scientist Satomi

School Kid Lydia

A

School Kid Carter

Entrance

■ B1F

Gym Leader Lenora

A

Nacrene City Gym Leader
Lenora

● **Normal-type Pokémon User**

Recommended Level for your Pokémon   Lv. 23

If you have a Fighting-type move, you can target the weakness of the two Pokémon

You advance in this Gym by doing research. Lenora's Pokémon are weak against Fighting-type moves. If you have a Pokémon that can learn TM94 Rock Smash, use it to target the weakness of Lenora's two Pokémon. If her Watchog uses the move Retaliate, your Pokémon will suffer serious damage, so be careful.

Lenora's Pokémon

◎ Herdier ♀	Lv. 18	● Moves to watch out for:
Normal		Take Down Normal

◎ Watchog ♀	Lv. 20	● Moves to watch out for:
Normal		Retaliate Normal

◎

◎

◎

◎

TM Received   TM **67** Retaliate

If an ally fainted in the previous turn, this attack's power is doubled.

Basic Badge

Pokémon up to Lv. 30, including those received in trades, will obey you.

After beating the Nacrene City Gym

Team Plasma steals the Dragon Skull

After you defeat Lenora in the Nacrene City Gym, Hawes rushes in. He says Team Plasma has raided the museum. In the museum, Team Plasma steals the Dragon Skull by using smoke screens and running off.

Team Plasma: To show you we're serious, we'll steal it right before your eyes!

After beating the Nacrene City Gym

Meet the Castelia City Gym Leader, Burgh

Lenora chases Team Plasma, and when you follow her, you run into the Castelia City Gym Leader, Burgh. Bianca and Cheren also join you. Lenora decides that she will check the east side of the city, and Bianca and Cheren will protect the museum.

He may not look like it, but he's Castelia City's Gym Leader!

After beating the Nacrene City Gym

Head to Pinwheel Forest with Burgh

Lenora asks you to search Pinwheel Forest with Burgh to bring back the Dragon Skull that Team Plasma stole. Head west through the city and hurry to Pinwheel Forest (p. 87)

Burgh and Trainer, you two search Pinwheel Forest!

After beating the Nacrene City Gym — Bianca gives you a Dowsing MCHN

When you are ready to go to Pinwheel Forest, Bianca stops you and gives you a Dowsing MCHN that can find hidden items (p. 43). Use this item right away in Pinwheel Forest.

Dowsing MCHN

After visiting the Relic Castle — Meet Professor Juniper in front of the museum

When you visit the Nacrene Museum after leaving the Relic Castle, Professor Juniper, Cedric Juniper, Bianca, and the Champion Alder are standing in front of the museum. Professor Juniper says you are caught up in something serious.

After visiting the Relic Castle — Lenora gives you the Light Stone (Dark Stone)

Lenora comes out of the Nacrene Museum and hands you the Light Stone (*Pokémon Black Version*) or Dark Stone (*Pokémon White Version*). Lenora says Team Plasma probably stole the Dragon Skull because they want to restore the Legendary Dragon-type Pokémon.

Light Stone   **Dark Stone**

After visiting the Relic Castle — Lenora thinks of ideal advisers

After you receive the Light Stone (Dark Stone), Alder speaks to you and asks if you are prepared to battle N if anything happens to him. Lenora remembers people who are familiar with the Legendary Dragon-type Pokémon.

After visiting the Relic Castle — Fly to Icirrus City and walk to Opelucid City

To follow Alder to Opelucid City, first use Fly to get to Icirrus City. Head northeast through Icirrus City to walk to Opelucid City along Route 8 (p. 154).

Pinwheel Forest

Pinwheel Forest is a dense forest. You can stick to the road for a straightforward path or explore the complicated maze of trees. You will battle many Pokémon Trainers, but a Nurse will heal your Pokémon.

Field Moves Needed — Surf

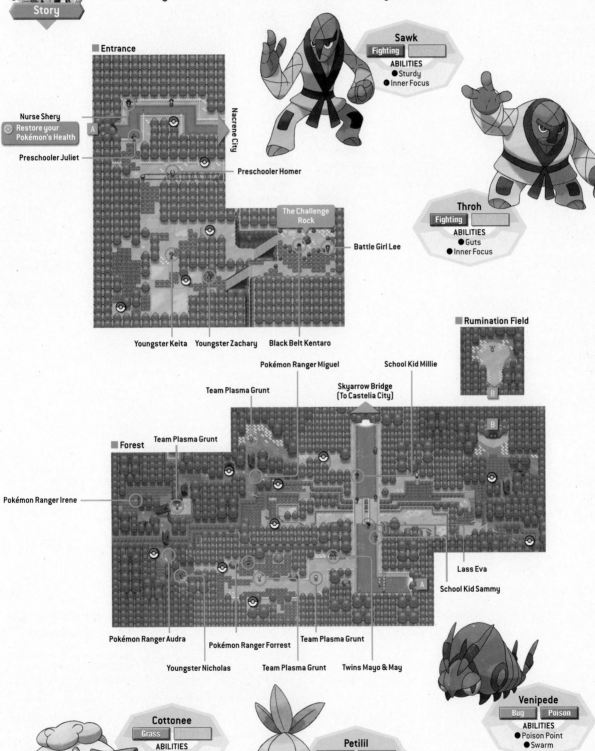

Entrance

Nurse Shery — Restore your Pokémon's Health
Preschooler Juliet
Preschooler Homer
Nacrene City

The Challenge Rock
Battle Girl Lee

Rumination Field

Youngster Keita
Youngster Zachary
Black Belt Kentaro

Pokémon Ranger Miguel
School Kid Millie

Team Plasma Grunt
Skyarrow Bridge (To Castelia City)

Forest
Team Plasma Grunt
Pokémon Ranger Irene

Lass Eva
School Kid Sammy

Pokémon Ranger Audra
Pokémon Ranger Forrest
Team Plasma Grunt
Youngster Nicholas
Team Plasma Grunt
Twins Mayo & May

Sawk
Fighting
ABILITIES
● Sturdy
● Inner Focus

Throh
Fighting
ABILITIES
● Guts
● Inner Focus

Venipede
Bug   Poison
ABILITIES
● Poison Point
● Swarm

Cottonee
Grass
ABILITIES
● Prankster
● Infiltrator

Petilil
Grass
ABILITIES
● Chlorophyll
● Own Tempo

UNOVA ADVENTURE WALKTHROUGH
PINWHEEL FOREST

Items

First visit
- ☐ Antidote ×2
- ☐ Big Root
- ☐ Dragon Skull
- ☐ Ether
- ☐ Great Ball
- ☐ Miracle Seed
- ☐ Moon Stone
- ☐ Net Ball
- ☐ Parlyz Heal
- ☐ Super Potion ×2
- ☐ TM86 Grass Knot
- ☐ TM94 Rock Smash

After defeating Pokémon Ranger Forrest
- ☐ Chesto Berry

After defeating Pokémon Ranger Audra
- ☐ Chesto Berry

After defeating Pokémon Ranger Irene
- ☐ Pecha Berry

After defeating Pokémon Ranger Miguel
- ☐ Pecha Berry

After getting Bicycle
- ☐ Hyper Potion
- ☐ TM22 SolarBeam

After getting Surf
- ☐ SilverPowder

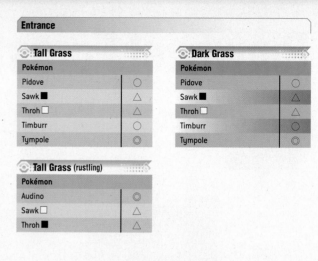

Entrance

Tall Grass
Pokémon	
Pidove	○
Sawk ■	△
Throh ☐	△
Timburr	○
Tympole	◎

Dark Grass
Pokémon	
Pidove	○
Sawk ■	△
Throh ☐	△
Timburr	○
Tympole	◎

Tall Grass (rustling)
Pokémon	
Audino	◎
Sawk ☐	△
Throh ■	△

Forest

Tall Grass
Pokémon	
Cottonee ■	◎
Petilil ☐	◎
Pidove	○
Sewaddle	◎
Venipede	○

Tall Grass (rustling)
Pokémon	
Audino	◎
Lilligant ☐	△
Panpour	△
Pansage	△
Pansear	△
Whimsicott ■	△

Dark Grass
Pokémon	
Cottonee ■	◎
Petilil ☐	◎
Swadloon	◎
Tranquill	○
Whirlipede	○

Water Surface
Pokémon	
Basculin (Blue-Striped Form) ☐	◎
Basculin (Red-Striped Form) ■	◎

Water Surface (ripples)
Pokémon	
Basculin (Blue-Striped Form) ■	◎
Basculin (Red-Striped Form) ☐	◎

■ After finishing the main story

Fishing
Pokémon	
Basculin (Blue-Striped Form) ☐	○
Basculin (Red-Striped Form) ■	○
Goldeen	◎

Fishing (ripples)
Pokémon	
Basculin (Blue-Striped Form) ■	○
Basculin (Red-Striped Form) ☐	○
Goldeen	◎
Seaking	△

Step 1 — Depart after preparing for status conditions

Pinwheel Forest is full of Pokémon that inflict special conditions in battle, such as Venipede and Cottonee (or Petilil). Before entering Pinwheel Forest, it's a good idea to buy several healing items such as Antidote, Parlyz Heal, and Awakening at Nacrene City's Pokémon Center.

Pinwheel Forest
Did you remember to pack an Antidote?

Find items with the Dowsing MCHN

The Dowsing MCHN, which you received from Bianca in Nacrene City, is a item that helps you find hidden items. There are many hidden items in Pinwheel Forest, so use it to find them.

Step 2 — A Nurse heals your Pokémon

Shery, the Nurse at the entrance to Pinwheel Forest, will heal your Pokémon if you defeat her in battle. Afterward, you can ask her to heal your Pokémon anytime, so if you run into trouble in Pinwheel Forest, talk to Nurse Shery.

Tough Trainer!
I will make your Pokémon healthy.

Can't enter Pinwheel Forest?

You can't go into the depths of Pinwheel Forest until you defeat the Nacrene City Gym Leader. If Team Plasma is blocking the way into the depths of the forest, go back to challenge the Nacrene City Gym.

UNOVA ADVENTURE WALKTHROUGH   ◉ PINWHEEL FOREST

Step 3 — Get Star Pieces by smashing the challenge rock

A challenge rock sits in the southern part of Pinwheel Forest. If you have a Fighting-type Pokémon in your party, it can hit the rock once a day. Chipping away at the challenge rock gives you a Star Piece that you can sell for a lot of money.

Catch a Fighting-type Pokémon

Visit Pinwheel Forest if you are having trouble with the Normal-type Pokémon used in the Nacrene City Gym. The forest is home to many Fighting-type Pokémon, which have an advantage against Normal-type Pokémon.

Step 4 — Go west from the Nurse

Pinwheel Forest is huge, and it's easy to run out of steam in the middle of the forest if you try to pass through in a single trip. First, battle the Pokémon Trainers around the entrance and gather some items. After you've had your Pokémon healed by Nurse Shery, go west and enter the forest.

Defeat Rangers to get Berries

Get Chesto Berries by defeating Pokémon Rangers Forrest and Audra in battle, and Pecha Berries by defeating Pokémon Rangers Irene and Miguel. Take the time to battle them while chasing Team Plasma, because the Berries can be useful!

Step 5 — Battle Team Plasma as you proceed into the forest

When you enter Pinwheel Forest from the east side, Burgh goes north to chase Team Plasma, and he asks you to go west to see if Team Plasma is hiding in that direction. Proceed through the forest while defeating the Team Plasma Grunts.

The mysterious moss-covered rock

A moss-covered rock sits deep in the western part of Pinwheel Forest. This rock is related to the evolution of a Pokémon that appears in a different region (p. 252).

Step 6 — Reclaim the Dragon Skull from Team Plasma

Venture even deeper into Pinwheel Forest while battling Pokémon Trainers and collecting items. You can reclaim the stolen Dragon Skull after defeating the last of the Team Plasma Grunts.

Dragon Skull

Step 7 — Meet Gorm, one of Team Plasma's Seven Sages

After you reclaim the Dragon Skull, Gorm, one of Team Plasma's Seven Sages, shows up. Gorm disappears after you talk to him, and Burgh leaves after telling you he will be waiting at the Castelia City Gym. Lenora gives you a Moon Stone as thanks after you return the Dragon Skull.

Step 8 — Look around Pinwheel Forest

Head east from the place where Lenora left, and you will reach a paved road. There are several Pokémon Trainers on this road, so challenge them to battle. The fence on the east side of the route has a gap in it—but an old man is blocking the path, so you can't go that way at this point.

Step 9 — Head north on the Skyarrow Bridge

Once you've had a look around Pinwheel Forest, go north on the paved road and head toward your destination, Castelia City. The Skyarrow Bridge, which has a fantastic view, links Pinwheel Forest to Castelia City.

After getting the Bicycle — You can now go where you couldn't go before

After you get the Bicycle in Nimbasa City, the old man who was blocking the gap in the fence is gone, and you can continue deeper into the forest. Also, if you use Surf, you can collect an extra item.

After capturing Cobalion — Meeting the Legendary Pokémon Virizion

After you meet the Legendary Pokémon Cobalion in Mistralton Cave (p. 143), the four seals disappear, and you can proceed to Rumination Field, the deepest part of Pinwheel Forest. The Legendary Pokémon Virizion is waiting for you there.

🔘 Capture Virizion!

First, use moves that do double damage, such as Fire-, Ice-, Poison-, and Psychic-type moves. After that, reduce its HP gradually with moves that aren't very effective, such as Water-, Grass-, Electric-, and Ground-type moves. Virizion has the Justified Ability, so if you use Dark-type moves against it, its Attack stat will go up. Be careful!

Virizion Lv. 42

| Grass | Fighting |

ABILITY ● Justified
MOVES ● Helping Hand
Retaliate
Giga Drain
Sacred Sword

The Skyarrow Bridge

Story

The Skyarrow Bridge connects Pinwheel Forest to Castelia City. The bridge has two levels, and trucks pass by on the lower level. As you cross the bridge, Castelia City's skyscrapers come closer in an impressive scene.

Field Moves Needed

Items
- [ ] Quick Claw

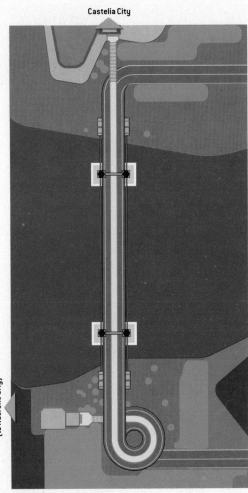

Castelia City

Pinwheel Forest
(to Nacrene City)

Step 1 — Cross the bridge to Castelia City

Across the Skyarrow Bridge is the Unova region's largest city, Castelia City (p. 92). Enjoy the beautiful scenery as you cross the bridge to discover what adventures await on the other side!

Think fast!

There's a Hiker in a gate on the Pinwheel Forest side. Talk to him to get the Quick Claw. When a Pokémon is holding this useful item, sometimes it will attack first in battle.

Castelia City

Story

Skyscrapers tall enough to pierce the clouds are clustered in Castelia City, and its many streets bustle with the comings and goings of many people. The elegant cruise ship, *The Royal Unova*, is moored at the port.

Field Moves Needed

Items

● First visit
☐ Fresh Water
☐ Hyper Potion
☐ Lemonade
☐ Quick Ball x3
☐ Revive
☐ Scope Lens
☐ Smoke Ball
☐ Timer Ball x3
☐ TM44 Rest
☐ TM45 Attract
☐ TM70 Flash
☐ Yache Berry
● When your answer to the man's question is Pansage
☐ Leaf Stone
● When your answer to the man's question is Pansear
☐ Fire Stone
● When your answer to the man's question is Panpour
☐ Water Stone
● After defeating Janitor Geoff
☐ Exp. Share
● After you've answered all of the surveys at Passerby Analytics HQ
☐ Soda Pop
● When your Pokédex's SEEN number is 20 Pokémon or more
☐ Eviolite
● When you've defeated the three Dancers
☐ Amulet Coin
● After winning the Castelia City Gym challenge
☐ Insect Badge
☐ TM76 Struggle Bug

Poké Mart
(Lower Clerk)

BridgeMail S	50
Favored Mail	50
Greet Mail	50
Inquiry Mail	50
Like Mail	50
Reply Mail	50
RSVP Mail	50
Thanks Mail	50
Heal Ball	300
Nest Ball	1,000
Net Ball	1,000

Vending Machine

Fresh Water	200
Soda Pop	300
Lemonade	350

Street with the Pokémon Gym

Castelia City Gym

Passerby Analytics HQ

Liberty Pier

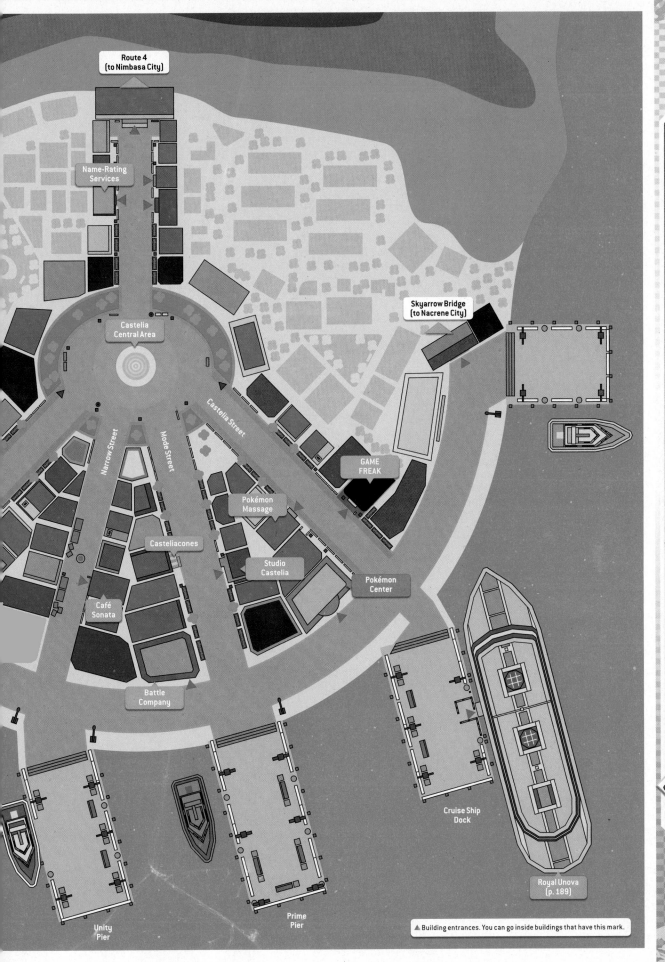

Route 4
(to Nimbasa City)

Name-Rating
Services

Skyarrow Bridge
(to Nacrene City)

Castelia
Central Area

Castelia Street

Narrow Street

Mode Street

GAME
FREAK

Pokémon
Massage

Casteliacones

Studio
Castelia

Pokémon
Center

Café
Sonata

Battle
Company

Cruise Ship
Dock

Unity
Pier

Prime
Pier

Royal Unova
(p. 189)

▲ Building entrances. You can go inside buildings that have this mark.

UNOVA ADVENTURE WALKTHROUGH

◎ CASTELIA CITY

Step 1 — Get a Pokémon-evolving item

Pass through the gate and walk into the viewing area that juts out into the ocean. Talk to the man there, and he will tell you that the Pokémon you received in the Dreamyard evolves by using a stone. He will give you a Leaf Stone if your answer to his question is Pansage, a Fire Stone if your answer is Pansear, or a Water Stone if it is Panpour.

Panpour...
Then, it's a Water Stone you need.

Step 2 — Register Zorua in your Pokédex

In the lobby of GAME FREAK's building on Castelia Street, a girl is reading a picture book to a small boy. "Zorua, who was left alone, wandered around looking for its mother..." If you listen to the story, Zorua will be registered in your Pokédex.

Step 3 — Visit GAME FREAK on the 22nd floor

In the GAME FREAK building, you can take the elevator up to the 22nd floor to visit the creators of *Pokémon Black Version* and *Pokémon White Version*. Talk to some of the people who made the game, like the Game Director and Graphic Designer.

Hi there!
I am the Game Director.

Step 4 — Get a massage for your Pokémon

Talk to a woman on the first floor of the building across from GAME FREAK's office, and she will give your Pokémon a massage. Letting one of your Pokémon get a massage will make that Pokémon a little more friendly toward you! Pokémon massages are available once per day.

▶ YES
NO

If you'd like, I will massage your Pokémon.

Step 5 — Get items by trading with many people

Talk to the man on the second floor of the Pokémon Center, and he will give you one of six items depending on the number of different people you've traded Pokémon with. If you've traded with 50 or more people, you'll get a Master Ball that will always capture any Pokémon.

Great!
I will give this to you!

Step 6 — No cruising on the *Royal Unova* yet

The cruise ship, the *Royal Unova*, is moored at the cruise ship dock. Although you might want to go inside, you can't ride it right now. You can ride the *Royal Unova* once you've completed the main story (p. 189).

We are working very hard to ready the ship for the best Pokémon Trainers.

It's not always rush hour

Traffic changes according to time in Castelia Street, Mode Street, and in front of the Route 4 gate. In mornings and evenings, the streets are very crowded. In the afternoons and nights, they are a little crowded, and late at night, there aren't many people. Visit at different times to observe the changes.

Is today your lucky day?

On Castelia City's Castelia Street, and in many other places throughout the Unova region, vending machines sell drinks. Vending machines have a little bonus. If you're lucky, you might get an extra drink for free!

Gifts you get for trading with people:

5 or more	Wide Lens
10 or more	Everstone
20 or more	Zoom Lens
30 or more	Choice Scarf
40 or more	PP Max
50 or more	Master Ball

Register your favorite Pokémon

Talk to the person standing in front of the computer at the Pokémon Center to hear about favorite Pokémon, and register the first Pokémon in your party. Then the favorite Pokémon is displayed in the Vs. Recorder's ranking screen.

Step 7 — Get Berries by showing Pokémon

Talk to the Harlequin in Studio Castelia. Every day he will ask to see a certain type of Pokémon. If you show him the type of Pokémon he wants to see, he will give you your choice of a Cheri Berry, Chesto Berry, Pecha Berry, Rawst Berry, or Aspear Berry.

Please show me a Pokémon that's Grass type!

Change your Pokémon's nickname

Name-Rating Services are available in a building on the road that continues to Route 4. If you want, you can change your Pokémon's nickname. However, you can't change the nickname of a Pokémon you've received in a trade.

Step 8 — Get TM70 Flash

Enter Narrow Street and continue down the road. A man in sunglasses pops out from behind a garbage bin and gives you TM70 Flash. If you teach Flash to a Pokémon, it can light up dark caves.

Trainer obtained a TM70 Flash!

Challenge the Gym before moving on

Continue north from the central area to get to Route 4. Until you defeat the Castelia City Gym Leader, a Worker will block your way, and you can't continue. Visit this area after you've obtained the Gym Badge.

Step 9 — Buy a Casteliacone on Tuesday

It's not easy to buy a Casteliacone, even if you can afford the 100 price tag. The Casteliacone stand on Mode Street is closed during the winter, and if you visit on any day but Tuesday, the last man in line will tell you they're sold out. But keep trying, because the Casteliacone is very useful— it can heal a Pokémon of all status conditions!

How about Castelia City's famous Casteliacone!

Step 10 — Get an Exp. Share at the Battle Company

The Battle Company on Mode Street is full of Pokémon Trainers, and you can enjoy Pokémon battling there. The Trainers get tougher as you approach the top, and if you defeat the Janitor on the 55th floor, he'll give you an Exp. Share (p. 37)!

Trainer obtained an Exp. Share!

Another Exp. Share!

You can receive a second Exp. Share, a very useful item that gives Experience Points to a Pokémon even if it isn't used in battle. Take a Pokémon you've raised to Icirrus City's Pokémon Fan Club (p. 148) to get it!

Step 11 — Visit Passerby Analytics HQ

When you enter the Passerby Analytics HQ and talk to the leader, he will appoint you as a statistician. Being a statistician lets you receive Passerby Survey requests. If you take your Nintendo DS to a place where other people are playing the game, you can enjoy Tag Mode with other Pokémon fans.

...Good! I will specially appoint you as a statistician!

Step 12 — Bring the three Dancers together

Dancer Mickey is in the central area by the fountain. He tells you he wants to form a dance team, and he asks you to talk to the other Dancers, Edmond on Narrow Street and Raymond on the Unity Pier, and battle them. When you talk to Mickey after that, he gives you the Amulet Coin.

If you invite both of them, the three of us can groove as a team!

Need cash?

The Amulet Coin you get from the dance team doubles your prize money when the Pokémon holding it joins a battle. Have a Pokémon hold this when you need more money.

CASTELIA CITY · UNOVA ADVENTURE WALKTHROUGH

Step 13 — Meet Cheren and Burgh at the Pokémon Gym

Cheren, who has just finished his Gym challenge, comes out of the Castelia City Gym when you try to enter for the first time. Gym Leader Burgh is right behind him. Burgh asks you to come with him to Prime Pier, because Team Plasma has shown up again.

Step 14 — Bianca's Pokémon is stolen by Team Plasma

When you get to Prime Pier, you see Burgh, Bianca, and a girl named Iris, from Opelucid City. Bianca is sad because Team Plasma stole one of her Pokémon. One member of Team Plasma comes back, but then sees Burgh and runs away. Chase after her!

Step 15 — A Team Plasma base—right near the Gym?!

It turns out Team Plasma has been hiding in a building right across from the Castelia City Gym! Defeat the Team Plasma Grunts at the entrance, go inside, and meet Ghetsis. At first, Ghetsis lectures Burgh, but then he backs down and returns Bianca's Munna.

Step 16 — Get a Yache Berry from Iris

Team Plasma leaves after giving Munna back. Bianca makes Iris her bodyguard, and says she's going to tour Castelia City. As thanks for your help against Team Plasma, Iris gives you a Yache Berry.

Gym battle 3 — Castelia City Gym Battle

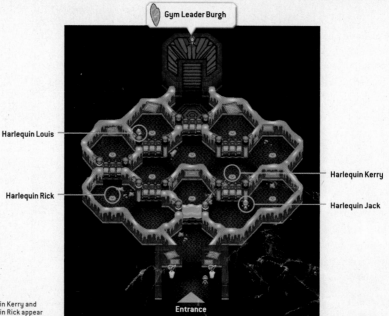

● Harlequin Kerry and Harlequin Rick appear when you step on a switch.

Castelia City Gym Leader
Burgh

● **Bug-type Pokémon User**

Recommended Level for your Pokémon	Lv. 26

Battle by lowering your opponent's accuracy to reduce the number of hits

In the Gym, proceed by passing through honeycomb-like walls. Burgh's Whirlipede is weak to Fire- and Flying-type moves, Dwebble is weak to Water- and Rock-type moves, and Leavanny is weak to Fire- and Flying-type moves. If you don't have any moves that can take advantage of these weaknesses, an effective tactic is using TM70 Flash to lower your opponent's accuracy.

Burgh's Pokémon

● Whirlipede ♂ Lv. 21 ● Moves to watch out for:
Bug Poison   Poison Tail Poison

● Dwebble ♂ Lv. 21 ● Moves to watch out for:
Bug Rock   Smack Down Rock

● Leavanny ♂ Lv. 23 ● Moves to watch out for:
Bug Grass   Struggle Bug Bug

TM Received **TM 76** Struggle Bug
Your opponent's Sp. Atk is lowered one stage with every hit.

Insect Badge
Pokémon up to Lv. 40, including those received in trades, will obey you.

After beating the Castelia City Gym
Bianca challenges you to a battle via the Xtransceiver

After you defeat the Gym Leader, Bianca calls you on the Xtransceiver to challenge you to a Pokémon battle. The two of you agree to meet at the gate to Route 4 on the north side of Castelia City.

Bianca ⊙◉ ... Trainer
Could you do me a favor?
Let's have a Pokémon battle!

Remember to heal up

Don't forget to visit the Pokémon Center and heal your Pokémon before meeting Bianca for a battle. Your Pokémon are probably tired after battling at the Castelia City Gym.

After beating the Castelia City Gym
Head for the gate that connects to Route 4

Take any street and go to the central area with the fountain, then head north to reach the gate to Route 4. Bianca comes up to you from behind once you enter the gate.

Battle your childhood friend Bianca! 3

She has two more Pokémon than last time, and two of her Pokémon have evolved.

● If you chose Snivy:

● Herdier ♀	Lv. 18	Normal	
● Dewott ♂	Lv. 20	Water	
● Munna ♀	Lv. 18	Psychic	
● Pansear ♂	Lv. 18	Fire	

● If you chose Tepig:

● Herdier ♀	Lv. 18	Normal	
● Servine ♂	Lv. 20	Grass	
● Munna ♀	Lv. 18	Psychic	
● Panpour ♂	Lv. 18	Water	

● If you chose Oshawott:

● Herdier ♀	Lv. 18	Normal	
● Pignite ♂	Lv. 20	Fire	Fighting
● Munna ♀	Lv. 18	Psychic	
● Pansage ♂	Lv. 18	Grass	

After beating the Castelia City Gym
Go north towards Route 4

Your next destination is Nimbasa City. Head north on Route 4 to reach Nimbasa City (p. 105). You can also get to the Desert Resort via Route 4. It's a good place to train your Pokémon, and you can get a Pokémon Fossil, so stop by.

Route 4

Story

Since there is always a sandstorm on Route 4, the route being built in the desert still isn't complete. There are two exits to the north: The eastern exit goes to Nimbasa City, and the western exit goes to the Desert Resort.

Field Moves Needed

Surf

Items

- ☐ Burn Heal
- ☐ Ether
- ☐ Great Ball
- ☐ Hyper Potion
- ☐ Super Potion
- ☐ TM28 Dig
- ☐ TM41 Torment
- ☐ Ultra Ball x10
- ☐ X Accuracy

Desert

Pokémon	
Darumaka	◎
Sandile	◎
Scraggy	○

Water Surface

Pokémon	
Frillish	◎

Water Surface (ripples)

Pokémon	
Alomomola	◎
Jellicent	△

■ After finishing the main story

Fishing

Pokémon	
Clamperl	○
Krabby	◎
Luvdisc	△

Fishing (ripples)

Pokémon	
Gorebyss ☐	△
Huntail ■	△
Kingler	△
Luvdisc	○
Relicanth	◎

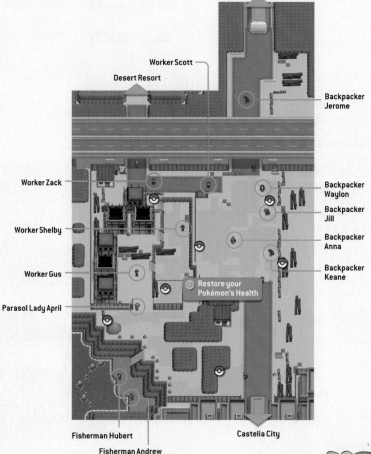

Nimbasa City

Worker Scott

Desert Resort

Backpacker Jerome

Worker Zack

Backpacker Waylon

Backpacker Jill

Worker Shelby

Backpacker Anna

Worker Gus

Backpacker Keane

Parasol Lady April

Restore your Pokémon's Health

Fisherman Hubert

Castelia City

Fisherman Andrew

Sandile

Ground	Dark

ABILITIES
- Intimidate
- Moxie

Darumaka

Fire	

ABILITIES
- Hustle
- Inner Focus

● Darumaka with the Hidden Ability Inner Focus don't appear in the wild.

Step 1 — **Battle Pokémon Trainers as you go**

On Route 4, Pokémon Trainers await not only on the paved road, but on the desert sands as well. If you head west after leaving Castelia City, you'll find a few more Trainers to battle by the water. Before heading to Nimbasa City, take the time to wander around the entire area and battle.

I'll have a battle with you using my freshly caught Pokémon!

The Sandstorm never stops

On Route 4, the weather is always Sandstorm during a battle. Pokémon that aren't Rock-, Ground-, or Steel-type will take damage from the Sandstorm every turn. Check frequently to make sure your Pokémon have enough HP left.

Step 2 — Meet Cheren after heading north

Head north from the Castelia City gate, and you will find Cheren waiting for you. He will talk to you when you approach him and challenge you to a Pokémon battle to see which of you is stronger. Challenge him after you've restored your Pokémon's HP in the prefab house.

And now it's time to see which one of us is the stronger Trainer!

Pokémon hide in the dark sand

As you travel through the desert, you'll notice the sand comes in different colors. When you walk in the darker sand, you can run into wild Pokémon. So if you want to catch Pokémon, walk in the dark sand...but if your team is worn out, stick to the pale sand to avoid battles.

Step 3 — Heal your Pokémon at the prefab house

There's a prefab house on the west side of the route after you leave Castelia City. If you talk to the woman inside the house, she will restore your Pokémon's health. If your Pokémon were hurt in the Sandstorm or in battles with Pokémon Trainers, heal them at the prefab house.

What? Are you worn out?
OK! Then rest here for a minute!

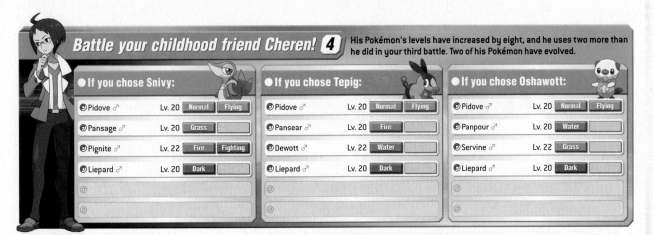

Battle your childhood friend Cheren! 4

His Pokémon's levels have increased by eight, and he uses two more than he did in your third battle. Two of his Pokémon have evolved.

● If you chose Snivy:

Pidove ♂	Lv. 20	Normal	Flying
Pansage ♂	Lv. 20	Grass	
Pignite ♂	Lv. 22	Fire	Fighting
Liepard ♂	Lv. 20	Dark	

● If you chose Tepig:

Pidove ♂	Lv. 20	Normal	Flying
Pansear ♂	Lv. 20	Fire	
Dewott ♂	Lv. 22	Water	
Liepard ♂	Lv. 20	Dark	

● If you chose Oshawott:

Pidove ♂	Lv. 20	Normal	Flying
Panpour ♂	Lv. 20	Water	
Servine ♂	Lv. 22	Grass	
Liepard ♂	Lv. 20	Dark	

Step 4 — A call from Professor Juniper

The Xtransceiver rings after you defeat Cheren in battle. It's from Professor Juniper. Bianca doesn't pick up, so there's no image for her. Professor Juniper says she will be waiting at the gate to Nimbasa City to the north of Route 4.

Professor   Cheren

Trainer

OK! I'll be waiting for you two in front of the gate to Nimbasa City!

Dig your way out of caves

Get TM28 Dig in the prefab house to the north. When you teach Dig to a Pokémon, you can use it to return instantly to the entrance of a cave you are in. It has the same effect as Escape Rope, so it is very useful.

Step 5 — Visit the Desert Resort

Route 4 has two exits on the north side, and you can visit the Desert Resort by taking the western exit. It's a good place to make your Pokémon stronger before heading to Nimbasa City. You can't get past the first floor of the Relic Castle yet (p. 102), though, so head back to Route 4 when you get there.

Ruins buried in the desert...
It's like a grand adventure in a story.

Step 6 — Get Ultra Balls from Professor Juniper

When you enter the gate to Nimbasa City, Professor Juniper is there, just like she said she'd be. The Professor gives both you and Cheren ten Ultra Balls. These high-performance balls catch Pokémon more easily than Great Balls.

Step 7 — Go north to Nimbasa City

Professor Juniper leaves to look for Bianca. Saying he's going to catch more Pokémon, Cheren returns to Route 4. Your next destination is Nimbasa City (p. 105). Continue north from the gate, and head for the next city!

Look at the electric bulletin board to see what's happening in Nimbasa City!

Thanks, Mom!

According to Cheren, your mom—and his mom, and Bianca's mom, too—asked Professor Juniper to give you the Pokédex. The three of you were set off on your adventure because your mothers wanted you to see the world!

Catch Pokémon in the water

You'll find a small beach at the west end of Route 4. If you have learned the hidden move Surf, visit this area to catch Pokémon. After finishing the main story, you become able to fish, and you can catch different types of Pokémon!

It is a popular place for tourists, but too harsh to be a resort

Desert Resort

Story

The Desert Resort is a huge desert with a small entrance area before the gate. The sandstorm always rages in the desert. At the back are the Relic Castle and the Relic Castle Tower. Ancient Pokémon statues are quietly watching the entrance of the castle.

Field Moves Needed

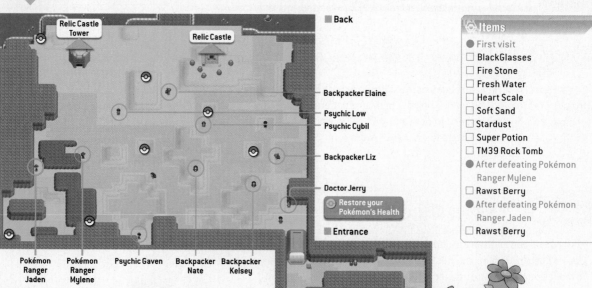

Relic Castle Tower

Relic Castle

■ Back

- Backpacker Elaine
- Psychic Low
- Psychic Cybil
- Backpacker Liz
- Doctor Jerry
  - Restore your Pokémon's Health

■ Entrance

Pokémon Ranger Jaden · Pokémon Ranger Mylene · Psychic Gaven · Backpacker Nate · Backpacker Kelsey

Items

● First visit
☐ BlackGlasses
☐ Fire Stone
☐ Fresh Water
☐ Heart Scale
☐ Soft Sand
☐ Stardust
☐ Super Potion
☐ TM39 Rock Tomb
● After defeating Pokémon Ranger Mylene
☐ Rawst Berry
● After defeating Pokémon Ranger Jaden
☐ Rawst Berry

Back — Desert	
Pokémon	
Darumaka	○
Dwebble	△
Maractus	△
Sandile	◎
Sigilyph	△

Entrance — Desert	
Pokémon	
Darumaka	○
Dwebble	△
Maractus	△
Sandile	◎
Scraggy	△

Route 4 (to Nimbasa City)

Maractus

Grass

ABILITIES
● Water Absorb
● Chlorophyll

1 ### Have Doctor Jerry heal your Pokémon

You'll find Doctor Jerry standing close to the entrance gate. After you beat him in a Pokémon battle, he'll heal all your Pokémon. Talk to him again after defeating him, and he'll always be willing to heal your Pokémon. If your Pokémon are hurt, take advantage of his kind offer.

Now, I will make your Pokémon healthy!

Get Berries from Trainers

Defeat the Pokémon Rangers Mylene and Jaden to receive Rawst Berries. Mylene and Jaden are in the southwest of the far side of the resort. Be sure to battle them, because Rawst Berries can come in very handy at times.

 2 ### Proceed while battling Trainers

A lot of Pokémon Trainers wait at the far side of the resort. Battle all the Trainers as you collect items. Pokémon can easily get low on HP due to Pokémon battles and the Sandstorm weather condition (p. 34). You'll want to make sure to heal your Pokémon frequently.

I am a Psychic, so just one look at you tells me that you are a Trainer!

You meet a traveler from the Hoenn region

There is a traveler from the Hoenn region near the center of the far side of the resort. He blurts out, "Go-Goggles." He's talking about goggles to protect your eyes from the sandstorm. Unlike the sandstorm in the Hoenn region, you don't have to wear goggles here, so don't worry.

Step **3** ### Enter the Relic Castle near the statues

Head for the far side of the resort, and you'll see the entrance to the Relic Castle. Ancient Pokémon statues surround the entrance. During your adventure, when you're on the way to Nimbasa City, you can explore only the first floor, but enter the castle anyway (p. 102).

You can't go further in the tower yet

On the west side of the Relic Castle entrance, you'll see a tower entrance. Go in if you want, but you won't be able to go downstairs because a ledge blocks you. You'll be able to travel further in after you finish the main story (p. 190).

After visiting Dragonspiral Tower ### Follow Cheren and enter the castle

When you're about to enter the Relic Castle, Cheren stops you. According to Cheren, Alder has already entered the castle. Follow after Alder in order to get a clue about the Light Stone (Dark Stone).

Alder went on ahead. Let's hurry.

Sigilyph

Psychic | Flying

ABILITIES
● Wonder Skin
● Magic Guard

Relic Castle

Story

The Relic Castle is comprised of ancient ruins buried in the sand. The floor has quicksand here and there, and if you try to run through it, you'll be caught in the sand and fall to the lower floor. At first, you can go only halfway because the deeper levels are buried in sand.

Field Moves Needed

Tower 1F

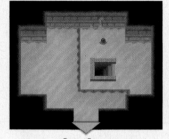

Desert Resort

● You can't reach the stairs from this entrance because they're on the wrong side of a one-way ledge.

1F

Psychic Dua

Psychic Perry

B1F

Desert Resort

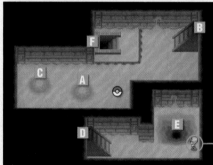

Team Plasma Grunt

B2F

Team Plasma Grunt

Team Plasma Grunt

B3F

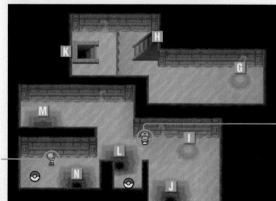

Team Plasma Grunt

Team Plasma Grunt

Team Plasma Grunt

Items

● First visit
☐ Cover Fossil / Plume Fossil
☐ Revive
● After visiting the Dragonspiral Tower
☐ Max Potion
☐ Max Revive
☐ PP Up
☐ Sun Stone
☐ TM30 Shadow Ball

1F • B1F • Tower 1F

Inside

Pokémon	
Sandile	◎
Yamask	◎

B2F–B5F

Inside

Pokémon	
Cofagrigus	◎
Krokorok	◎

■ B4F

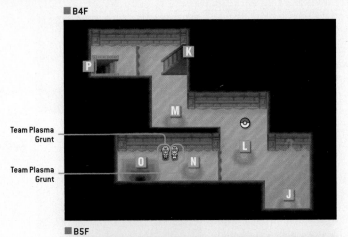

Team Plasma Grunt

Team Plasma Grunt

■ B5F

Yamask

Ghost

ABILITY
● Mummy

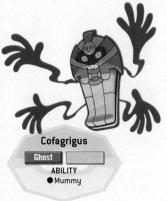

Cofagrigus

Ghost

ABILITY
● Mummy

1 You can enter here after finishing the main story (p. 190).

Step 1 Fall through quicksand to reach B1F

You can reach B1F through the quicksand on 1F. If you walk to the center or try to run through it, you will be caught in the quicksand. If you want to pass without getting caught in the quicksand, walk along the edge. After picking up the item on B1F, go back to 1F again and proceed.

Step 2 Get a Pokémon Fossil

Speak to a Backpacker on the west side of 1F. She will give you a Cover Fossil or Plume Fossil. The Cover Fossil can be restored to Tirtouga, and the Plume Fossil can be restored to Archen. Choose whichever one you want, and it's yours!

▶ Cover Fossil
  Plume Fossil
  Cancel

Would you take one of them off my hands?

Have a Pokémon Fossil restored

The Cover Fossil or Plume Fossil that you received can be restored to a Pokémon at the Nacrene Museum in Nacrene City. Make room in your party, go to the museum, and speak to a woman on the right side of the reception counter.

Tirtouga

Archen

Step 3 — You can't move further yet

During your adventure, on the way to Nimbasa City, a Worker in front of the stairs stops you if you approach the stairs on the west side. You can't go deeper yet, because the rest of the castle is buried in the sand. Head back to Route 4 and continue on to Nimbasa City (p. 98).

Trainer! You still can't move ahead 'cause there is so much sand!

After visiting Dragonspiral Tower — Move on while battling Team Plasma

Come back again after visiting Dragonspiral Tower, and you will be able to proceed to B1F using the stairs. Fall through the quicksand and head down to B5F. Team Plasma Grunts are waiting for you on the way. Keep heading down while battling them and collecting items.

We will see if you can defeat Team Plasma!

After visiting Dragonspiral Tower — Ghetsis is waiting for you on B5F

When you arrive at B5F, Alder and Ghetsis are there. Ghetsis tells you that the Light Stone (Dark Stone) is not here. Ghetsis leaves after telling you to find the other Legendary Pokémon so you can fight the king.

But it appears the Light Stone you seek is not here.

After visiting Dragonspiral Tower — Return to the entrance with Alder and Cheren

After Ghetsis has left, Alder reveals his concerns about battling N as a Champion and about the Light Stone (Dark Stone). Cheren suggests going outside. Alder keeps worrying about the situation.

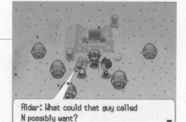

Alder: What could that guy called N possibly want?

Why does Alder continue his journey?

According to Ghetsis, after Alder lost a Pokémon (one that had been his partner for many years) to illness, he ordered the Elite Four to protect the Pokémon League, and he's been traveling in the Unova region ever since. What's on his mind in his travels?

After visiting Dragonspiral Tower — A call from Professor Juniper

When you're talking with Alder and Cheren at the entrance of the Relic Castle, your Xtransceiver rings. It's an urgent call from Professor Juniper, asking you to come to the museum in Nacrene City immediately.

Professor — Trainer

Come to the museum in Nacrene City immediately! Right away, got it?

After visiting Dragonspiral Tower — Head to Nacrene City using Fly

After the call from Professor Juniper, Alder heads straight for Nacrene City. Cheren decides to stay and check the Relic Castle one more time. You'll want to head for Nacrene City using Fly (p. 86).

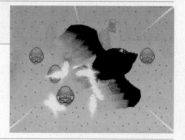

You can go further after finishing the main story

On B5F in the Relic Castle, you'll find an entrance to the inner part of the castle. However, as the entrance is above the ground, you can't go further at this time. You'll be able to go further after finishing the main story, because the sand will be piled up by then (p. 190).

Nimbasa City

Story

Nimbasa City is a huge city of leisure, with various facilities such as the Battle Subway, the Musical Theater, and an amusement park. Come here to get your fourth Gym Badge.

Field Moves Needed

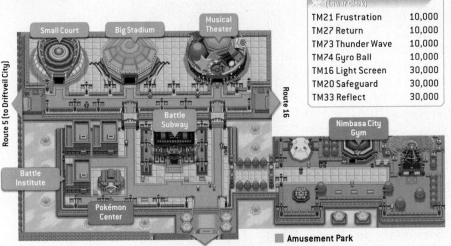

Poké Mart (Lower Clerk)	
TM21 Frustration	10,000
TM27 Return	10,000
TM73 Thunder Wave	10,000
TM74 Gyro Ball	10,000
TM16 Light Screen	30,000
TM20 Safeguard	30,000
TM33 Reflect	30,000

Items

- ● First visit
- ☐ Bicycle
- ☐ Fresh Water
- ☐ HM04 Strength
- ☐ Macho Brace
- ☐ Prop Case
- ☐ Sun Stone
- ☐ TM49 Echoed Voice
- ☐ Vs. Recorder
- ☐ X Attack
- ● If your friendship with the Pokémon at the head of your party is strong
- ☐ Soothe Bell
- ● After defeating the Nimbasa City Gym
- ☐ Bolt Badge
- ☐ TM72 Volt Switch

UNOVA ADVENTURE WALKTHROUGH ◎ NIMBASA CITY

Step 1 — Get a Bicycle from the Day-Care Man

When you arrive at the city, Team Plasma Grunts are attacking the Day-Care Man right in front of you. Challenge a Team Plasma Grunt to battle so you can rescue the Day-Care Man! If you win, the Day-Care Man gives you a Bicycle as a token of his gratitude. You can travel a lot faster by Bicycle than by running!

Bicycle

Step 2 — You meet Bianca, who's visiting the city

After you rescue the Day-Care Man from Team Plasma, Bianca tells you that there are many facilities in Nimbasa City, then goes on her way to see the Musical Theater. Catch up with Bianca later.

You can leave two Pokémon at the Pokémon Day Care

After you help the Day-Care Man, you can leave two Pokémon at the Pokémon Day Care on Route 3 (p. 76). If you leave the right sort of Pokémon, a Pokémon Egg may be found.

Step 3 — Get a Vs. Recorder at the Battle Subway

When you are about to enter the Battle Subway, a woman jumps out of the building. She gives you a Vs. Recorder. It enables you to record a video of a battle in the Battle Subway or a Link Battle with a friend.

Vs. Recorder

Step 4 Challenge the Battle Subway

In the Battle Subway, you can get on a real winning streak battling Pokémon Trainers. For every seven Trainers you defeat, you'll get Battle Points (BP). Exchange Battle Points for items useful in battles. The more Trainers you challenge, the more BP you can collect!

You can take the Battle Subway from Gear Station!

There is a train to Anville Town, too

In the Gear Station of the Battle Subway, there is a train to Anville Town, a small town located at the west end of the Unova region (p. 109). Take a train and visit Anville Town!

Step 5 Visit the Battle Institute

You can take a Battle Test in the Battle Institute on the west side of the Pokémon Center. However, the test is available only after you finish the main story. For now, continue your adventure, finish the main story, then come back and visit the Battle Institute again (p. 203).

I will judge your battles in a Battle Test!

Step 6 Get Strength from a guy in a house

Go to a house on the north side of the Battle Institute and talk to a guy in the house. He'll give you HM04 Strength. It's a hidden move that lets a Pokémon push a big boulder, and even drop a boulder into a hole. Don't miss it!

Trainer obtained an HM04 Strength!

Use Strength to get an item

You can get an item by using Strength on Route 2 (p. 66) Once you get Strength, zip over to Route 2 to get a Rare Candy.

Step 7 Visit Big Stadium

Baseball, soccer, and football are played in Big Stadium on the north side of the city. Which sport is played depends on the day (p. 6). You can also enjoy battles with Pokémon Trainers on the field during practice. Visit there to train your Pokémon.

Join the training of our Pokémon Eleven!

You can battle Trainers every day

In Big Stadium and Small Court, the level of your foe's Pokémon goes up (and the Pokémon get stronger) after you get three, five, and seven Gym Badges, and after finishing the main story. Also, the number of Trainers increases. Keep yourself fighting fit by going there every day.

Step 8 Visit Small Court

Tennis and basketball are played in Small Court to the west of Big Stadium. Tennis and basketball alternate, depending on the day (p. 6). On the court during practice, you can enjoy Pokémon battles with athletes and Pokémon Trainers.

I'll improve by having a lot of Pokémon battles!

You can't battle during a game

In Big Stadium and Small Court, there are games at certain times every day. During these periods, you can't battle with Trainers in the practice area. The timing of a game depends on which sport is being played, so check the calendar (p. 6) when planning your challenges.

Step 9 Get a Prop Case from the owner of the Musical Theater

When you enter the Musical Theater, Bianca is waiting for you. Go with Bianca to the back of the theater. The owner of the Musical Theater will give you a Prop Case. You can use it to store Props to Dress Up your Pokémon.

Trainer obtained the Prop Case!

Prop Case

Step 10 — Try the Pokémon Musical

At the Pokémon Musical, you can Dress Up your Pokémon with Props and let it participate in a musical. When the show ends, you can receive a Prop. Participate in the musical many times, collect many Props, and enjoy the fun of Dressing Up your Pokémon.

Would you like to participate?

Bianca stops you if you try to leave the city

If you try to get out of the city before visiting the Musical Theater, Bianca will stop you, and you two will go to the Musical Theater. Leave the city after visiting the Musical Theater.

Step 11 — Meet Bianca's very worried dad

When you leave the Musical Theater, you'll see Bianca's dad waiting outside. He's been worrying about Bianca's welfare, and has come to take her back home. The Gym Leader Elesa can't stand watching them quarrel. She intervenes, and in the end, persuades Bianca's dad that Bianca will be fine.

Bianca's Dad: I've come to take you back home, of course!

Step 12 — Go to the amusement park to see N again

At the amusement park on the east side of the city, you'll run into N. He asks you to ride the Ferris wheel. When you take a ride with him, he reveals that he is the king of Team Plasma. He's ready to battle you to buy time for some Team Plasma Grunts to flee.

First, I must tell you...
I am the king of Team Plasma.

N's title changes

After N reveals that he is the king of Team Plasma, his title changes from Pokémon Trainer to Team Plasma. You'll pick up on this if you pay close attention next time you start a Pokémon battle with N.

Battle with Team Plasma's N! [3]

N uses Pokémon that have different weaknesses. For Sandile, Water- and Fighting-type moves; for Darumaka, Water-, Ground-, and Rock-type moves; for Sigilyph, Electric- and Rock-type moves; and for Scraggy, Fighting- and Flying-type moves are effective.

● N's Pokémon

Pokémon		Level	Type	Type
◎ Sandile ♂		Lv. 22	Ground	Dark
◎ Darumaka ♂		Lv. 22	Fire	
◎ Sigilyph ♂		Lv. 22	Psychic	Flying
◎ Scraggy ♂		Lv. 22	Dark	Fighting
◎				
◎				

Step 13 — Get a Macho Brace from an Infielder

Go to the gate to Route 16 on the east side of the city, and speak to an Infielder in the gate. He will give you a Macho Brace. If you let a Pokémon hold it, it reduces Speed temporarily, but promotes strong growth.

Trainer obtained a Macho Brace!

⟪ UNOVA ADVENTURE WALKTHROUGH

◎ NIMBASA CITY ◎

Step 14 — Train your Pokémon before going to the Pokémon Gym

Before challenging the Nimbasa City Gym, spend a little time on Route 16 (p. 110). You can get your Pokémon ready for the Gym battle ahead by facing off against the Pokémon Trainers you'll encounter. When you're done exploring Route 16 and Lostlorn Forest, head back to Nimbasa City.

You can go to the Driftveil Drawbridge after defeating the Nimbasa City Gym

You can take Route 5 even before you challenge the Nimbasa City Gym. However, you can't cross Driftveil Drawbridge on the west side of Route 5 until you beat Nimbasa City Gym.

Gym battle 4 — Nimbasa City Gym Battle

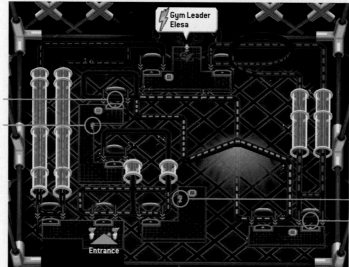

Gym Leader Elesa

Rich Boy Rolan

Rich Boy Cody

Lady Magnolia

Lady Colette

Entrance

● Rich Boy Rolan and Lady Colette will arrive in the roller coaster cars.

Nimbasa City Gym Leader
Elesa

● Electric-type Pokémon User

Recommended Level for your Pokémon	Lv. 30

If your Pokémon have Rock-, Ice-, and Ground-type moves, you'll have the advantage.

In this Gym, you'll ride the roller coasters and proceed by pressing the switches to change the path. Elesa's Zebstrika is weak against Ground-type moves, and her two Emolga are weak against Ice- and Rock-type moves but immune to Ground-type moves. If you don't have any of these moves, use TMs to teach your Pokémon Rock Tomb or Dig. And watch out for the new move called Volt Switch—after the user attacks, it immediately changes places with another Pokémon on Elesa's team!

Elesa's Pokémon

◎ Emolga ♂	Lv. 25	● Moves to watch out for:
Electric / Flying		Aerial Ace — Flying

◎ Emolga ♀	Lv. 25	● Moves to watch out for:
Electric / Flying		Pursuit — Dark

◎ Zebstrika ♂	Lv. 27	● Moves to watch out for:
Electric		Volt Switch — Electric

TM Received — TM 72 Volt Switch

It lets the Pokémon switch with a different Pokémon in the party after attacking.

Bolt Badge

Pokémon up to Lv. 50, including those received in trades, will obey you.

After beating the Nimbasa City Gym — Go west toward Route 5

The next destination is Driftveil City, where you can get your fifth Gym Badge. Head west from Nimbasa City, passing through the gate on the west side of the city and over to Route 5 (p. 112).

You can ride the Ferris wheel with a Trainer

After you defeat the Nimbasa City Gym, a Pokémon Trainer will show up in front of the Ferris wheel. After you defeat the Trainer, you can ride the Ferris wheel together. The Trainer changes depending on the season and your gender, so you'll get to enjoy different conversations during your Ferris wheel rides.

Anville Town

Anville Town is a small town. You can get there by riding a train from the Gear Station in Nimbasa City. There is a turntable to change the direction of trains at the center of the town. The town gets lively with tourists on Saturdays and Sundays, when the trains come through.

Field Moves Needed

Items

- [ ] Calcium
- [ ] Carbos
- [ ] Elixir
- [ ] Full Restore
- [ ] HP Up
- [ ] Iron
- [ ] Max Revive
- [ ] Protein
- [ ] Rare Candy
- [ ] Zinc

● A Depot Agent in Anville Town will give you items depending on your success in the Battle Subway. If you have a seven-win streak in the Battle Subway, you'll get a different item. If you have two or more seven-win streaks, the number of items increases. The Depot Agent can give you as many as 10 items at once!

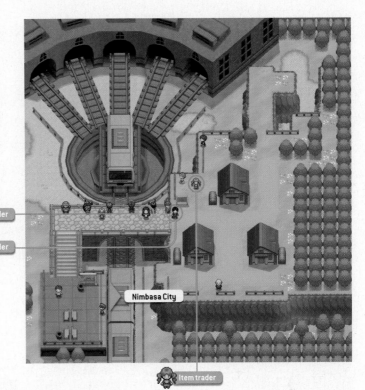

Item trader

Item trader

Nimbasa City

Item trader

Step 1 — Visit on weekends to trade items

On Saturdays and Sundays, people who trade items visit the town. One person gives you a Revive in exchange for two Escape Ropes; another gives you a PP Up in exchange for a Star Piece; and another gives you a Full Restore in exchange for 20 Poké Balls.

Will you trade your 2 Escape Ropes for my 1 Revive?

▶ YES
   NO

Listen to the flute player

On the bridge above the turntable, a woman is playing a flute. Move toward the woman, and the sound will be louder. If you walk away from her, the sound will be softer.

● Flute

Route 16 • Lostlorn Forest

Story

Route 16 is a short road connecting Nimbasa City and Marvelous Bridge. Through a break in the trees on the north side, you'll find Lostlorn Forest. It is said that people get lost there somehow, although the forest is not very big.

Field Moves Needed

Cut Surf Strength Waterfall

Route 16

Items

- ☐ Charcoal
- ☐ Rare Candy
- ☐ TM66 Payback

Tall Grass

Pokémon	
Gothita ■	○
Liepard	○
Minccino	○
Solosis ☐	○
Trubbish	○

Tall Grass (rustling)

Pokémon	
Audino	◎
Cinccino	△
Emolga	△

Dark Grass

Pokémon	
Gothita ■	○
Liepard	○
Minccino	○
Solosis ☐	○
Trubbish	○

Whimsicott

Grass

ABILITIES
- ● Prankster
- ● Infiltrator

Lostlorn Forest

Items

- ● First visit
- ☐ Big Mushroom
- ● After getting Surf and Waterfall
- ☐ Rare Candy

Tall Grass

Pokémon	
Cottonee ■	◎
Petilil ☐	○
Swadloon	◎
Tranquill	○
Venipede	○

Dark Grass

Pokémon	
Cottonee ■	○
Petilil ☐	○
Swadloon	◎
Tranquill	○
Venipede	○

Tall Grass (rustling)

Pokémon	
Audino	◎
Emolga	△
Leavanny	△
Lilligant ☐	△
Pansage	△
Pansear	△
Panpour	△
Unfezant	△
Whimsicott ■	△

Water Surface

Pokémon	
Basculin (Blue-Striped Form) ☐	◎
Basculin (Red-Striped Form) ■	◎

Water Surface (ripples)

Pokémon	
Basculin (Blue-Striped Form) ■	◎
Basculin (Red-Striped Form) ☐	◎

■ Route 16

A

Nimbasa City

1

Policeman Daniel Backpacker Stephen Cyclist Krissa Backpacker Peter Backpacker Lora Cyclist Hector

1 You can visit after finishing the main story (p. 201).

■ Lostlorn Forest

A

UNOVA ADVENTURE WALKTHROUGH

ROUTE 16 • LOSTLORN FOREST

Lostlorn Forest

■ After finishing the main story

◉ **Fishing**

Pokémon	
Basculin (Blue-Striped Form) ☐	○
Basculin (Red-Striped Form) ■	○
Goldeen	◎

◉ **Fishing** (ripples)

Pokémon	
Basculin (Blue-Striped Form) ■	○
Basculin (Red-Striped Form) ☐	○
Goldeen	◎

Step 1 ## Head east while battling Pokémon Trainers

Route 16 is a short road, but six Pokémon Trainers are waiting to battle you there. One of them is behind a boulder that can be moved by using Strength. Battle all the Trainers and make your Pokémon strong in preparation for the Nimbasa City Gym Battle.

I will have a Pokémon battle at this speed!

Step 2 ## A mysterious woman lives in Lostlorn Forest

Head through the trees to the north to find the entrance to Lostlorn Forest. You'll come to a camper parked at the north end, but the woman inside won't respond if you speak to her. According to the nearby Backpacker, she seems to think living quietly by herself is important.

Step 3 ## You can't go to Marvelous Bridge yet

There is an entrance to Marvelous Bridge on the east side of Route 16. However, you can't enter because the bridge is being checked. You can go to Marvelous Bridge after finishing the main story (p. 201).

They said Marvelous Bridge is being checked!

Come back later for a Rare Candy

If you go back to Lostlorn Forest after getting HM06 Waterfall on Route 18, you can get a Rare Candy by climbing the waterfall. Don't forget to go back for it!

Step 4 ## Go back to Nimbasa City

Go back to Nimbasa City after exploring Route 16 and Lostlorn Forest. Now, you can challenge the Nimbasa City Gym at last (p. 108). Head to the Gym after visiting the Pokémon Center to heal your Pokémon.

Lilligant

Grass

ABILITIES
● Chlorophyll
● Own Tempo

Route 5

Story

Route 5 is a short road connecting Nimbasa City and Driftveil Drawbridge, but it is very lively because a lot of performers gather there. This is where you'll meet the Champion of the Unova region, Alder.

Field Moves Needed

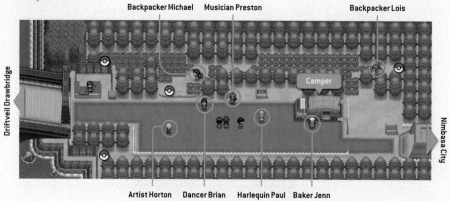

Backpacker Michael Musician Preston Backpacker Lois

Camper

Driftveil Drawbridge

Nimbasa City

Artist Horton Dancer Brian Harlequin Paul Baker Jenn

Items
- ☐ Great Ball
- ☐ Hyper Potion
- ☐ Revive
- ☐ Zinc

Props
- ● After defeating Musician Preston
- ☐ Electric Guitar

Tall Grass

Pokémon	
Gothita ■	○
Liepard	○
Minccino	○
Solosis ☐	○
Trubbish	○

Dark Grass

Pokémon	
Gothita ■	○
Liepard	○
Minccino	○
Solosis ☐	○
Trubbish	○

Tall Grass (rustling)

Pokémon	
Audino	◎
Cinccino	△
Emolga	△

● Items that the Maid in the camper buys

Items	Price	Items	Price	Items	Price	Items	Price
Aguav Berry	20	Liechi Berry	20	Yache Berry	20	Spelon Berry	500
Apicot Berry	20	Lum Berry	20	Sweet Heart	100	TinyMushroom	500
Aspear Berry	20	Mago Berry	20	Fresh Water	200	Watmel Berry	500
Babiri Berry	20	Occa Berry	20	Leftovers	200	Wepear Berry	500
Charti Berry	20	Oran Berry	20	Lucky Egg	200	Berry Juice	1,500
Cheri Berry	20	Passho Berry	20	Stick	200	Casteliacone	2,000
Chesto Berry	20	Payapa Berry	20	Soda Pop	300	Lava Cookie	4,000
Chilan Berry	20	Pecha Berry	20	Lemonade	350	Old Gateau	4,000
Chople Berry	20	Persim Berry	20	Belue Berry	500	Big Mushroom	5,000
Coba Berry	20	Petaya Berry	20	Bluk Berry	500	RageCandyBar	6,000
Colbur Berry	20	Pomeg Berry	20	Cornn Berry	500	Shoal Salt	7,000
Figy Berry	20	Qualot Berry	20	Durin Berry	500	Rare Candy	10,000
Ganlon Berry	20	Rawst Berry	20	Honey	500	BalmMushroom	25,000
Grepa Berry	20	Rindo Berry	20	Magost Berry	500	Custap Berry	30,000
Haban Berry	20	Salac Berry	20	Moomoo Milk	500	Enigma Berry	30,000
Hondew Berry	20	Shuca Berry	20	Nanab Berry	500	Jaboca Berry	30,000
Iapapa Berry	20	Sitrus Berry	20	Nomel Berry	500	Lansat Berry	30,000
Kasib Berry	20	Tamato Berry	20	Pamtre Berry	500	Micle Berry	30,000
Kebia Berry	20	Tanga Berry	20	Pinap Berry	500	Rowap Berry	30,000
Kelpsy Berry	20	Wacan Berry	20	Rabuta Berry	500	Starf Berry	30,000
Leppa Berry	20	Wiki Berry	20	Razz Berry	500		

UNOVA ADVENTURE WALKTHROUGH · ROUTE 5

Step 1 — Cheren challenges you to battle

When you head west from Nimbasa City, Cheren catches up with you. It seems Cheren also got a Bolt Badge in Nimbasa City. He wants to see which of you is stronger, so he challenges you to battle.

Let's test who's stronger—you or me! This time, I'm going to win!

Battle your childhood friend Cheren! 5

All Pokémon's levels have increased by four since the fourth battle, and Pidove has evolved to Tranquill.

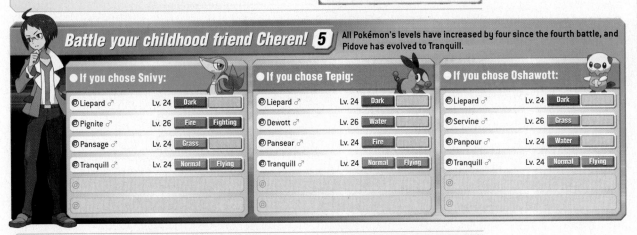

If you chose Snivy:

Liepard ♂	Lv. 24	Dark
Pignite ♂	Lv. 26	Fire / Fighting
Pansage ♂	Lv. 24	Grass
Tranquill ♂	Lv. 24	Normal / Flying

If you chose Tepig:

Liepard ♂	Lv. 24	Dark
Dewott ♂	Lv. 26	Water
Pansear ♂	Lv. 24	Fire
Tranquill ♂	Lv. 24	Normal / Flying

If you chose Oshawott:

Liepard ♂	Lv. 24	Dark
Servine ♂	Lv. 26	Grass
Panpour ♂	Lv. 24	Water
Tranquill ♂	Lv. 24	Normal / Flying

Step 2 — Meet the Champion of the Unova region

When you head west with Elesa as your guide, you meet a man with red hair. He is the Champion of the Unova region, Alder. Cheren tells Alder that the purpose of his journey is to become the Champion, but he can't answer why he wants to become the Champion.

Alder: Hm. Traveling with a goal in mind is a commendable thing.

Step 3 — Team up with Cheren to have a Tag Battle

Cheren can't find a purpose for his journey other than striving to become stronger, so Alder asks you and Cheren to have a battle with two Preschoolers. Team up with Cheren and battle. Afterwards, Alder teaches Cheren that some people are happy just being with Pokémon.

Cheren: OK, let's battle.

Have your Pokémon healed before moving forward

After the Tag Battle with the Preschoolers, go back to Nimbasa City before battling Pokémon Trainers on Route 5. Drop by the Pokémon Center to restore your Pokémon's health.

Step 4 — Thanks to Elesa, the drawbridge is lowered

When you head west with Elesa as a guide, she contacts somebody at the foot of the bridge and asks them to lower the drawbridge. Once the drawbridge is lowered and people can cross, Cheren leaves for Driftveil City.

It's me, Elesa. Please lower the drawbridge.

Calling Clay

Elesa contacted the Driftveil City Gym Leader, Clay. As the Gym Leader, Clay is also a manager of Driftveil Drawbridge.

Step 5 — Explore Route 5

Before going to Driftveil Drawbridge, battle Pokémon Trainers and collect items on Route 5. Battle all seven Trainers and make your Pokémon strong to prepare for the next Gym Battle.

As my mind roams, as the wind blows, destiny has brought us to this battle.

Get a Prop for a Musical

Defeat Musician Preston, and he will give you an Electric Guitar Prop. Props are used to Dress Up Pokémon in the Pokémon Musical in Nimbasa City.

Step 6 — Sell a lot of food to the Maid

The Maid in the camper buys various food items from you. "Food" includes Berries and other items with food-like names. Check the list and sell various items to the Maid (p. 112).

Do you have a wonderful ingredient in your Bag?

It's a better deal than a Poké Mart

Except BalmMushroom, you can sell items that the Maid buys in a Poké Mart, too. However, the prices that the Maid pays for the items are much higher than a Poké Mart. It's a much better deal to sell items to the Maid.

Step 7 — Head west and cross Driftveil Drawbridge

If you go west on Route 5, you'll see the Driftveil Drawbridge that was just lowered. Driftveil City, located on the west side of the drawbridge, has the fifth Pokémon Gym. Cross Driftveil Drawbridge to head to Driftveil City.

A drawbridge raises and lowers, depending on the ship schedules

Driftveil Drawbridge

Story

Driftveil Drawbridge is a bridge that raises and lowers depending on the ship schedules. Driftveil Drawbridge is managed by the Driftveil City Gym Leader, Clay. Above the bridge, flying Pokémon come and go.

Field Moves Needed

Driftveil City · A · Route 5 (to Nimbasa City)

A

🔅 Pokémon shadow

Pokémon	
Ducklett	◎

Ducklett

Water · Flying

ABILITIES
● Keen Eye
● Big Pecks

Step 1 — Cross the bridge to Driftveil City

Thanks to Elesa and Clay, Driftveil Drawbridge is now lowered. Cross the bridge to head west. Once you finish crossing the bridge, you are right in front of Driftveil City (p. 116). The bridge is very long and you have to travel far. Ride your Bicycle to cross the bridge quickly.

Step on a shadow of a flying Pokémon

You can see shadows of flying Pokémon on the bridge. Step on these shadows. You will get various kinds of Wings (p. 29) and Ducklett may jump out. If you see a shadow, make sure to step on it.

Pokémon That Learn Many of the Field Moves

Some Pokémon can learn a variety of field moves such as Strength and Surf. With these Pokémon on your team, you'll have no trouble getting anywhere in the Unova region. Take them with you and let them support your journey.

Use these Pokémon to make travel easy

Watchog

Usable field moves

Flash	Normal
Cut	Normal
Strength	Normal

Watchog is found on Route 7. You could also raise a Patrat found on Route 1 up to Lv. 20, when it evolves.

Basculin (Red-Striped Form / Blue-Striped Form)

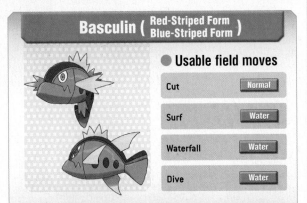

Usable field moves

Cut	Normal
Surf	Water
Waterfall	Water
Dive	Water

You can get Basculin from a boy in a house in Driftveil City in exchange for Minccino.

Ducklett

Usable field moves

Fly	Flying
Surf	Water
Dive	Water

You may find Ducklett when you step on a Pokémon shadow on Driftveil Drawbridge.

Tirtouga

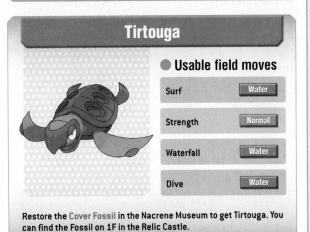

Usable field moves

Surf	Water
Strength	Normal
Waterfall	Water
Dive	Water

Restore the Cover Fossil in the Nacrene Museum to get Tirtouga. You can find the Fossil on 1F in the Relic Castle.

Frillish

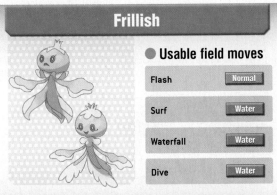

Usable field moves

Flash	Normal
Surf	Water
Waterfall	Water
Dive	Water

Frillish may be found when you use Surf on Route 17 and on the water surface of Route 4.

Haxorus

Usable field moves

Cut	Normal
Surf	Water
Strength	Normal

You can get Haxorus by leveling up the Fraxure found on Victory Road to Lv. 48.

Driftveil City

Story

Driftveil City is a port where various goods are distributed. There is a market in the city where you can buy items that you can't buy anywhere else. Come here to earn your fifth Gym Badge.

Field Moves Needed

Surf

Items

- **First visit**
- ☐ Big Pearl
- ☐ Repeat Ball x3
- ☐ Ultra Ball
- **When your Pokédex's SEEN number is 50 or more Pokémon**
- ☐ Shell Bell
- **If you have a Pokémon at Lv. 30 or more in your party**
- ☐ Expert Belt
- **After visiting the Cold Storage**
- ☐ Fresh Water
- **After defeating the Driftveil City Gym**
- ☐ Quake Badge
- **After defeating Bianca**
- ☐ HM02 Fly
- **After getting Surf**
- ☐ Water Stone

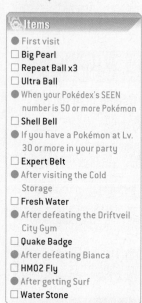

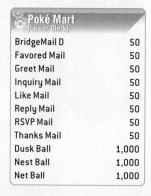

Route 6 (to Mistralton City)

Driftveil City Gym

Pokémon Center

Trade: Basculin (Receive Basculin in exchange for Minccino)

Driftveil Market

Move Tutor's House

Driftveil Drawbridge (to Nimbasa City)

Cold Storage

Motorcyclist Charles

Driftveil Market

Heal Powder	450
EnergyPowder	500
Moomoo Milk	500
Energy Root	800
Revival Herb	2,800

Poké Mart
(Lower Clerk)

BridgeMail D	50
Favored Mail	50
Greet Mail	50
Inquiry Mail	50
Like Mail	50
Reply Mail	50
RSVP Mail	50
Thanks Mail	50
Dusk Ball	1,000
Nest Ball	1,000
Net Ball	1,000

Water Surface

Pokémon	
Frillish	◎

Water Surface (ripples)

Pokémon	
Alomomola	◎
Jellicent	△

■ After finishing the main story

Fishing

Pokémon	
Chinchou	○
Krabby	◎
Luvdisc	△

Fishing (ripples)

Pokémon	
Chinchou	◎
Kingler	△
Lanturn	△
Luvdisc	○

Step 1 Clay asks you to find Team Plasma

When you enter the city, the Gym Leader Clay and Cheren are standing there. Clay is upset because when they lowered the bridge, the Team Plasma guys they had caught escaped. Clay asks you to find Team Plasma.

Yer both talented Trainers, aren't ya?

Sometimes it rains

Driftveil City's weather changes depending on the date and season. Rain can fall during spring, summer, and autumn, and snow or hail will sometimes fall during winter. When you visit the city, observe the changes in weather (p. 206).

Dewott

Servine

Pignite

Step 2 Learn a special move in the Move Tutor's House

In the Move Tutor's House, if you have a strong bond with any of the three starter Pokémon, he will teach that Pokémon a battle-combo move. If these moves are used at the same time in a Double Battle or a Triple Battle, their power increases and they create a special effect.

A special move...
Should I teach it a battle-combo move?

● Battle-combo moves that can be learned and Pokémon in the Unova Pokédex that can learn those moves

Move	Effect	Pokémon
Grass Pledge	When combined with Water Pledge or Fire Pledge, the power and effect will change.	Snivy
	If combined with Water Pledge, the power will be 150 and it becomes a Grass-type move. It lowers the Speed of your foe's Pokémon for three turns.	Servine
	If combined with Fire Pledge, the power will be 150 and it becomes a Fire-type move. It damages all types except Fire for three turns.	Serperior
Fire Pledge	When combined with Water Pledge or Grass Pledge, the power and effect will change.	Tepig
	If combined with Water Pledge, the power will be 150 and it becomes a Water-type move. It boosts your team's chances of added move effects.	Pignite
	If combined with Grass Pledge, the power will be 150 and it becomes a Fire-type move. It damages all types except Fire for three turns.	Emboar
Water Pledge	When combined with Fire Pledge or Grass Pledge, the power and effect will change.	Oshawott
	If combined with Fire Pledge, the power will be 150 and it becomes a Water-type move. It boosts your team's chances of added move effects.	Dewott
	If combined with Grass Pledge, the power will be 150 and it becomes a Grass-type move. It lowers the Speed of your foe's Pokémon for three turns.	Samurott

Step 3 Show a Pokémon she wants to see and get a Heart Scale

When you speak to a woman in a house on the west side of the Pokémon Center, she says that she wants to see a Pokémon that knows a certain move. If you show her a Pokémon she wants to see, she will give you a Heart Scale. You can speak to her every day to get a Heart Scale.

I would like to see a Pokémon that has learned a move called Struggle Bug.

Your Pokémon can re-learn moves in Mistralton City

A Heart Scale is an item necessary to let your Pokémon remember one of the moves it has forgotten. If you want your Pokémon to remember one of the moves it has forgotten, go to the Move Family's House in Mistralton City and speak to the reminder girl (p. 130)

Step 4 Learn Rotation (Triple) Battle

Charles is riding a motorcycle on the west side of the Driftveil Market. Speak to Charles. He will teach you Rotation (Triple) Battle, and you can also battle with him. Try out this new battle format!

Its name... Rotation Battle!
Want to learn about it?

Two new battle formats

Motorcyclist Charles teaches you Rotation Battle in *Pokémon Black Version* and Triple Battle in *Pokémon White Version*.

Step 5 Enjoy shopping in the Driftveil Market

In the Driftveil Market, you can buy items that you can't buy anywhere else. These include Moomoo Milk and medicinal herbs such as Heal Powder and EnergyPowder. You can buy Moomoo Milk by the dozen!

₱ 157200

► One bottle
One dozen
No thanks!

Moomoo Milk—one bottle for ₱500.
Would you like some for your trip?

Get a Shell Bell

An elderly man in a house on the east side of the Pokémon Center gives you a Shell Bell if your Pokédex's SEEN number is 50 or more. It restores the user's HP by one-eighth of the damage taken by the target.

Step 6 — Go to the Cold Storage to find Team Plasma

Clay asked you to find Team Plasma, and they seem to have fled into the Cold Storage on the south side of the city. You can't challenge the Driftveil City Gym to battle unless you find Team Plasma. Head south through the city and go to the Cold Storage (p. 121).

After visiting the Cold Storage — Ghetsis takes Team Plasma away

When you arrive at the Driftveil City Gym, Ghetsis is in front of the Gym demanding the handover of the Team Plasma members. Ghetsis threatens Clay, saying they have many, many more members around them. Clay has no choice but to comply with the demand, so Ghetsis leaves with the Team Plasma members.

Get an Expert Belt

If you have a Pokémon at Lv. 30 or more in your party, a man with sunglasses in the Driftveil Market will give you an Expert Belt. This item boosts the power of supereffective moves.

The inside of the market is different

The fruit and flowers in the Driftveil Market are different between *Pokémon Black Version* and *Pokémon White Version*. If your friend is playing a different version, take a peek to see the changes!

Gym battle 5 — Driftveil City Gym

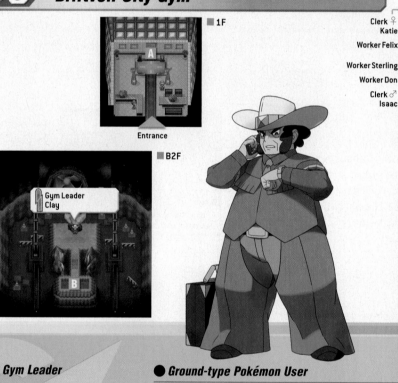

■ 1F

A

Entrance

■ B2F

Gym Leader Clay

B

■ B1F

Clerk ♀ Katie
Worker Felix
Worker Sterling
Worker Don
Clerk ♂ Isaac

A

Driftveil City Gym Leader
Clay

● Ground-type Pokémon User

Recommended Level for your Pokémon	Lv. 34

Inflict great damage using Water-, Fighting-, and Grass-type moves

Take the elevators up and down to move through the Gym. Clay's Krokorok is weak against Grass-, Water-, and Fighting-type moves, Excadrill is weak against Water- and Fighting-type moves, and Palpitoad is weak against Grass-type moves. If your Pokémon can learn Grass Knot and Scald, use these moves to target their weaknesses.

Clay's Pokémon

◉ Krokorok ♂	Lv. 29	● Moves to watch out for:	
Ground	Dark	Swagger	Normal

◉ Excadrill ♂	Lv. 31	● Moves to watch out for:	
Ground	Steel	Rock Slide	Rock

◉ Palpitoad ♂	Lv. 29	● Moves to watch out for:	
Water	Ground	Muddy Water	Water

Quake Badge

Pokémon up to Lv. 60, including those received in trades, will obey you.

● Unlike the other Gym Leaders, Clay won't give you a TM right after the battle. You'll get it when you meet him at the Chargestone Cave entrance (p. 126).

After beating the Driftveil City Gym — Bianca stops you and challenges you to a battle

When you are heading west to Mistralton City, Bianca stops you. At first, Bianca is distracted because she is so impressed by the fact that you won the Gym battle and got a Quake Badge. Then she regains her focus and challenges you to a Pokémon battle.

I'm also a Trainer!
At times like this you battle, right?

Battle your childhood friend Bianca! 4

Her Pokémon's levels have increased by eight from your third battle. Munna has evolved into Musharna.

● If you chose Snivy:

Herdier ♀	Lv. 26	Normal
Pansear ♂	Lv. 26	Fire
Dewott ♂	Lv. 28	Water
Musharna ♀	Lv. 26	Psychic

● If you chose Tepig:

Herdier ♀	Lv. 26	Normal
Panpour ♂	Lv. 26	Water
Servine ♂	Lv. 28	Grass
Musharna ♀	Lv. 26	Psychic

● If you chose Oshawott:

Herdier ♀	Lv. 26	Normal
Pansage ♂	Lv. 26	Grass
Pignite ♂	Lv. 28	Fire / Fighting
Musharna ♀	Lv. 26	Psychic

After beating the Driftveil City Gym — Get HM02 Fly from Bianca

Win the battle with Bianca and she will give you HM02 Fly. This item allows you to fly instantly to any place you have already visited. Teach the move to a Pokémon right away so that you can move around the Unova region easily.

Trainer obtained an HM02 Fly!

After beating the Driftveil City Gym — Go west towards Route 6

The next destination is Mistralton City, where the sixth Pokémon Gym is located. You can get there by taking Route 6 on the west side of Driftveil City and passing the Chargestone Cave. Take Route 6 to Mistralton City (p. 124).

Use Surf to get an item

After getting HM03 Surf, you can go to an island with a lighthouse on the water. You can get an item there, so after you find Surf, visit Driftveil City again.

People Who Look After Pokémon

During your travels in Unova, you'll meet people who help you by raising your Pokémon's friendship, changing your Pokémon's nicknames, teaching your Pokémon moves, and more. If you forget where to find one of these people, check this page.

These people will help you every day...

By raising your Pokémon's friendship

Where Pokémon Massage in Castelia City

Speak to a woman on the first floor of a building on Castelia Street, and she will raise the friendship of a Pokémon in your party.

(p. 94)

If you'd like, I will massage your Pokémon.

By changing your Pokémon's nicknames

Where Name Rater in Castelia City

Speak to an elderly man on the first floor of a building on the path to Route 4, and he will change your Pokémon's nickname.

(p. 95)

Want me to rate the nicknames of your Pokémon?

By rating your friendship with your Pokémon

Where Pokémon Fan Club in Icirrus City

Speak to a woman in the Pokémon Fan Club, and she will rate your friendship with one of the Pokémon in your party.

(p. 148)

Shall I check how friendly your Pokémon is toward you?

By helping your Pokémon forget the moves they know

Where Move Family's House in Mistralton City

Speak to the Move Deleter at the Move Family's House, and he will let your Pokémon forget any move, including an HM.

(p. 129)

You've come to make me force your Pokémon to forget some moves?

By helping your Pokémon remember moves they've forgotten

Where Move Family's House in Mistralton City

Give one Heart Scale to the reminder girl at the Move Family's House, and she will help your Pokémon remember a forgotten move.

(p. 130)

Should a move be remembered?

By teaching your Pokémon battle-combo moves

Where Move Tutor's House in Driftveil City

If Snivy, Tepig, Oshawott, or their evolved form has a strong bond with you, he will teach you a battle-combo move.

(p. 117)

A special move... Should I teach it a battle-combo move?

By teaching your Pokémon ultimate moves

Where Ultimate Move Tutor's House on Route 13

If you are good friends with Serperior, Emboar, or Samurott, he will teach it an ultimate move.

(p. 222)

Shall I teach them to your Pokémon?

By teaching the strongest Dragon-type move to your Dragon-type Pokémon

Where Drayden's House in Opelucid City

If a Dragon-type Pokémon, such as Druddigon or Fraxure, has a strong bond with you, Iris (Drayden) will teach that Pokémon the move Draco Meteor.

(p. 196)

Fun, huh? Want me to teach your Pokémon this move?

Cold Storage

Story

Cold Storage is where a lot of goods are stored before they are distributed in Driftveil City. Stretches of tall grass grow in this area, and you will find various kinds of Pokémon. Search this area to find Team Plasma.

Field Moves Needed

■ Cold Storage Area

Driftveil City · Youngster Kenneth · Youngster Albert

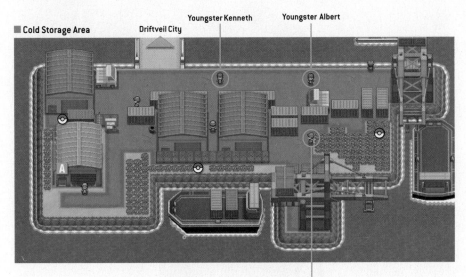

Worker Eddie

Items

- ● First visit
- ☐ Ether
- ☐ Heart Scale
- ☐ Hyper Potion
- ☐ Ice Heal
- ☐ Net Ball
- ☐ NeverMeltIce
- ☐ Protein
- ☐ Rocky Helmet
- ☐ TM55 Scald
- ● After finishing the main story
- ☐ TM01 Hone Claws

Cold Storage Area

Tall Grass	
Pokémon	
Herdier	◎
Minccino	○
Timburr	○
Vanillite	○

Tall Grass (rustling)	
Pokémon	
Audino	◎
Cinccino	△
Stoutland	△

Dark Grass	
Pokémon	
Herdier	◎
Minccino	○
Timburr	○
Vanillite	○

Herdier

Normal

ABILITIES
- ● Intimidate
- ● Sand Rush

■ Storage Building

Worker Ryan

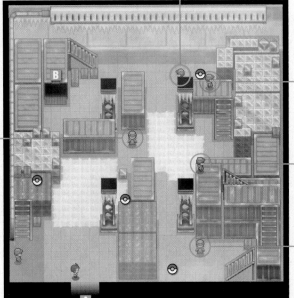

Worker Victor

Worker Glenn

Worker Filipe

Worker Patton

Vanillite

Ice

ABILITY
- ● Ice Body

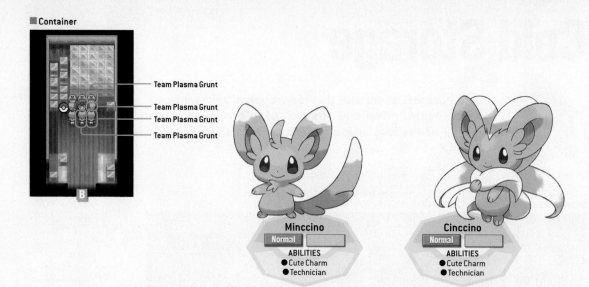

■ Container

Team Plasma Grunt

Team Plasma Grunt
Team Plasma Grunt

Team Plasma Grunt

B

Minccino

Normal

ABILITIES
● Cute Charm
● Technician

Cinccino

Normal

ABILITIES
● Cute Charm
● Technician

Step 1 — Collect items while battling Trainers

Three Pokémon Trainers are waiting at the Cold Storage area. Before you enter the storage building, battle these Trainers and collect items. Some Pokémon in the tall grass here are difficult to find elsewhere. Catch and register them in your Pokédex.

The pure chill of the Cold Storage! Taste how cold it is!

Find items with the Dowsing MCHN

The Cold Storage area has many hidden items. If you use the Dowsing MCHN, you can find these items!

Step 2 — Cheren shows up in front of the storage building

When you approach the west end of the Cold Storage area, Cheren shows up. He will check the inside of the storage building with you. Enter the building. If your Pokémon are hurt, go back to the Pokémon Center in Driftveil City to restore their health first.

Cheren: All right, Trainer. Let's get this over with.

Step 3 — The icy floor makes walking tricky

The floor in the storage building is frozen and icy. Once you step on the ice, you can't stop until you hit a wall or an obstacle. Think carefully about how to get where you want to go before moving.

some places are frozen, so you go sliding around!

You can't get anywhere from the container by the entrance

There is a ladder to the roof of a container just north of the storage entrance. It looks like you can proceed from here, but you can't because of the ice floor. Use the ladder to exit the storage building after catching Team Plasma.

Step 4 — Proceed while battling Trainers

You can't move freely in the storage building because the floor is covered with ice. There is a single path through the building, so slide on the ice floor and battle Pokémon Trainers along the way. The direction you should aim is the container on the west end. You'll meet five Trainers in total.

Let's warm up with a Pokémon battle!

Step 5 — Team Plasma hiding in a container

Enter the container in the west end of the storage building and you'll find the hiding place of Zinzolin, one of the Seven Sages. Zinzolin has been keeping warm by huddling in the middle of a group of Team Plasma Grunts. When he notices you and Cheren coming in, he commands the Grunts to attack you.

Zinzolin: All of you—huddle around me! I can't take this cold...

Step 6 — Battle the Team Plasma Grunts

The eight Team Plasma Grunts who were surrounding Zinzolin stand right in front of you. Cheren takes care of the four on the left side. Speak to each of the four on the right side and challenge them to a battle. Defeat the four Team Plasma Grunts, and Team Plasma will surrender.

Cheren: Trainer, you take care of those guys over there!

Use items to heal your Pokémon

You will battle the Team Plasma Grunts one by one, so you can heal your Pokémon between the battles. If your Pokémon are hurt, don't push them too hard. Instead, restore their HP by using items before battling the next Grunt.

Step 7 — Clay takes Team Plasma away

When you beat Team Plasma, Clay enters the container with a lot of Workers. The Workers take Team Plasma away. Clay tells you to come challenge his Gym as he promised, and then leaves.

You guys take these Pokémon robbers!

Step 8 — Go back to Driftveil City and challenge the Gym

Now that you've defeated Team Plasma, you can finally challenge the Gym. Head north from the Cold Storage and have your Pokémon healed in the Pokémon Center. After your Pokémon are healed, visit the Driftveil City Gym on the north side of the city (p. 118).

Route 6

Story

Route 6 is a road surrounded by rich nature with a flowing river and green trees. The Season Research Lab stands at the center. The Scientists are conducting research on Pokémon whose form changes depending on the season.

Field Moves Needed

Surf

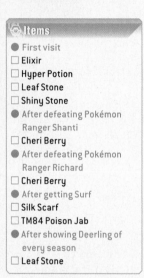

Items

- ● First visit
- ☐ Elixir
- ☐ Hyper Potion
- ☐ Leaf Stone
- ☐ Shiny Stone
- ● After defeating Pokémon Ranger Shanti
- ☐ Cheri Berry
- ● After defeating Pokémon Ranger Richard
- ☐ Cheri Berry
- ● After getting Surf
- ☐ Silk Scarf
- ☐ TM84 Poison Jab
- ● After showing Deerling of every season
- ☐ Leaf Stone

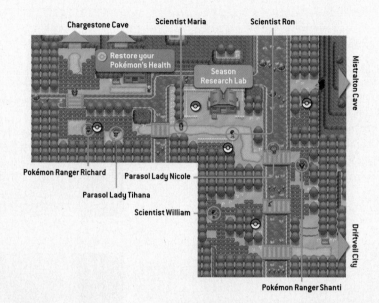

Chargestone Cave • Scientist Maria • Scientist Ron

Restore your Pokémon's Health

Season Research Lab

Mistralton Cave

Pokémon Ranger Richard • Parasol Lady Nicole

Parasol Lady Tihana

Scientist William

Driftveil City

Pokémon Ranger Shanti

Spring Summer Autumn

Tall Grass

Pokémon	
Deerling	◎
Foongus	○
Karrablast	○
Swadloon	△
Tranquill	○

Tall Grass (rustling)

Pokémon	
Audino	◎
Emolga	○
Leavanny	△
Unfezant	△

Dark Grass

Pokémon	
Deerling	◎
Foongus	○
Karrablast	○
Swadloon	△
Tranquill	○

Winter

Tall Grass

Pokémon	
Deerling	◎
Foongus	○
Karrablast	○
Swadloon	△
Vanillite	○

Tall Grass (rustling)

Pokémon	
Audino	◎
Emolga	○
Leavanny	△

Dark Grass

Pokémon	
Deerling	◎
Foongus	○
Karrablast	○
Swadloon	△
Vanillite	○

All Seasons

Water Surface

Pokémon	
Basculin (Blue-Striped Form) ☐	◎
Basculin (Red-Striped Form) ■	◎

Water Surface (ripples)

Pokémon	
Basculin (Blue-Striped Form) ■	◎
Basculin (Red-Striped Form) ☐	◎

■ After finishing the main story

Fishing

Pokémon	
Basculin (Blue-Striped Form) ☐	○
Basculin (Red-Striped Form) ■	○
Poliwag	◎
Poliwhirl	△

Fishing (ripples)

Pokémon	
Basculin (Blue-Striped Form) ■	○
Basculin (Red-Striped Form) ☐	○
Poliwhirl	◎
Politoed	△

Karrablast

Bug

ABILITIES
- ● Swarm
- ● Shed Skin

Step 1 — Stop by the Season Research Lab

At the Season Research Lab, research is being conducted on Deerling, which changes form depending on the season (p. 248). The researcher on the left will ask you to assist him with his research when you talk to him. Put a Deerling in your party and show it to him. You can catch Deerling on Route 6.

haven't really had a chance to catch many Deerling to study. ▼

Show Deerling's four forms to the researchers

Show the researcher at the Season Research Lab Deerling's four forms—Spring Form, Summer Form, Autumn Form, and Winter Form—and he will give you a Leaf Stone as a thank you.

Step 2 — Heal your Pokémon on the way

Keep heading west and talk to the woman in a house on Route 6. She will heal your Pokémon. Feel free to stop by and heal the Pokémon in your party when they are hurt during battles in the area with Pokémon Trainers or wild Pokémon.

You can't go anywhere when you're not feeling well. ▼

Get Berries by defeating Trainers

Defeat the Pokémon Rangers Shanti and Richard in battle to get Cheri Berries. Shanti is on the eastern part of Route 6 and Richard is on the west side. Be sure to battle them and get Cheri Berries.

Step 3 — Head for Chargestone Cave

Your next destination, Mistralton City, lies just beyond Chargestone Cave. Continue north from the westernmost part of Route 6 and you will reach the entrance to Chargestone Cave (p. 126). Heal your Pokémon at the house, and continue on your way north.

Don't be fooled by Foongus!

Sometimes, when you check items that have fallen on the ground, a Foongus will pop out and surprise you. With their Poké Ball caps, the Foongus look just like fallen items! The battle comes out of nowhere, so be ready for a battle whenever picking up an item.

After getting Surf — Head for Mistralton Cave after gathering items

If you use Surf to cross the water, you can reach Mistralton Cave on the easternmost part of the route (p. 143). After you collect the items in places that can only be reached if you use Surf, head for Mistralton Cave, where a legendary Pokémon is rumored to reside.

Look for items every time you visit

Use the Dowsing MCHN every time you visit Route 6. Even if you collect all of the items here, new TinyMushrooms sprout after a couple of days. Try to find the other locations in the Unova region where items are hidden.

Chargestone Cave

Story

Chargestone Cave is where electrically charged stones wait around every corner. Pathways are blocked by stones, and there are ledges as well. The exit will lead you to Mistralton City.

Field Moves Needed

■ 1F

Scientist Ronald · Ace Trainer Jared · Hiker Hardy · Scientist Orville · Ace Trainer Corky · Mistralton City

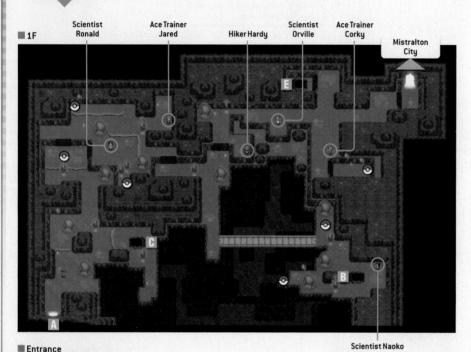

Scientist Naoko

Items

● First visit
- ☐ BrightPowder
- ☐ Heal Ball
- ☐ Hyper Potion ×2
- ☐ Iron
- ☐ Lucky Egg
- ☐ Magnet
- ☐ Nugget ×2
- ☐ Parlyz Heal
- ☐ Rare Candy
- ☐ Revive
- ☐ Thunderstone
- ☐ Timer Ball
- ☐ TM78 Bulldoze

● After finishing the main story
- ☐ TM69 Rock Polish

■ Entrance

Route 6
(To Driftveil City)

■ B1F

Team Plasma Grunt · Team Plasma Grunt

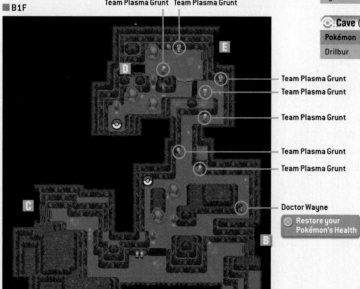

Team Plasma Grunt
Team Plasma Grunt

Team Plasma Grunt

Team Plasma Grunt
Team Plasma Grunt

Doctor Wayne
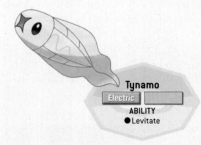
Restore your Pokémon's Health

1F • B1F	
Cave	
Pokémon	
Boldore	△
Ferroseed	○
Joltik	◎
Klink	○
Tynamo	▲

Cave (dust cloud)	
Pokémon	
Drilbur	◎

B2F	
Cave	
Pokémon	
Boldore	△
Ferroseed	○
Joltik	◎
Klink	○
Tynamo	△

Cave (dust cloud)	
Pokémon	
Drilbur	◎

Tynamo
Electric

ABILITY
● Levitate

Joltik

Bug | Electric

ABILITIES
● Compoundeyes
● Unnerve

Klink

Steel |

ABILITIES
● Plus
● Minus

■ B2F

Ace Trainer Allison

Ace Trainer Stella

Step 1 — Have Clay clear the way

As you approach the Chargestone Cave, a Galvantula web is blocking the entrance. Clay comes right along and removes it for you. He'll give you TM78 Bulldoze, which he should have given you after your Gym battle, then heads off on his way

> if there are folks havin' problems, th' Gym Leader's th' one ta fix it.

No way in before the Gym battle

Even if you visit Chargestone Cave before you get the Quake Badge from the Driftveil Gym, you can't go in the cave. This is because Clay, who can break the web blocking the entrance, will not come along to save the day. If you don't have it yet, get that Gym Badge and come back.

Step 2 — Meet N and the Shadow Triad

Three dark figures will surround you when you enter the cave, then take you to N. They are members of the Shadow Triad—members of Team Plasma picked by Ghetsis himself. N tells you that Team Plasma is waiting ahead to test you.

> My lord N, we brought the one you wanted.

Step 3 — Reunite with Bianca and Professor Juniper

Continue into the cave, and Bianca and Professor Juniper will approach you. The professor is here to research Klink, while Bianca is acting as her bodyguard. Bianca tells you that you can move the floating stones by pushing them. Professor Juniper will hand you the Lucky Egg.

> Trainer obtained a Lucky Egg!

Give a Pokémon the Lucky Egg to hold

Here in this dark cave, Professor Juniper is kind enough to give you the Lucky Egg. When a Pokémon holds this item, it receives more Experience Points after battle, so have the first Pokémon in your party hold it (p. 37).

UNOVA ADVENTURE WALKTHROUGH

CHARGESTONE CAVE

Step 4 — Continue into the cave while pushing stones

Clear the way forward by moving the stones blocking the path, just like Bianca showed you. The stones are electrically charged, so they will stick to boulders. If you try and push a stone in a direction with no boulders, it can't move. When you want to move a stone, push it while facing in the direction of a nearby boulder.

Go to a different floor if you make a mistake

If you push a stone in the wrong direction, you can head to another floor and it will return to where it was before. You can start over as many times as you need to, so don't worry too much when moving the stones.

Step 5 — Have the Doctor heal your Pokémon

Doctor Wayne is on the path in B1F. After you defeat the Doctor in a Pokémon battle, he will heal all of your Pokémon. Talk to him again after defeating him, and he will heal your Pokémon whenever you need it. It's good to have a Doctor in the house!

Now, as I promised, I will make your Pokémon healthy.

A cave that affects Pokémon evolution

Chargestone Cave is connected to the evolution of Pokémon that come from other regions. The environment here has a special effect on the evolution of two particular species of Pokémon (p. 252).

Step 6 — N waits near the exit

When you take a different set of stairs up to 1F after looking around the lower floors, you are almost to the exit to Mistralton City. But N is waiting for you, saying he wants to see what kind of dream you have. N will then challenge you to a battle.

I'll learn just what kind of dream you have—in battle!

Meet the Nugget brothers

Just to the west of where you enter B1F are the Nugget brothers. There is an older and younger brother, and they each give you a Nugget. These are valuable items!

Battle with Team Plasma's N! 4

N sends out a variety of Pokémon. They have different types, but many share a common weakness. Boldore, Klink, and Ferroseed are all weak to Fighting-type moves. You can also attack Joltik, Klink, and Ferroseed's weaknesses to Fire-type moves.

● N's Pokémon			
◎ Boldore ♂	Lv. 28	Rock	
◎ Joltik ♂	Lv. 28	Bug	Electric
◎ Klink	Lv. 28	Steel	
◎ Ferroseed ♂	Lv. 28	Grass	Steel
◎			
◎			

Step 7 — Continue north to Mistralton City

After you defeat N in battle, Bianca and Professor Juniper show up. N expresses his hostility toward Professor Juniper for being a Pokémon researcher, then leaves. After seeing off Bianca and the professor, you continue north to the exit into Mistralton City.

But I hope he'll spend a little time trying to understand how others feel.

Find items with the Dowsing MCHN

Chargestone Cave has many hidden items. Use the Dowsing MCHN to find them.

Mistralton City

Story

Most of Mistralton City is taken up by a giant runway for cargo planes. The area around the runway is surrounded by greenhouses (or fields). The vegetables harvested here are carried to other regions by cargo planes. It's time for you to earn your sixth Gym Badge.

Field Moves Needed

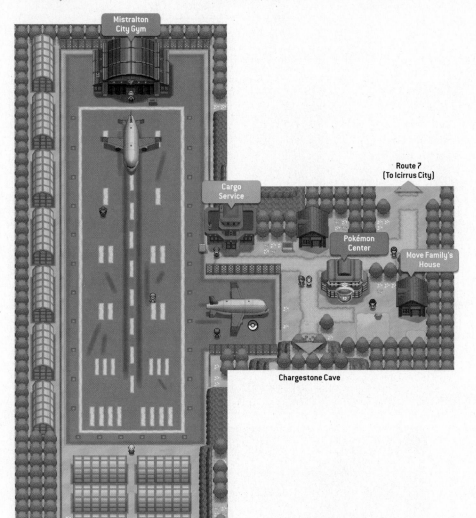

Mistralton City Gym

Cargo Service

Route 7 (To Icirrus City)

Pokémon Center

Move Family's House

Chargestone Cave

● The image above is from *Pokémon Black Version*.
In *Pokémon White Version*, fields surround the runway instead of greenhouses.

Items

First visit
- [ ] Sharp Beak
- [ ] TM58 Sky Drop

● After investigating the Celestial Tower
- [ ] Fresh Water

● After defeating the Gym Leader
- [ ] Jet Badge
- [ ] TM40 Aerial Ace
- [ ] TM62 Acrobatics

Poké Mart
(Lower Clerk)

TM07 Hail	50,000
TM11 Sunny Day	50,000
TM18 Rain Dance	50,000
TM37 Sandstorm	50,000

Step 1 — Seek the help of the Move Deleter

The Move Deleter in the Move Family's House can make your Pokémon forget a learned move. He can even make them forget a move that can't normally be forgotten, like an HM. When you want a Pokémon to forget a learned move, talk to the Move Deleter.

You've come to make me force your Pokémon to forget some moves?

Sometimes the weather is rainy

Mistralton City's weather changes depending on the date and season. Rain can fall during the spring, summer, and autumn, and snow or hail will sometimes fall during the winter. When you visit the city, check the changes in weather (p. 206).

Step 2 — Have the reminder girl make your Pokémon remember moves

The reminder girl in the Move Family's House will make your Pokémon remember a forgotten move in exchange for one Heart Scale. The reminder girl can even make a Pokémon remember a move it knew at Level 1.

Should a move be remembered?

Learn the type of Hidden Power

Talk to the man inside the Pokémon Center to have him tell you what type Hidden Power will be when you teach it to a Pokémon. It's good info to have before you teach this move to a Pokémon.

Step 3 — Meet Professor Juniper's father

A man approaches you as you continue north on the road directly west of the Pokémon Center. The man calls himself Juniper. It's Professor Juniper's dad! Cedric Juniper upgrades your Pokédex to commemorate your first meeting.

In honor of our meeting, I'm going to upgrade your Pokédex!

Check out your new Pokédex!

When your Pokédex is upgraded, you can check the different forms of a Pokémon or see your Shiny Pokémon. Also, new search features have been added. Open the Pokédex and have a look around (p. 39).

Step 4 — The Celestial Tower waits on Route 7

The Gym Leader, Skyla, is walking behind Cedric Juniper. Skyla says she is going to check on a weakened Pokémon at the top of the Celestial Tower and leaves. In order to reach the Celestial Tower, you'll need to head for Route 7 (p. 132).

I'm leaving for Route 7's Celestial Tower. You can come along if you want.

Gym battle 6 — *Mistralton City Gym Battle*

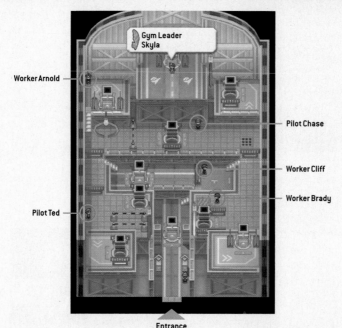

Gym Leader Skyla

Worker Arnold

Pilot Chase

Worker Cliff

Worker Brady

Pilot Ted

Entrance

Mistralton City Gym Leader
Skyla

● *Flying-type Pokémon User*

Recommended Level for your Pokémon **Lv. 38**

Attack your opponents' weak points with Electric- and Rock-type moves

In the Gym, proceed by using the cannons to launch yourself from platform to platform. All of Skyla's Pokémon are weak to Electric- and Rock-type moves. If you don't have any of these moves, use TMs to teach your Pokémon moves like Volt Switch or Rock Slide. Her Swanna uses Aerial Ace, which always hits without fail. Defeat Swanna quickly before it can do big damage.

Skyla's Pokémon

Pokémon	Lv.	Moves to watch out for:
Swoobat ♀ Psychic Flying	Lv. 33	● Heart Stamp Psychic
Unfezant ♀ Normal Flying	Lv. 33	● Razor Wind Normal
Swanna ♀ Water Flying	Lv. 35	● Aerial Ace Flying

TM Received | Received **62** Acrobatics
If the user isn't holding an item, this attack does double damage.

Jet Badge
Pokémon up to Lv. 70, including those received in trades, will obey you.

After Investigating the Celestial Tower
Challenge the Mistralton City Gym

After you've returned from the Celestial Tower on Route 7, stop by the Pokémon Center first to heal your Pokémon and stock up on items. After you're fully prepared, follow the runway north to the Mistralton City Gym.

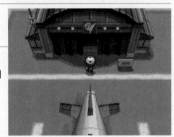

Exchange Sweet Hearts for Heart Scales

If you give the girl in Cargo Service ten Sweet Hearts, she will give you one Heart Scale. Get lots of Sweet Hearts by doing Feeling Checks on the C-Gear with your friends.

After beating the Mistralton City Gym
N tells you about the Legendary Dragon-type Pokémon

After you emerge victorious from your battle with Skyla, N is waiting for you. Before he leaves, N announces that he is going to resurrect and befriend the Legendary Dragon-type Pokémon, then the world will recognize him as the hero.

Dragon-type Pokémon from one of these stones, and become its friend.

After beating the Mistralton City Gym
Find the kid's buried treasure by the runway

After defeating the Gym Leader, visit the house to the north of the Pokémon Center. After talking to the kid inside, you can find TM40 Aerial Ace near the south end of the runway. When you find it, the kid comes to meet you and gives you Aerial Ace as a gift.

Oh! You found our treasure!

Find items with the Dowsing MCHN

Many items are hidden near the greenhouses (or fields) to the south and west of the runway. Use the Dowsing MCHN to find these hidden items.

After beating the Mistralton City Gym
Pass through Route 7 to reach Twist Mountain

The location of the seventh Gym is Icirrus City, past Route 7 and Twist Mountain. Head north to Route 7 and continue to the east side, where there are Harlequins standing on the raised walkways. If you continue north from there, you will reach the entrance to Twist Mountain (p. 136).

Route 7

Story

Route 7 is thick with patches of tall grass. Pokémon Trainers are hidden in the tall grass so you can only see their heads. There are raised walkways everywhere, so if you like, you can use them to proceed without walking through the tall grass. The grass here is too thick for your Bicycle to navigate, so you'll have to walk to explore these areas.

Field Moves Needed

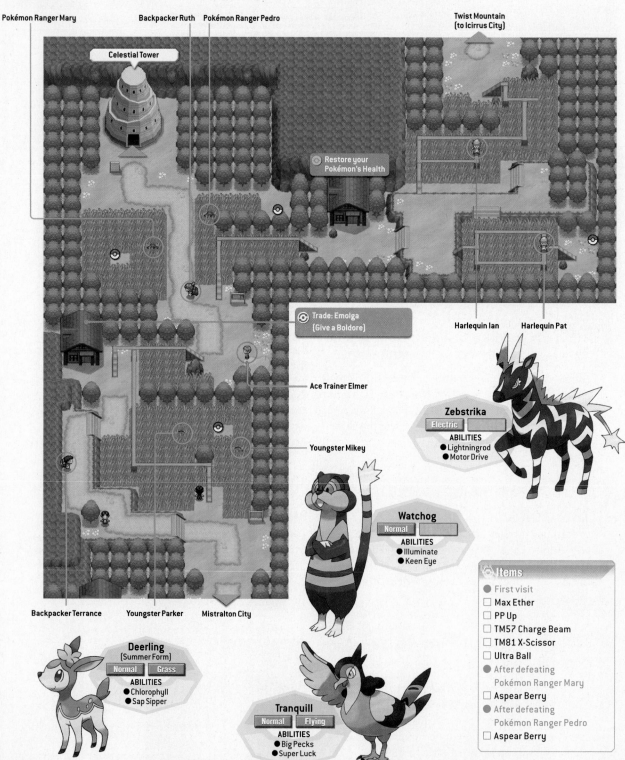

Pokémon Ranger Mary

Backpacker Ruth   Pokémon Ranger Pedro

Twist Mountain (to Icirrus City)

Celestial Tower

Restore your Pokémon's Health

Trade: Emolga (Give a Boldore)

Harlequin Ian   Harlequin Pat

Ace Trainer Elmer

Youngster Mikey

Backpacker Terrance   Youngster Parker   Mistralton City

Zebstrika

Electric

ABILITIES
- Lightningrod
- Motor Drive

Watchog

Normal

ABILITIES
- Illuminate
- Keen Eye

Deerling
(Summer Form)

Normal   Grass

ABILITIES
- Chlorophyll
- Sap Sipper

Tranquill

Normal   Flying

ABILITIES
- Big Pecks
- Super Luck

Items

- First visit
- ☐ Max Ether
- ☐ PP Up
- ☐ TM57 Charge Beam
- ☐ TM81 X-Scissor
- ☐ Ultra Ball
- After defeating Pokémon Ranger Mary
- ☐ Aspear Berry
- After defeating Pokémon Ranger Pedro
- ☐ Aspear Berry

Spring Summer Autumn

Tall Grass

Pokémon	
Deerling	○
Foongus	△
Tranquill	○
Watchog	○
Zebstrika	○

Dark Grass

Pokémon	
Deerling	○
Foongus	△
Tranquill	○
Watchog	◎
Zebstrika	○

Tall Grass (rustling)

Pokémon	
Audino	◎
Emolga	△
Unfezant	△

Winter

Tall Grass

Pokémon	
Cubchoo	○
Deerling	○
Foongus	△
Watchog	○
Zebstrika	○

Dark Grass

Pokémon	
Cubchoo	○
Deerling	○
Foongus	△
Watchog	◎
Zebstrika	○

Tall Grass (rustling)

Pokémon	
Audino	◎
Emolga	△

Step 1 — A new way to battle Trainers

A little north of Mistralton City, Ace Trainer Elmer challenges you to a Rotation Battle in *Pokémon Black Version* or a Triple Battle in *Pokémon White Version*. Before taking this challenge, check to make sure the three Pokémon that will appear in battle are ready to go.

Rotation Battles are new Pokémon battles

Sometimes the weather is Rain

Route 7's weather changes depending on the day. It can rain in spring, summer, and autumn. When the weather is Rain, the power of Water-type moves goes up, and the power of Fire-type moves goes down. Consider this when choosing moves to use when battling.

Step 2 — Heal your Pokémon at the house

Continue north from Mistralton City, and you'll find a house where the route turns east. If you talk to the woman inside the house, she'll restore your Pokémon's health. Stop by and get your Pokémon healed when they're low on HP from battles with Trainers or wild Pokémon.

It seems all worn out. Rest for just a moment now!

Stop on the raised walkway, and you'll come tumbling down

If you miss a step on the raised walkways, you will fall down to the tall grass below. Even if you stop, you can eventually fall, so cross slowly and carefully.

Step 3 — Twist Mountain is to the east

Head east from the house where you can heal your Pokémon, then continue north to reach the entrance to Twist Mountain. But right now, your destination is the Celestial Tower, where Skyla went. Visit Twist Mountain after defeating Skyla at the Mistralton City Gym (p. 136).

Check in with Mom

When you proceed east on Route 7, your mom calls on the Xtransceiver. It's been a while since you've talked to your mom. Go home to Nuvema Town every now and again to see her so she won't worry too much.

Step 4 — Go north to reach the Celestial Tower

To reach the Celestial Tower, go straight north from Mistralton City. Skyla went there to rescue a weakened Pokémon. After battling Pokémon Trainers and collecting items, heal your Pokémon at the house, and continue north to reach the tower.

Get Berries by defeating Trainers

Defeat the Pokémon Rangers Mary and Pedro to get Aspear Berries. Mary and Pedro are in the tall grass next to the Celestial Tower.

UNOVA ADVENTURE WALKTHROUGH ROUTE 7

After you've heard about the storm in Opelucid City — Meet the Pokémon that roams Unova

During the storm, when you pass by the front of the house where you can heal your Pokémon, an old woman lets you inside. When you go back outside after hearing her story, Tornadus (Thundurus) appears and then goes flying away. After this, Tornadus (Thundurus) moves around the Unova region.

Apparently it's that Pokémon's doing!

Check the electric bulletin board

A massive storm is proof that Tornadus (Thundurus) is nearby. By checking the electric bulletin boards at every gate, you can see the location of the massive storm. Run to that area to catch Tornadus (Thundurus).

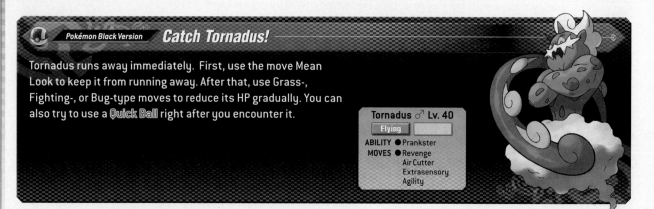

Pokémon Black Version *Catch Tornadus!*

Tornadus runs away immediately. First, use the move Mean Look to keep it from running away. After that, use Grass-, Fighting-, or Bug-type moves to reduce its HP gradually. You can also try to use a Quick Ball right after you encounter it.

Tornadus ♂ Lv. 40
Flying
ABILITY ● Prankster
MOVES ● Revenge
Air Cutter
Extrasensory
Agility

Pokémon White Version *Catch Thundurus!*

Thundurus ♂ Lv. 40
Electric Flying
ABILITY ● Prankster
MOVES ● Revenge
Shock Wave
Heal Block
Agility

Thundurus runs away immediately. First, use the move Mean Look to keep it from running away. After that, use Grass-, Fighting-, or Flying-type moves to reduce its HP gradually. Using a Quick Ball right after you encounter it is also effective.

After you've heard about the storm in Opelucid City — Fly back to Opelucid City

Your next destination is the true test that stands between you and the Pokémon League—Victory Road. Victory Road is north of Opelucid City past Route 10. Use Fly to return to Opelucid City (p. 163, 167)

Celestial Tower

Story

The Celestial Tower is a five-story tower built as a memorial to lost Pokémon. A bell whose tones are said to comfort spirits is placed on the top of the tower at the fifth floor.

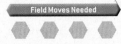

■ 2F

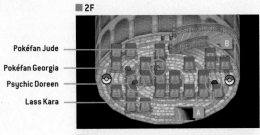

Pokéfan Jude
Pokéfan Georgia
Psychic Doreen
Lass Kara

■ 1F

Route 7 (To Mistralton City)

■ 5F

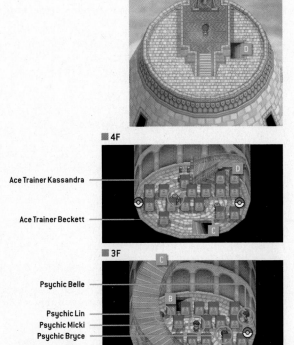

■ 4F

Ace Trainer Kassandra

Ace Trainer Beckett

■ 3F

Psychic Belle

Psychic Lin
Psychic Micki
Psychic Bryce

Nurse Sachiko

⊙ Restore your Pokémon's Health

Litwick
| Ghost | Fire |

ABILITIES
● Flash Fire
● Flame Body

🔧 Items

- ☐ Hyper Potion
- ☐ Revive
- ☐ Spell Tag
- ☐ TM61 Will-O-Wisp
- ☐ TM65 Shadow Claw

2F
🔾 Inside

Pokémon	
Litwick	◎

3F/4F
🔾 Inside

Pokémon	
Elgyem	○
Litwick	◎

5F
🔾 Roof

Pokémon	
Elgyem	◎
Litwick	◎

Step 1 — **Climb the tower while battling Trainers**

There are no Pokémon Trainers on the first floor, and wild Pokémon do not appear. Pokémon Trainers wait for you between the tombstones on the second floor and up. Pass through the gaps while battling Pokémon Trainers, and keep climbing towards the top.

what we do is, of course,
engage in a Pokémon battle, don't we? ▼

Meet Ghost- and Psychic-type Pokémon

The Ghost-type Pokémon Litwick appears on the second through fifth floors of the Celestial Tower. This Pokémon can only be found here. The only place you can find Elgyem is on floors three through five in this tower. Catch them both if you can!

Step 2 — Have the Nurse heal your Pokémon on 3F

Nurse Sachiko stands right before the stairs to the fourth floor. After you defeat her in a Pokémon battle, she will heal all of your Pokémon. If you talk to her again after defeating her, she will always heal your Pokémon. If your Pokémon are hurt, talk to her and have her heal them.

OK! Then...
Time to give your Pokémon some energy!

Step 3 — Skyla is waiting on the top floor

Skyla is already on the top floor when you get there and has already helped the weakened Pokémon. She invites you to ring the bell, so walk up to the bell and choose "Yes." After listening to the sound of the bell, Skyla says you are a kind and strong person.

▸ YES
NO

It's the Celestial Tower bell...
Will you ring the bell?

Ringing the bell soothes spirits

The bell on the fifth floor is said to soothe the spirits of Pokémon. The sound of the bell is a tone so pure it feels as if it cleanses the spirit. After you ring the bell, take a moment to listen.

Step 4 — Return to Mistralton City to challenge the Gym

After you ring the bell, Skyla will return to Mistralton City. Now it's time to return to Mistralton City to challenge the Gym (p. 131). Use Fly from the top of the Celestial Tower so you can get back to the city in an instant.

It has a reputation as a mine littered with valuable ore

Twist Mountain

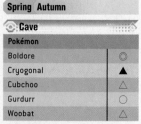

Story

Twist Mountain is a mine with caves designed to make it easy to extract minerals from the mountain. It is split up into an upper, middle, lower, and lowest level, and you can move down into the dip in the center with each level.

Field Moves Needed

Spring Autumn

Cave

Pokémon	
Boldore	◎
Cryogonal	▲
Cubchoo	△
Gurdurr	○
Woobat	△

Summer

Cave

Pokémon	
Boldore	◎
Cryogonal	▲
Cubchoo	△
Gurdurr	○
Woobat	○

Winter

Cave

Pokémon	
Boldore	○
Cryogonal	△
Cubchoo	◎
Gurdurr	△
Woobat	△

All Seasons

Cave (dust cloud)

Pokémon	
Drilbur	◎

Items

Any season	When the season is spring, summer, or autumn
☐ Ether	
☐ Full Heal	☐ Ultra Ball
☐ HM03 Surf	**When the season is winter**
☐ Max Potion	☐ Metal Coat
☐ Moon Stone	☐ TM90 Substitute
☐ Nugget	
☐ PP Up	
☐ Revive	
☐ TM91 Flash Cannon	

■ Middle Level 2

Worker Cairn

■ Lower Level 1

■ Lowest Level 1

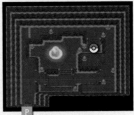

■ Upper Level 1

Hiker Terrell

■ Entrance

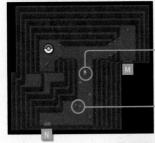

Route 7 (to Mistralton City)

■ Outside (Spring/Summer/Autumn)

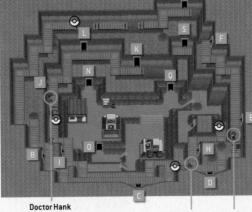

Doctor Hank

◎ Restore your Pokémon's Health

Ace Trainer Caroll · Worker Brand

■ Upper Level 3

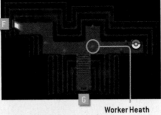

Worker Heath

■ Middle Level 1

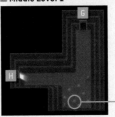

Worker Rob

■ Middle Level 4

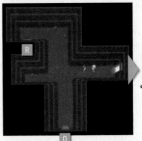

Black Belt Teppei
(Can't be battled during winter)

Worker Rich
(Can't be battled during winter)

■ Upper Level 2

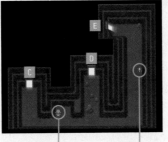

Hiker Darrell · Battle Girl Sharon

■ Lower Level 2

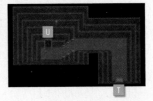

Icirrus City

■ Upper Level 4
(Only accessible in winter)

■ Middle Level 3

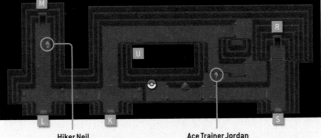

Hiker Neil
(Can't be battled during winter)

Ace Trainer Jordan
(Winter only)

■ Outside (during winter)

■ Lowest Level 2
(Only accessible in winter)

Cubchoo
Ice
ABILITY
● Snow Cloak

Step 1 Cheren challenges you to battle

Continue north from Route 7, and when you reach the entrance, Cheren arrives. Cheren also beat the Mistralton City Gym and received the Jet Badge. Saying he wants to see which of you is stronger, he challenges you to battle.

Since we both hold the Jet Badge now, let's see which of us is stronger!

No entrance before the Gym battle

If you visit before beating the Mistralton City Gym, a Worker blocks the entrance to the mountain and won't let you inside. Also, you can't meet Cheren or Alder. Visit after beating the Mistralton City Gym.

Battle your childhood friend Cheren! 6

His Pokémon are nine levels higher than in your fifth battle, and Tranquill and Pansage/Pansear/Panpour have evolved.

● If you chose Snivy:			
◎ Unfezant ♂	Lv. 33	Normal	Flying
◎ Pignite ♂	Lv. 35	Fire	Fighting
◎ Simisage ♂	Lv. 33	Grass	
◎ Liepard ♂	Lv. 33	Dark	

● If you chose Tepig:		
◎ Unfezant ♂	Lv. 33	Normal	Flying
◎ Dewott ♂	Lv. 35	Water	
◎ Simisear ♂	Lv. 33	Fire	
◎ Liepard ♂	Lv. 33	Dark	

● If you chose Oshawott:		
◎ Unfezant ♂	Lv. 33	Normal	Flying
◎ Servine ♂	Lv. 35	Grass	
◎ Simipour ♂	Lv. 33	Water	
◎ Liepard ♂	Lv. 33	Dark	

Step 2 Get the HM Surf from Alder

When you defeat Cheren, Alder comes out of Twist Mountain. Alder teaches you that what you do with the power you obtained by becoming stronger is important, and he gives you HM03 Surf. Surf is a move that lets you travel over the water's surface.

Trainer obtained an HM03 Surf!

Visit places Surf makes accessible

After you get Surf from Alder and before entering Twist Mountain, return to the places you skipped before where you now can use Surf. You can access Routes 17 and 18 (p. 140). If you use Surf on Route 6, you can go to Mistralton Cave (p. 143).

Step 3 Meet Clay

When you enter Twist Mountain, you run into Clay checking up on the mountain. Clay is concerned because he hasn't seen Team Plasma lately, and he can't figure out the location of their base. He says that kids should just enjoy their travels, and he leaves.

Th' two of ya seem a bit more rugged than the last time I saw ya.

Sometimes the weather is rainy

Twist Mountain's weather changes depending on the date and season. The weather doesn't influence the inside of the cave, but it does influence the entrance and outside. Rainy weather makes Water-type moves stronger and Fire-type moves weaker.

Step 4 — Proceed while battling Trainers

Pokémon Trainers are waiting inside the caves and along the walls of Twist Mountain. Some of these Trainers are even hiding under clumps of dirt in the path. Battle the Trainers to raise your Pokémon's level while continuing deeper into the cave.

At work, we do our best.
That is my, and my Pokémon's, way of life! ▼

Does the ice-covered rock hold a secret?

On Lowest Level 1, you'll find an ice-covered rock. This rock is related to the evolution of a Pokémon from a different region (p. 252).

Step 5 — Doctor Hank heals your Pokémon

You can find Doctor Hank by the wall on the west side of Twist Mountain's outdoor area. After you defeat him in a Pokémon battle, he will heal all of your Pokémon. If you talk to him again after defeating him, he will always heal your Pokémon. If your Pokémon are hurt, have him heal them.

After a Pokémon battle,
let them recover slowly. ▼

Come back to visit the Worker

There's a Worker by the corner in Lower Level 1. Talk to him after finishing the main story, and you can get one Pokémon Fossil per day (p. 194).

Step 6 — Cheren argues with Team Plasma

When you reach Lower Level 2, Cheren is arguing with a member of Team Plasma. Another Team Plasma Grunt shows up, and as they leave he says "that item" has been found and they should go to the tower. What could "that item" be?

But taking people's Pokémon by force
is not right. ▼

Step 7 — Exit leads to Icirrus City

When you leave using the exit east of where Cheren and Team Plasma were arguing, you are in Icirrus City, where the seventh Gym is located. Explore the rest of Twist Mountain while battling Pokémon Trainers and collecting items. Then continue east to Icirrus City (p. 146)

Visit again when it snows

During winter, Twist Mountain is covered in snow, and you can reach places you couldn't during spring, summer, or autumn. Visit again during winter to collect items and battle Pokémon Trainers.

Route 17 • Route 18 • P2 Laboratory

To reach Route 17, you must travel over water from Route 1. To the west is the beach island containing Route 18, and to the north stands the small research lab, P2 Laboratory. The ocean current is very fast, so you must proceed carefully.

Field Moves Needed

Surf　Strength

■ Route 18

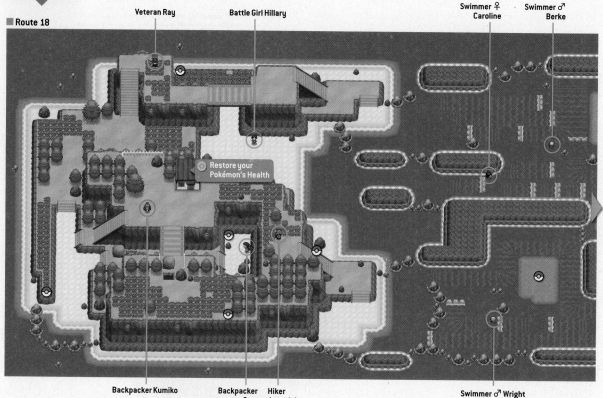

Veteran Ray　Battle Girl Hillary　Swimmer ♀ Caroline　Swimmer ♂ Berke

Restore your Pokémon's Health

Backpacker Kumiko　Backpacker Sam　Hiker Jeremiah　Swimmer ♂ Wright

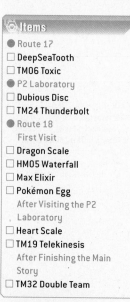

⚙ Items

- ● Route 17
- ☐ DeepSeaTooth
- ☐ TM06 Toxic
- ● P2 Laboratory
- ☐ Dubious Disc
- ☐ TM24 Thunderbolt
- ● Route 18
  - First Visit
- ☐ Dragon Scale
- ☐ HM05 Waterfall
- ☐ Max Elixir
- ☐ Pokémon Egg
  - After Visiting the P2 Laboratory
- ☐ Heart Scale
- ☐ TM19 Telekinesis
  - After Finishing the Main Story
- ☐ TM32 Double Team

● Item the man in the prefab house will buy

Item	Price
Rare Bone	10,000

Route 18

⚙ Tall Grass

Pokémon	
Dwebble	○
Sawk ■	△
Scraggy	◎
Throh ☐	△
Watchog	○

⚙ Tall Grass (rustling)

Pokémon	
Audino	◎
Sawk ☐	△
Throh ■	△

⚙ Dark Grass

Pokémon	
Crustle	○
Sawk ■	△
Scraggy	◎
Throh ☐	△
Watchog	○

⚙ Water Surface

Pokémon	
Frillish	◎

⚙ Water Surface (ripples)

Pokémon	
Alomomola	◎
Jellicent	△

■ After finishing the main story

⚙ Fishing

Pokémon	
Chinchou	▲
Finneon	◎
Horsea	◎

⚙ Fishing (ripples)

Pokémon	
Kingdra	△
Lumineon	△
Qwilfish	◎
Seadra	◎

Crustle

| Bug | Rock |

ABILITIES
● Sturdy
● Shell Armor

Scientist Nathan
■ P2 Laboratory ■ Route 17

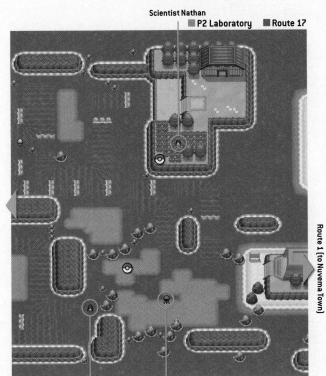

Swimmer ♀ Joyce   Fisherman Lydon

Route 1 (to Nuvema Town)

P2 Laboratory

Tall Grass

Pokémon	
Herdier	◎
Klink	○
Scraggy	○
Watchog	◎

Tall Grass (rustling)

Pokémon	
Audino	◎
Stoutland	△

Route 17/P2 Laboratory

Water Surface

Pokémon	
Frillish	◎

Water Surface (ripples)

Pokémon	
Alomomola	◎
Jellicent	△

■ After finishing the main story

Fishing

Pokémon	
Finneon	◎
Horsea	◎

Fishing (ripples)

Pokémon	
Kingdra	△
Lumineon	△
Qwilfish	○
Seadra	◎

Alomomola

| Water | |

ABILITIES
● Healer
● Hydration

Step 1   Ride the rapids

Use Surf on Route 1 and continue west over the water, and once you get past the gate, you are on Route 17. The water surrounding the area flows rapidly in one direction, and two rapid flows on the west side of the shallows will carry you further west. If you ride the bottom rapid flow, you can continue to Route 18.

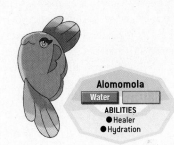

Step 2   The girl in the prefab house heals your Pokémon

Head north on Route 18 and you will find a prefab house. If you talk to the girl inside the house, she will restore your Pokémon's health. Stop by the prefab house and get your Pokémon healed when they're hurt by battles with Trainers or wild Pokémon.

Aren't your Pokémon a bit tired? Here, don't be shy! Let them rest! ▼

Find items with the Dowsing MCHN

Many items are hidden in Route 17, Route 18, and the P2 Laboratory. Use the Dowsing MCHN to find hidden items.

UNOVA ADVENTURE WALKTHROUGH

ROUTE 17 • ROUTE 18 • P2 LABORATORY ◉

Step 3 — Get a Pokémon Egg from the treasure hunter

Talk to the treasure hunter in the prefab house and he will give you the Pokémon Egg. If you have space in your party, you can receive the Egg. Walk around with the Egg in your party, and in time it will hatch.

Would you like to receive this Pokémon Egg and raise it?

Larvesta hatches from the Egg

A treasure hunter gives you a Larvesta Egg. Larvesta does not appear in the wild. Make sure to get the Egg, and register Larvesta in the Pokédex.

Step 4 — Sell your Rare Bone

The sunglasses-wearing man in the corner of the prefab house will pay a lot for the item Rare Bone. Very rarely, a wild Crustle in the dark grass will be holding a Rare Bone. If you get one, sell it here.

What's up?
Did you find something cool for me?

Step 5 — Get HM05 Waterfall

Continue west to the prefab house on Route 18, go down the stairs, and when you reach the plateau on the west side you can find an item that has fallen on the outcropping to the south. It's HM05 Waterfall. Teach this HM to a Pokémon, and you can climb up and down waterfalls. Make sure to get it.

Collect items in the Lostlorn Forest

Visit the waterfall to the north of the Lostlorn Forest on Route 16 and use Waterfall to climb it. At the top, you can collect an item. Go to the Lostlorn Forest once you have Waterfall (p. 110).

Step 6 — Get items at the P2 Laboratory

Ride the rapids on the north side of Route 18 to the east to reach the P2 Laboratory. The P2 Laboratory is an island with a small research lab, but you will find a Pokémon Trainer and some items there, as well as tall grass where wild Pokémon appear. Make sure to have a look at everything.

Step 7 — Go to Route 18 from the P2 Laboratory

Use Surf from the P2 Laboratory. Be careful not to ride the rapids, and pass through the gaps between them. Continue west to reach the beach in the center of Route 18. You can't reach this place from Route 17.

Step 8 — Visit Mistralton Cave

Once you've looked around Route 17, Route 18, and the P2 Laboratory, use Fly to go to Driftveil City. Go west to Route 6 and use Surf from the tall grass in the north to cross the river and go east. Then, you can reach Mistralton Cave.

Mistralton Cave

Story

Mistralton Cave is a cave deep within Route 6. Somewhere in its depths, the Legendary Pokémon Cobalion lives in hiding. It is said that Cobalion saved the Pokémon of the Unova region from a sea of fire in the distant past.

Field Moves Needed

Flash   Strength

■ 1F

Hiker Clarke

Route 6 (to Driftveil City)

A

Hiker Hugh

Items

- ☐ Dusk Stone
- ☐ Hard Stone
- ☐ Hyper Potion
- ☐ Iron
- ☐ Max Repel
- ☐ Rare Candy
- ☐ Revive
- ☐ TM80 Rock Slide

1F/2F/Guidance Chamber

Cave

Pokémon	
Axew	○
Boldore	○
Woobat	○

Cave (dust cloud)

Pokémon	
Drilbur	○

Axew

Dragon	

ABILITIES
- ● Rivalry
- ● Mold Breaker

Drilbur

Ground	

ABILITIES
- ● Sand Rush
- ● Sand Force

■ 2F

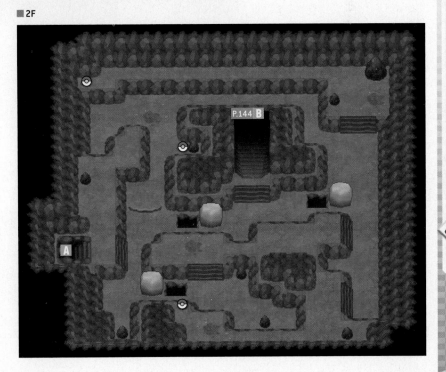

P.144 B

A

■ Guidance Chamber

P.143 **B**

Step 1 ### Head to Mistralton Cave from Route 6

The entrance to Mistralton Cave is in the eastern part of Route 6. Go west from Driftveil City and head toward Chargestone Cave on Route 6 until you reach the house. Go east from that house and then use Surf. Keep going east to the cave.

Find items with the Dowsing MCHN

Many items are hidden in Mistralton Cave. Use the Dowsing MCHN to find hidden items.

Step 2 ### Use Flash to brighten up the area

The inside of the cave is pitch-black. Only the area around you is lit up, so you can't see what's going on inside. Teach TM70 Flash to a Pokémon and use the move in the cave. The lit area expands, and it is easier to explore the cave.

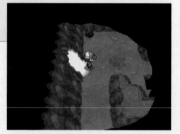

Get Flash

Get TM70 Flash from the sunglasses-wearing man who pops out from behind the garbage bin in Castelia City's Narrow Street. If you don't have it yet, visit Castelia City (p. 95).

Step 3 ### Proceed while collecting items

Inside the caves, rocks sometimes block the path. You can move them aside with Strength. Push the rocks into the holes, and continue deep into the caves. Many items have been dropped in the cave. Check every corner to collect all of the items.

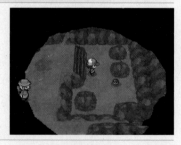

Step 4 — Listen to the old man in the Guidance Chamber

On the eastern side of the Guidance Chamber, an old man offers to tell you an old story when you approach him. If you say "YES," he will tell you how Cobalion, Terrakion, and Virizion saved the Pokémon from a sea of fire.

Cobalion and the others have lost faith in humanity

Cobalion, Terrakion, and Virizion rescued Pokémon from a fire started by a war between humans. After that, they refused to associate with humans, and they hid themselves far from people.

Step 5 — Discover the Legendary Pokémon Cobalion

In the Guidance Chamber, go west from the old storyteller. Use Strength to push the rock into the hole, and keep going west until you reach Cobalion. When you talk to it, the battle begins. Capture it in order to complete your Pokédex.

🔴 Capture Cobalion!

Cobalion's Ability, Justified, makes Cobalion's attack rise one level when it is hit by a Dark-type attack. When its Attack goes up, the move Sacred Sword becomes very powerful, so be careful. Lower its HP with Normal-, Grass-, and Ice-type moves.

Cobalion Lv. 42

| Steel | Fighting |

ABILITY ● Justified
MOVES ● Helping Hand
● Retaliate
● Iron Head
● Sacred Sword

Step 6 — Now you can capture the other two

When you meet Cobalion, the seals in Pinwheel Forest and Victory Road are removed and you can capture Virizion and Terrakion. First, hurry over to Pinwheel Forest and capture Virizion (p. 90).

Virizion

Terrakion

Step 7 — Leave the cave and return to Twist Mountain

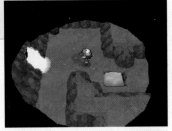

Once you've captured Cobalion, return to your quest to collect the Gym Badges. When you leave the cave, use Fly to return to Mistralton City. Head to Route 7 to the east, then north on Route 7, and enter Twist Mountain (p. 138).

Icirrus City

Icirrus City is a city with wetlands where Pokémon appear. It has the Pokémon Fan Club and Aha's House, where you can win prizes at a quiz. Come here to earn your seventh Gym Badge.

Field Moves Needed

Surf

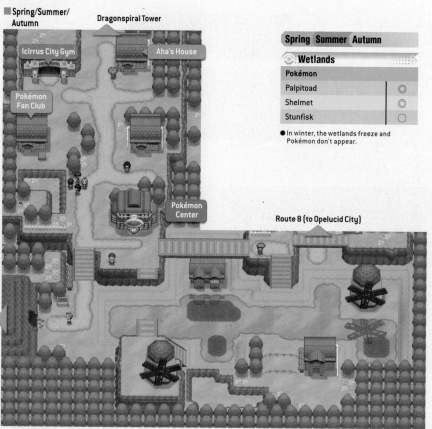

■ Spring/Summer/Autumn

Dragonspiral Tower

Icirrus City Gym

Aha's House

Pokémon Fan Club

Pokémon Center

Route 8 (to Opelucid City)

Twist Mountain (to Mistralton City)

Spring	Summer	Autumn
Wetlands		
Pokémon		
Palpitoad		◎
Shelmet		◎
Stunfisk		○

● In winter, the wetlands freeze and Pokémon don't appear.

Shelmet

Bug

ABILITIES
● Hydration
● Shell Armor

Items

- ● First Visit
- ☐ Fresh Water
- ☐ TM31 Brick Break
- ● After you show the Pokémon Fan Club Chairman a Pokémon you raised 25 to 49 levels
- ☐ Exp. Share
- ● After you show the Pokémon Fan Club Chairman a Pokémon you raised 50 to 98 levels
- ☐ Cleanse Tag
- ● After you show the Pokémon Fan Club Chairman a Pokémon you raised 99 levels
- ☐ King's Rock
- ● After beating the Icirrus City Gym
- ☐ Freeze Badge
- ☐ TM79 Frost Breath
- ● During winter
- ☐ RageCandyBar
- ☐ Rare Candy

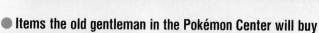

● Items the old gentleman in the Pokémon Center will buy

Items	Price	Items	Price	Items	Price
Blue Shard	200	Red Shard	200	Dusk Stone	3,000
Bug Gem	200	Rock Gem	200	Fire Stone	3,000
Dark Gem	200	Steel Gem	200	Moon Stone	3,000
Dragon Gem	200	Water Gem	200	Shiny Stone	3,000
Electric Gem	200	Yellow Shard	200	Sun Stone	3,000
Fighting Gem	200	Hard Stone	500	Thunderstone	3,000
Fire Gem	200	Damp Rock	1,000	Water Stone	3,000
Flying Gem	200	Everstone	1,000	Shoal Shell	7,000
Ghost Gem	200	Float Stone	1,000	Big Pearl	7,500
Grass Gem	200	Heat Rock	1,000	Star Piece	9,800
Green Shard	200	Icy Rock	1,000	Nugget	10,000
Ground Gem	200	Smooth Rock	1,000	Pearl String	25,000
Ice Gem	200	Pearl	1,400	Big Nugget	30,000
Normal Gem	200	Oval Stone	1,500	Comet Shard	60,000
Poison Gem	200	Stardust	2,000		
Psychic Gem	200	Dawn Stone	3,000		

Poké Mart
(Lower Clerk)

TM14 Blizzard	70,000
TM25 Thunder	70,000
TM38 Fire Blast	70,000

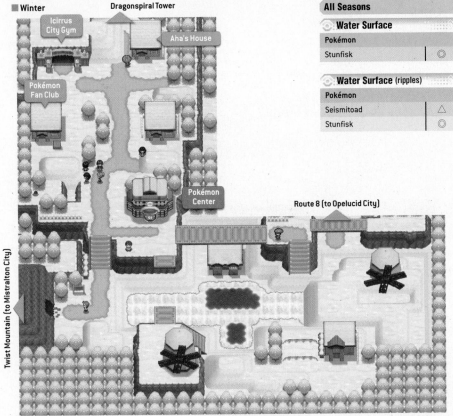

■ Winter

Dragonspiral Tower

Icirrus City Gym

Aha's House

Pokémon Fan Club

Pokémon Center

Route 8 (to Opelucid City)

Twist Mountain (to Mistralton City)

All Seasons	
◎ Water Surface	
Pokémon	
Stunfisk	◎

◎ Water Surface (ripples)	
Pokémon	
Seismitoad	△
Stunfisk	◎

■ After finishing the main story

◎ Fishing	
Pokémon	
Barboach	◎
Stunfisk	○

◎ Fishing (ripples)	
Pokémon	
Barboach	◎
Stunfisk	○
Whiscash	△

Step 1

Listen to Cedric Juniper's story about Dragonspiral Tower

Cedric Juniper comes to talk to you when you enter Icirrus City from Twist Mountain. According to him, Dragonspiral Tower just outside of Icirrus City is the place where the Legendary Pokémon came to life and now sleeps.

> YES
> NO

Say, I just had a thought—have you heard of Dragonspiral Tower?

Changes in the weather

Icirrus City's weather changes depending on the date and season. Rain can fall during spring, summer, and autumn, and snow or blizzards will sometimes fall during winter. When you visit the city, observe the changes in weather (p. 206).

Step 2

Pokémon appear in the wetlands

Wetlands sprawl east of Twist Mountain's exit. Walking through the swamp water can make wild Pokémon appear. But in winter, the swamp is frozen and you can't catch any Pokémon here. Catch them in spring, summer, or autumn.

Step 3 — Sell many different stones

The old gentleman in the Pokémon Center buys many stones from you. He buys gems and shards from you, in addition to stones and items with similar names, such as the Fire Stone or Water Stone. Refer to the list when you are selling an item (p. 146).

Don't you have an adorable ore that shakes my core?

Listen carefully to the background music

Four people are dancing in a circle to the west of the Pokémon Center. When you approach them, clapping is added to the background music. Listen carefully to the music when you approach the dancing people.

● Rhythmic clapping and dancing

Step 4 — Learn how friendly your Pokémon is

Talk to the girl in the Pokémon Fan Club, and she will offer to see how well you are getting along with your Pokémon. If you answer "YES" and choose one of your party Pokémon, the girl will tell you how friendly that Pokémon is toward you.

▶ YES
  NO

Shall I check how friendly your Pokémon is toward you?

Step 5 — Get three items from the Pokémon Fan Club Chairman

Talk to the chairman of the Pokémon Fan Club and show him a well-raised Pokémon to get an item. Show him a Pokémon you raised 25 to 49 levels to get an Exp. Share, 50 to 98 levels to get a Cleanse Tag, and 99 levels to get a King's Rock.

▶ YES
  NO

how you are raising your Pokémon with loving care?

Get one more item in winter

You can't reach the item by the south side of the Pokémon Fan Club during spring, summer, or autumn. However, in winter, snowdrifts make it possible to cross the ledge and get the item.

Step 6 — Win prizes for answering the quiz

Take the Pep Quiz at Aha's House. You can challenge it once per day. Aha asks the questions. Use the hints Wye gives to answer the questions. A correct answer gets you an Antidote, and an incorrect one gets you a Parlyz Heal.

Wye: Exciting! Thrilling! Zippy! Chilling! It's "Pep Quiz"!

Meet a former member of Team Rocket

During winter, snow piles up, and you can reach the house to the south of the wetlands. A former member of Team Rocket lives in the house with his family. Talk to his wife to get a RageCandyBar.

Step 7 — Take on the Pokémon Gym

The Icirrus City Gym is to the north of the Pokémon Fan Club. Heal your Pokémon at the Pokémon Center, and buy any items you may need at the Poké Mart. Then, head for the Gym to get your seventh Badge.

Hear stories about the Legendary Dragon-type Pokémon

Talk to the woman on the northern side of the Pokémon Center to hear about the Legendary Dragon-type Pokémon. If you are playing *Pokémon Black Version*, the story will be about Reshiram. If you are playing *Pokémon White Version*, it will be about Zekrom.

Gym battle 7　Icirrus City Gym Battle

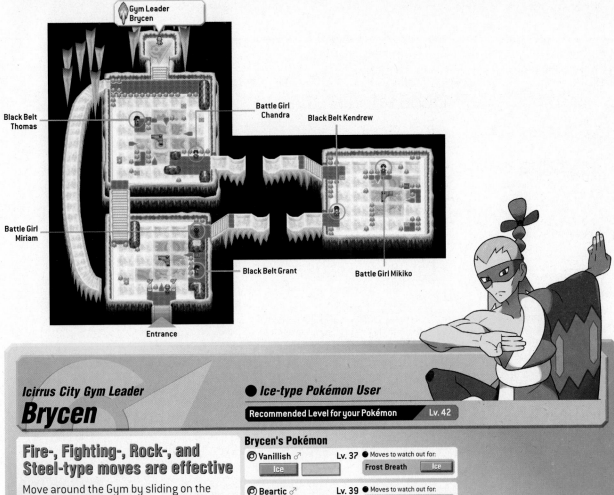

- Gym Leader Brycen
- Black Belt Thomas
- Battle Girl Chandra
- Black Belt Kendrew
- Battle Girl Miriam
- Black Belt Grant
- Battle Girl Mikiko
- Entrance

Icirrus City Gym Leader
Brycen

Fire-, Fighting-, Rock-, and Steel-type moves are effective

Move around the Gym by sliding on the ice floor. Brycen's Pokémon are weak to Fire-, Fighting-, Rock-, and Steel-type moves. If you don't have any Pokémon that know these moves, use TMs to teach your Pokémon Brick Break or Flash Cannon. If you use Grass-, Ground-, Flying-, or Dragon-type Pokémon, which are weak to Ice-type moves, you will take massive damage.

● **Ice-type Pokémon User**

Recommended Level for your Pokémon	Lv. 42

Brycen's Pokémon

			● Moves to watch out for:	
◎ Vanillish ♂	Lv. 37		Frost Breath	Ice
	Ice			
◎ Beartic ♂	Lv. 39		Icicle Crash	Ice
	Ice			
◎ Cryogonal	Lv. 37		Aurora Beam	Ice
	Ice			
◎				
◎				
◎				

TM Received	TM **79** Frost Breath
	A move that always results in a critical hit.

Freeze Badge

Pokémon up to Lv. 80, including those received in trades, will obey you.

After beating the Icirrus City Gym　Depart for Dragonspiral Tower

With your Gym battle over, you leave the Gym. Cheren and Bianca are waiting. The Shadow Triad appear and tell you Ghetsis wants you to come to Dragonspiral Tower. Then they disappear. Go north from the Gym, and head for Dragonspiral Tower (p. 151).

Ghetsis has a message for you: come to Dragonspiral Tower.

Trade Pokémon with People in the City

One of the great things about Pokémon trading is that it can be done with family, friends, and other players all over the world. You'll even encounter people during your journey who will want to trade Pokémon with you!

Trade for hard-to-get Pokémon

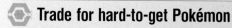

Pokémon Black Version

Trade 1 The girl in the house in Nacrene City

The Petilil you get by trading a Cottonee is a Pokémon that doesn't appear in the wild in *Pokémon Black Version*. You can easily catch a Cottonee in Pinwheel Forest, so this is a great trade!

Give	Receive
Cottonee	Petilil Lv. 15
● Main Habitat	● Held Item
Pinwheel Forest	Cheri Berry

Pokémon White Version

Trade 1 The girl in the house in Nacrene City

The Cottonee you get by trading a Petilil is a Pokémon that doesn't appear in the wild in *Pokémon White Version*. You can easily catch a Petilil in Pinwheel Forest, so this is a great trade!

Give	Receive
Petilil	Cottonee Lv. 15
● Main Habitat	● Held Item
Pinwheel Forest	Cheri Berry

Trade 2 The boy in the house in Driftveil City

The Basculin you get by trading a Minccino is the Red-Striped Form in *Pokémon Black Version* and the Blue-Striped Form in *Pokémon White Version*. You can catch a Minccino to trade on Route 16.

Give	Receive
Minccino	Basculin Lv. 25
● Main Habitat	● Held Item
Route 16	Sitrus Berry

Trade 3 The Hiker in the house on Route 7

The Emolga you get by trading a Boldore can be tough to find in the wild, because it only appears in the rustling grass. You can catch a Boldore in Twist Mountain, so be sure to make this trade!

Give	Receive
Boldore	Emolga Lv. 30
● Main Habitat	● Held Item
Twist Mountain Upper Level	Lum Berry

Trade 4 The woman in the trailer on Route 15

The Rotom you get by trading a Ditto is a hard-to-get Pokémon that doesn't appear in the Unova region. Catch a Ditto in the Giant Chasm to make this trade.

Give	Receive
Ditto	Rotom Lv. 60
● Main Habitat	● Held Item
Crater Forest in the Giant Chasm	Max Elixir

Trade 5 The man in the villa in Undella Town

This trader visits Undella Town during the summer. To get the Cinccino he wants, you can use a Shiny Stone to evolve a Minccino. Trade it to the man for a Munchlax, which is hard to find in the Unova region!

Give	Receive
Cinccino	Munchlax Lv. 60
● Main Habitat	● Held Item
Use a Shiny Stone on Minccino	Leftovers

Dragonspiral Tower

Story

Dragonspiral Tower is said to be the oldest structure built in the Unova region. Stories say the Legendary Dragon-type Pokémon is waiting on the top floor for the person who pursues truth or ideals.

Field Moves Needed

Surf   Strength

Ace Trainer Jamie

■ **Entrance (Spring/Summer/Autumn)**

Icirrus City

■ **Entrance (Winter)**

Icirrus City

■ **1F Outside**

Ace Trainer Jesse

■ **1F**

Pokémon	
Druddigon	○
Golett	◎
Mienfoo	○

■ **1F**

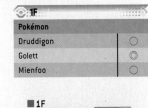

P. 152 C

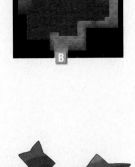

B

Entrance (Spring/Summer/Autumn)

Tall Grass

Pokémon	
Deerling	○
Druddigon	△
Mienfoo	○
Tranquill	○

Tall Grass (rustling)

Pokémon	
Audino	◎
Emolga	△
Unfezant	△

1F Outside (Spring/Summer/Autumn)

Tall Grass

Pokémon	
Deerling	○
Druddigon	△
Mienfoo	○
Tranquill	○

Tall Grass (rustling)

Pokémon	
Audino	◎
Emolga	△
Unfezant	△

Dark Grass

Pokémon	
Druddigon	△
Mienfoo	○
Sawsbuck	○
Tranquill	○

1F Outside (Winter)

Tall Grass

Pokémon	
Cubchoo	△
Deerling	○
Mienfoo	○
Vanillite	○

Tall Grass (rustling)

Pokémon	
Audino	◎
Emolga	△

Dark Grass

Pokémon	
Beartic	△
Mienfoo	○
Sawsbuck	○
Vanillish	○

Entrance (Winter)

Tall Grass

Pokémon	
Cubchoo	△
Deerling	○
Mienfoo	○
Vanillite	○

Tall Grass (rustling)

Pokémon	
Audino	◎
Emolga	△

Dark Grass

Pokémon	
Beartic	△
Mienfoo	○
Sawsbuck	○
Vanillish	○

Items

- ● First visit
- ☐ Dragon Fang
- ☐ Hyper Potion
- ☐ Max Elixir
- ☐ Old Gateau
- ☐ Revive
- ☐ Shiny Stone
- ☐ Star Piece
- ☐ Stardust x2
- ☐ TM63 Embargo
- ● In winter
- ☐ Nugget

Druddigon

Dragon

ABILITIES
● Rough Skin
● Sheer Force

1F Outside

Water Surface

Pokémon		
Basculin [Blue-Striped Form] ☐		◎
Basculin [Red-Striped Form] ■		◎

Water Surface (ripples)

Pokémon		
Basculin [Blue-Striped Form] ■		◎
Basculin [Red-Striped Form] ☐		◎

■ **After finishing the main story**

Fishing

Pokémon		
Basculin [Blue-Striped Form] ☐		○
Basculin [Red-Striped Form] ■		○
Dragonair		△
Dratini		◎

Fishing (ripples)

Pokémon		
Basculin [Blue-Striped Form] ■		○
Basculin [Red-Striped Form] ☐		○
Dragonair		△
Dragonite		▲
Dratini		◎

■ 5F

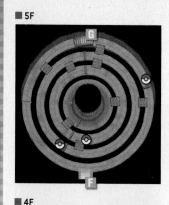

■ 6F

Team Plasma Grunt

Team Plasma Grunt

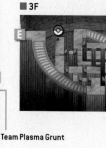

Team Plasma Grunt

Team Plasma Grunt

Team Plasma Grunt

■ 7F

Team Plasma Grunt

Sawsbuck
(Winter Form)

| Normal | Grass |

ABILITIES
● Chlorophyll
● Sap Sipper

■ 4F

Team Plasma Grunt

■ 3F

■ 2F

Team Plasma
Grunt

Team Plasma
Grunt

Team Plasma
Grunt

Team Plasma Grunt

P. 151 C

Step 1 — Cedric Juniper is waiting by the tower entrance

Cedric Juniper is waiting at the entrance to Dragonspiral Tower. Bianca introduces herself to Cedric, and he tells you he saw Cheren and Brycen chase after a large group of Team Plasma members that broke through the tower wall and went inside.

Are you going to go after Team Plasma like your friend did?

Changes in the weather

The weather changes in the area outside the first floor of the Dragonspiral Tower depending on the date and season. When the weather is rainy, the power of Water-type moves goes up, and the power of Fire-type moves goes down.

Step 2 — Climb the tower while collecting items

Enter Dragonspiral Tower and pass through the first floor. When you reach the second floor, Cheren is waiting by the exit. He chases Team Plasma further into the tower. Gather the items, and follow Cheren toward the third floor.

Climb the snow for an extra item

There is an item by a ledge to the west of the entrance. If the season is spring, summer, or autumn, you can't climb the ledge, so you can't get the item. In winter, the snow piles up and you can climb up to where the item is. Come back during winter to get the item.

Step 3 — Continue on the ramps

The third floor is covered with one-way launch ramps. You can jump over them in one direction, but you can't go back the other way. If you go the wrong direction, you'll end up heading back toward the entrance. Don't get frustrated— just think about which direction you're going, and you can reach the stairs to the fourth floor.

Battle Trainers outside the tower

Outside the tower, you can use Surf to cross the water and battle the two Pokémon Trainers in the tall grass to the east. There is an item left in the tall grass for you to pick up.

Step 4 — Brycen and Cheren lend a hand

When you reach the fourth floor, Brycen and Cheren are battling a large group of Team Plasma members. Brycen tells you to go on ahead while they hold the rest of the Team Plasma Grunts there. Head for the next floor and battle the Team Plasma members that try to stop you on the way.

You go on ahead!

Step 5 — Aim for the top while battling Team Plasma

Battle with Team Plasma as you climb the tower. Use the stairs to the north to climb to the fifth floor of the tower. On the fifth floor, there are four circular paths around the tower. Cross the bridges connecting the paths and continue toward the stairs to the sixth floor while picking up items.

Step 6 — Giallo makes a stand

When you reach the sixth floor, Giallo of the Seven Sages is standing there with four Team Plasma Grunts. Giallo sends them to stop you, and you'll have to defeat all four in a row before you can climb the stairs to the seventh floor.

Now! Stop that Trainer! For our lord N!

You can't recover until you beat four Grunts in a row

In this challenge, each Team Plasma Grunt will battle you one after another, without giving you a moment's rest. You won't have time to heal your Pokémon between battles. If your Pokémon's HP goes down, heal them during battle by using items.

Step 7 — N gets Zekrom (Reshiram)

On the seventh floor, N is befriending the Legendary Pokémon Zekrom (Reshiram). The Legendary Pokémon recognizes N as a hero. N tells you to look for the other Legendary Pokémon and leaves riding Zekrom (Reshiram).

Now, Zekrom and I will head to the Pokémon League and defeat the Champion! ▾

Step 8 — Go to the Desert Resort to look for a clue

When you return to the entrance, the Champion Alder arrives. Alder tells you the Relic Castle may hold a clue about the other Legendary Dragon-type Pokémon. Use Fly to return to Nimbasa City, then go through Route 4 to reach the Relic Castle (p. 104).

Let's head to the Relic Castle. Trainer, everyone, I'm going! ▾

A worried Cheren finds his answer

Cheren had been worrying about the reason he was trying to get stronger. After you visit Dragonspiral Tower, Cheren finally finds his answer, and realizes that being able to help someone out when they're in trouble is true strength.

Route 8 • Moor of Icirrus

Story

Route 8 is covered in marshes and water. Constant rain means the route is always mucky. To the north is the Moor of Icirrus, where a marsh has formed from water that has collected in uneven ground.

Field Moves Needed

Surf · Strength

■ Route 8

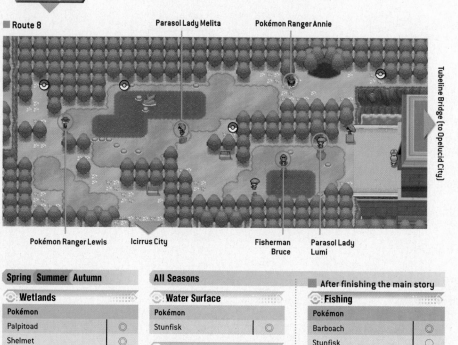

Parasol Lady Melita · Pokémon Ranger Annie

Tubeline Bridge (to Opelucid City)

Pokémon Ranger Lewis · Icirrus City · Fisherman Bruce · Parasol Lady Lumi

Spring	Summer	Autumn

Wetlands

Pokémon	
Palpitoad	◎
Shelmet	◎
Stunfisk	○

● In winter, the swamp freezes and Pokémon don't appear.

All Seasons

Water Surface

Pokémon	
Stunfisk	◎

Water Surface (ripples)

Pokémon	
Seismitoad	△
Stunfisk	◎

■ **After finishing the main story**

Fishing

Pokémon	
Barboach	◎
Stunfisk	○

Fishing (ripples)

Pokémon	
Barboach	◎
Stunfisk	○
Whiscash	△

■ Moor of Icirrus

Pokémon Ranger Harry

Pokémon Ranger Chloris

Parasol Lady Mariah · Fisherman Damon

Items

● Route 8
  First Visit
☐ Full Heal
☐ Poison Barb
☐ TM36 Sludge Bomb
☐ TM42 Facade
☐ Ultra Ball
  After defeating
  Pokémon Ranger Lewis
☐ Pecha Berry
  After defeating
  Pokémon Ranger Annie
☐ Pecha Berry
  After defeating Bianca
☐ Full Restore
● Moor of Icirrus
  First Visit
☐ Carbos
☐ Max Elixir
☐ Max Potion
☐ Max Revive
☐ Ultra Ball
  After defeating
  Pokémon Ranger Chloris
☐ Sitrus Berry
  After defeating
  Pokémon Ranger Harry
☐ Sitrus Berry

Palpitoad
Water · Ground
ABILITIES
● Swift Swim
● Hydration

Stunfisk
Ground · Electric
ABILITIES
● Static
● Limber

Step 1 ▶ Proceed while battling Trainers

First, head north when you enter Route 8 from Icirrus City. Use Surf from where Pokémon Ranger Lewis is and head east. Battle the Pokémon Trainers along the way and head for the Moor of Icirrus.

Sometimes the weather is rainy

Route 8's weather changes depending on the date and season. Rain can fall during spring, summer, and autumn, and snow or hail will sometimes fall during winter. Pay attention to changes in weather (p. 206).

Step 2 ▶ Investigate the Moor of Icirrus

In the Moor of Icirrus north of Route 8, Pokémon pop out of the marshes and water covering the area. Have battles with Pokémon Trainers and wild Pokémon. Make sure to check every last corner and gather items.

 Step 3 ▶ Use HMs to see everything

To see everything in the Moor of Icirrus, you need the HMs Surf and Strength. Use Surf to go around the east side, and then use Strength to push the rock on the west side into the hole and open up a path. Once you've seen everything, return to Route 8.

Get Berries by defeating Rangers

Get Pecha Berries by defeating Pokémon Rangers Lewis and Annie in Pokémon battles. Get Sitrus Berries by defeating Pokémon Rangers Harry and Chloris in the Moor of Icirrus.

Step 4 ▶ Return to Route 8 and head to its end

When you return to Route 8 from the Moor of Icirrus, go south through the marsh. When you reach the Trainer Tips sign, turn east. Continue on to the Tubeline Bridge while battling Trainers.

Step 5 ▶ Get items from the Parasol Lady

Get an item once a day from the Parasol Lady behind the sign. The item she gives you changes depending on the time of day (p. 49). She gives you a Damp Rock in the morning, a Heat Rock during the afternoon, a Smooth Rock in the evening, and an Icy Rock at night.

Defeat Bianca and get an item

Defeat Bianca in a Pokémon battle, and she will give you a Full Restore. It's a useful item that both restores HP and heals status conditions. After you get your eighth Gym Badge, you can buy them at the Poké Mart.

Step 6 ▶ Bianca calls to you from behind

When you try to enter the Tubeline Bridge to go east, Bianca appears and starts talking to you. She says that there is a lot she wants to do, but first she needs to know more about Pokémon, and then she challenges you to a battle. Accept Bianca's challenge.

UNOVA ADVENTURE WALKTHROUGH

ROUTE 8 • MOOR OF ICIRRUS • TUBELINE BRIDGE

Battle your childhood friend Bianca! **5**

Her Pokémon's levels have increased by 12 from your fourth battle. Her Pokémon (except Musharna) have all evolved.

● If you chose Snivy:

⊙ Stoutland ♀	Lv. 38	Normal
⊙ Simisear ♂	Lv. 38	Fire
⊙ Samurott ♂	Lv. 40	Water
⊙ Musharna ♀	Lv. 38	Psychic
⊙		
⊙		

● If you chose Tepig:

⊙ Stoutland ♀	Lv. 38	Normal
⊙ Simipour ♂	Lv. 38	Water
⊙ Serperior ♂	Lv. 40	Grass
⊙ Musharna ♀	Lv. 38	Psychic
⊙		
⊙		

● If you chose Oshawott:

⊙ Stoutland ♀	Lv. 38	Normal
⊙ Simisage ♂	Lv. 38	Grass
⊙ Emboar ♂	Lv. 40	Fire / Fighting
⊙ Musharna ♀	Lv. 38	Psychic
⊙		
⊙		

Step 7 — Head to the Tubeline Bridge

When you defeat Bianca in battle, she gives a few words of encouragement as she leaves. Your next goal is Opelucid City, where you'll find the eighth Pokémon Gym and hints about the Legendary Dragon-type Pokémon. First, head to the Tubeline Bridge.

Team Plasma blocks your way

You can explore Route 8 even before you beat the Icirrus City Gym. However, Team Plasma is blocking the entrance to the Tubeline Bridge. Once you beat the Icirrus City Gym, head for the Tubeline Bridge. If you haven't been to Relic Castle (p. 102) yet, you'll need to visit before they'll let you through.

A sturdy steel bridge that won't budge an inch when trains cross it

Tubeline Bridge

Story

Tubeline Bridge is a strong bridge made of steel. Subway trains constantly pass through the lower part of the bridge. On Friday nights, a group of toughs appear out of nowhere and ride their bikes around the bridge.

Field Moves Needed

⊙ Items
☐ TM43 Flame Charge

Route 9 (to Opelucid City)

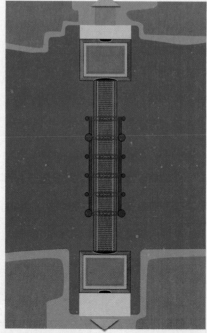

Route 8 (to Icirrus City)

Step 1 Hear Ghetsis's story and head for Route 9

Ghetsis is waiting near the exit. He compliments you on obtaining the Light Stone (Dark Stone). Then he lectures you about his plans and leaves. Go north toward Route 9.

We alone will be able to use Pokémon!

On Fridays, thugs take over the bridge

Every Friday evening and night, lots of Bikers and Roughnecks appear on the bridge (p. 49). If you beat the underling Morgann and the boss Jeremy, they'll change the name of their group to the name of your lead Pokémon.

This paved road attracts those who love bikes

Route 9

Route 9 is a paved road that cuts through a wooded area. On the north side is Shopping Mall Nine, which boasts the greatest variety of goods in Unova.

Field Moves Needed

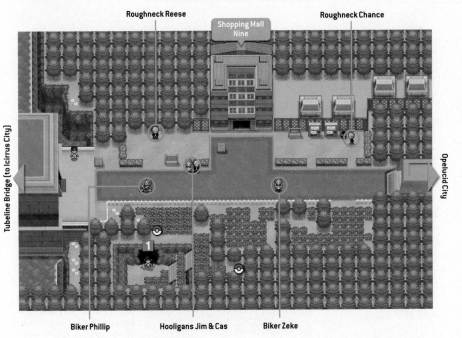

Roughneck Reese

Shopping Mall Nine

Roughneck Chance

Tubeline Bridge (to Icirrus City)

Opelucid City

1

Biker Phillip

Hooligans Jim & Cas

Biker Zeke

🔍 Items
- ☐ Full Restore
- ☐ HP Up
- ☐ PP Up
- ☐ Thunderstone
- ☐ TM56 Fling

🔍 Tall Grass

Pokémon	
Duosion ☐	○
Garbodor	○
Gothorita ■	○
Liepard	△
Minccino	○
Pawniard	○○

🔍 Tall Grass (rustling)

Pokémon	
Audino	◎
Cinccino	△
Emolga	△
Gothitelle ■	△
Reuniclus ☐	△

🔍 Dark Grass

Pokémon	
Duosion ☐	○
Garbodor	○○
Gothorita ■	○
Liepard	△
Minccino	○
Pawniard	○○

Gothorita

Psychic

ABILITY
● Frisk

Duosion

Psychic

ABILITIES
● Overcoat
● Magic Guard

1 You can visit after completing the main story (p. 195).

Step 1 — TM56 Fling is flung at you

When you enter Route 9 from the Tubeline Bridge, an Infielder close to the gate throws TM56 Fling to you. The Dark-type move Fling is an attack that lets the user throw its held item at the target.

What I just threw was TM56 Fling!

Scary-looking Trainers gather here

Several scary-looking guys riding around on motorcycles gather on Route 9. Sometimes, a Biker and a Roughneck will team up as a pair of Hooligans and challenge you to a Double Battle.

Step 2 — Stop by Shopping Mall Nine

Go east on Route 9 and you will see Shopping Mall Nine on the north side. This convenient store is well-stocked with a variety of items. Some of these items aren't available at Poké Marts, so be sure to stop by (p. 159).

Welcome to Shopping Mall Nine! It's called Nine because it's on Route 9.

Shopping Mall Nine

Shopping Mall Nine is a famous mall. It's on Route Nine, so that's where it got its name.

Step 3 — You can't enter the Challenger's Cave yet

Challenger's Cave is to the west, past the tall grass that spreads out through the south side of the route. However, the Black Belt standing in front of the entrance will not let you in. You can enter this cave after finishing the main story (p. 195).

goes in for training, but you aren't ready for this challenge.

Battle Trainers inside the mall too

Inside the shopping mall, four Pokémon Trainers are waiting for you. You can battle them by talking to them, so defeat all of them to make your Pokémon stronger.

Step 4 — Head east to Opelucid City

On the other side of the gate to the east is Opelucid City, where the eighth Gym is located (see p. 160 if you are playing *Pokémon Black Version*, and p. 164 if you are playing *Pokémon White Version*). Pass through the gate to go after your final Gym Badge.

What's the secret of the room with the appliances?

On the first floor of the Shopping Mall is a warehouse with a pile of appliances in cardboard boxes. This place has a special meaning for a Pokémon from a different region (p. 249).

UNOVA ADVENTURE WALKTHROUGH

ROUTE 9

Buy a variety of items at Shopping Mall Nine

Shopping Mall Nine sells a variety of items on each of its three floors. Some items indispensable for raising Pokémon, such as Protein and Iron, can only be purchased here.

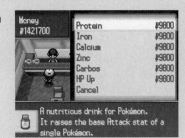

Protein	₽9800
Iron	₽9800
Calcium	₽9800
Zinc	₽9800
Carbos	₽9800
HP Up	₽9800
Cancel	

Money ₽1421700

A nutritious drink for Pokémon. It raises the base Attack stat of a single Pokémon.

Shopping Mall Nine
Floor Guide

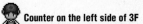

Counter on the left side of 3F

Items	Price
Calcium	9,800
Carbos	9,800
HP Up	9,800
Iron	9,800
Protein	9,800
Zinc	9,800

Counter on the left side of 2F

Items	Price
Favored Mail	50
Greet Mail	50
Inquiry Mail	50
Like Mail	50
Reply Mail	50
RSVP Mail	50
Thanks Mail	50
Poké Ball	200
Heal Ball	300
Great Ball	600
Dusk Ball	1,000
Nest Ball	1,000
Net Ball	1,000
Quick Ball	1,000
Timer Ball	1,000
Ultra Ball	1,200

Waiter Bert   Lady Isabel

Rich Boy Manuel

Waitress Flo

Entrance

Counter on the right side of 3F

Items	Price
X Sp. Def	350
X Special	350
X Speed	350
X Attack	500
X Defend	550
Dire Hit	650
Guard Spec.	700
X Accuracy	950

Counter on the right side of 2F

Items	Price
TM15 Hyper Beam	90,000
TM68 Giga Impact	90,000

 Information

Counter on the left side of 1F

Items	Price	Items	Price
Antidote	100	Escape Rope	550
Parlyz Heal	200	Full Heal	600
Awakening	250	Max Repel	700
Burn Heal	250	Super Potion	700
Ice Heal	250	Poké Toy	1,000
Potion	300	Hyper Potion	1,200
Repel	350	Revive	1,500
Super Repel	500	Max Potion	2,500

Opelucid City

Story

Opelucid City is a modern city packed with buildings. You can enjoy Rotation Battles in the Battle House. You visit this city to obtain information related to the Legendary Pokémon and take on the Gym.

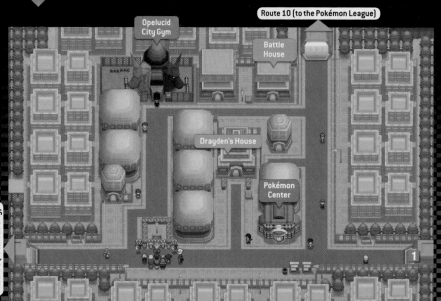

Route 10 (to the Pokémon League)

Opelucid City Gym

Battle House

Drayden's House

Pokémon Center

Route 9 (to Icirrus City)

Route 8 (to Icirrus City)

1

1 You can visit after completing the main story (p. 231).

Items

● **First visit**
☐ Destiny Knot
☐ Float Stone
☐ Fresh Water
☐ Ring Target

● **After showing a Pokémon caught in *Pokémon White Version* that knows the move Charge**
☐ Cell Battery

● **After Beating the Gym Leader**
☐ Legend Badge
☐ Master Ball
☐ TM82 Dragon Tail

Poké Mart
(Lower Clerk)

BridgeMail T	50
Favored Mail	50
Greet Mail	50
Inquiry Mail	50
Like Mail	50
Reply Mail	50
RSVP Mail	50
Thanks Mail	50
Dusk Ball	1,000
Quick Ball	1,000
Timer Ball	1,000

Props

☐ Big Bag
☐ Fluffy Beard
☐ Gift Box
☐ Scarlet Hat

Step 1 — Ghetsis is giving a speech to the people of the city

Ghetsis is giving a speech in front of a Trainer Tips sign when you enter the city and go east. He says that N has joined forces with the Legendary Pokémon and is going to make a new country, and you'd better set your Pokémon free. His speech puts the people of the city into turmoil.

We herald the return of the hero of Unova, founder of this region.

Hero?

Legend!

Dragon?

Step 2 — Alder introduces you to Drayden and Iris

After Ghetsis leaves, two people upset by his speech remain. They are Drayden and Iris, who hold a clue to the Legendary Pokémon. Drayden and Iris invite you to Drayden's house to talk. Visit Drayden's house after looking around the city.

to set the two Dragon-type Pokémon against each other in battle

You met Iris in Castelia City

You've already met Iris, the girl with Drayden, in Castelia City. She helped you when Team Plasma stole one of Bianca's Pokémon, and she acted as Bianca's bodyguard.

Step 3 — Get Props from the old man

An old man who loves the Pokémon Musical lives in the house to the west of the Trainer Tips sign. Talk to him every day to get a Prop to use when you Dress Up your Pokémon. He will give you four different Props. Visit four days in a row to get all the Props.

Would you like a new Prop to use in the musical?

Check how well you've raised your Pokémon

The girl in the first floor of a house will tell you how strong the first Pokémon in your party is. If she says, "It put in a great effort!" that's proof that your Pokémon has experienced many battles.

Step 4 — Have Rotation Battles at the Battle House

The Battle House is two doors east of the Opelucid City Gym. Here, you can enjoy Rotation Battles with two Pokémon Trainers once a day. Also, if you ask the man on the first floor, he will teach you the detailed rules.

As the name suggests, this is the place to enjoy Rotation Battles.

Step 5 — Show a Pokémon caught in *Pokémon White Version*

A man on the second floor of the house on the north side of the Pokémon Center asks you to loan him a Pokémon that knows the move Charge. Trade with someone who has *Pokémon White Version* for a Pokémon such as Blitzle, Zebstrika, or Klink. The man will give you the Cell Battery as thanks.

If you're able, would you be willing to lend me a Pokémon like that?

Step 6 — You can't proceed to Route 11

The gate on the east side of the city is connected to Route 11. But you can't go to Route 11 until you complete the main story (p. 231). If you enter the gate and try to go east, a guard will block your way.

There is something ahead, and the road is closed now.

Visit everyone to get items

If you talk to the people on the second floor of Drayden's house, or the people on the first floor of the house directly to the west of the Battle House, they will give you items. Visit all of the homes, talk to people, and collect items.

Step 7 — Learn about the Legendary Pokémon from Drayden

Go to Drayden's house, and you will hear the story of the Legendary Pokémon. This Pokémon became involved in a battle between the two heroes that split its body into two parts: Reshiram and Zekrom. But even Drayden doesn't know how to awaken the Pokémon.

Light Stone, and Zekrom, who is already awake, were once the same Pokémon.

Step 8 — Take on the Opelucid City Gym

After telling you about the Legendary Pokémon, Drayden—who, it turns out, is the Opelucid City Gym Leader—says he will accept your challenge. Go west from Drayden's house, and turn north at the Trainer Tips sign, and you will reach the Gym.

What's the price of Fresh Water?

Talk to Clyde at the entrance of the Opelucid City Gym after beating the Gym, and he will ask to be paid for all of the Fresh Water he has given you! (Luckily, he's joking.)

Gym battle 8 — *Opelucid City Gym Battle*

Gym Leader Drayden

Ace Trainer Jose

Ace Trainer Tom

Ace Trainer Clara

Ace Trainer Olwen

Ace Trainer Dara

Veteran Hugo

Veteran Kim

Ace Trainer Webster

Entrance

Opelucid City Gym
Drayden

● **Dragon-type Pokémon User**

Recommended Level for your Pokémon	Lv. 46

Hit extra hard with Ice- or Dragon-type moves

In this Gym, you proceed by changing the route with switches. Drayden's Pokémon are all weak to Ice- and Dragon-type moves. If you don't have any of these moves, use a TM to teach your Pokémon Frost Breath or Blizzard. The move Dragon Dance raises Attack and Speed one level. If it is used several times, you could be in danger of taking big damage, so defeat the opposing Pokémon as quickly as you can.

Drayden's Pokémon

			Moves to watch out for:	
⊙ Fraxure ♂	Dragon	Lv. 41	● Dragon Dance	Dragon
⊙ Druddigon ♂	Dragon	Lv. 41	● Revenge	Fighting
⊙ Haxorus ♂	Dragon	Lv. 43	● Dragon Tail	Dragon
⊘				
⊘				
⊘				

TM Received — [TM] **82** Dragon Tail

In a battle with a Trainer, this move forces another Pokémon to be switched in.

Legend Badge

All Pokémon, including those received in trades, will obey you.

After beating the Opelucid City Gym

Professor Juniper meets you outside the Gym

Professor Juniper is waiting for you when you leave the Gym after defeating Drayden. She was planning to tell you how to reawaken Reshiram, but she hasn't figured out how to do it yet. The Professor guides you to the road that will take you to the Pokémon League.

Oh, I came to report on how to resurrect the legendary Reshiram. ▼

After beating the Opelucid City Gym

Get the Master Ball from Professor Juniper

Just before the gate to Route 10, Professor Juniper asks if you regret going on your journey. When you answer, she gives you the Master Ball. It is the ultimate ball that can catch any Pokémon without fail.

Trainer obtained a Master Ball! ▼

After beating the Opelucid City Gym

Hear about the storm on Route 7

At the entrance of the gate to Route 10, the guide tells you about the storm striking Route 7. What could be going on? Use Fly to get to Mistralton City and head for Route 7 (p. 134).

I just heard this on the Xtransceiver. There's a big storm on Route 7! ▼

Meet the Pokémon that roams around Unova

When you visit the stormy Route 7, you'll meet Tornadus. It's a Pokémon that roams around the Unova region. Use the information displayed on the electric bulletin boards to chase it.

After visiting Route 7

Go north to Route 10

Heal your Pokémon at the Pokémon Center, and then head for Route 10 (p. 168). Route 10 begins just beyond the gate in the north of Opelucid City. Beyond that you'll find the Badge Check Gates and Victory Road.

Lend an ear to the synth's sound

There is a person playing a synthesizer close to the Pokémon Center. Get close to hear the sound.

● Synthesizer

UNOVA ADVENTURE WALKTHROUGH ◉ OPELUCID CITY (*POKÉMON BLACK VERSION*)

Opelucid City

Story

Opelucid City is a city that values its past, so its appearance hasn't changed much over the years. You can enjoy Triple Battles in the Battle House. You'll visit this city to obtain information related to the Legendary Pokémon and take on the Gym.

Field Moves Needed

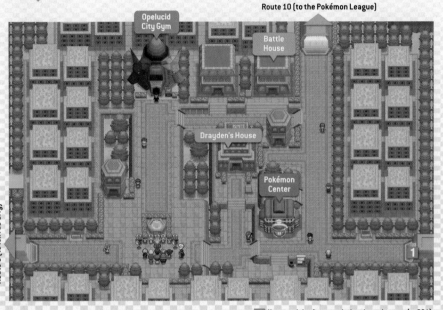

Items

- First visit
  - ☐ Destiny Knot
  - ☐ Float Stone
  - ☐ Fresh Water
  - ☐ Ring Target
- After lending a Pokémon caught in *Pokémon Black Version* that knows Charge
  - ☐ Cell Battery
- After defeating the Opelucid Gym
  - ☐ Legend Badge
  - ☐ Master Ball
  - ☐ TM82 Dragon Tail

1 You can visit after completing the main story (p. 231).

Props

- ☐ Big Bag
- ☐ Fluffy Beard
- ☐ Gift Box
- ☐ Scarlet Hat

Poké Mart (Lower Clerk)

BridgeMail T	50
Favored Mail	50
Greet Mail	50
Inquiry Mail	50
Like Mail	50
Reply Mail	50
RSVP Mail	50
Thanks Mail	50
Dusk Ball	1,000
Quick Ball	1,000
Timer Ball	1,000

Step 1 — Ghetsis is giving a speech to the people of the city

Ghetsis is giving a speech in front of a fountain when you enter the city and go east. He says that N has joined forces with the Legendary Pokémon and is going to create a new world, and advises everyone to set their Pokémon free. His speech puts the people of the city into turmoil.

Step 2 — Alder introduces you to Drayden and Iris

After Ghetsis leaves, two people upset by his speech remain. They are Drayden and Iris, who hold a clue to the legendary Pokémon. Drayden and Iris invite you to Drayden's house to talk. Visit Drayden's house after looking around the city.

You met Iris in Castelia City

You've already met Iris in Castelia City. She helped you when Team Plasma stole one of Bianca's Pokémon, and she acted as Bianca's bodyguard.

UNOVA ADVENTURE WALKTHROUGH

OPELUCID CITY (POKÉMON WHITE VERSION)

UNOVA ADVENTURE WALKTHROUGH ◦ OPELUCID CITY (*POKÉMON WHITE VERSION*)

Step 3 — Get Props from the old man

An old man who loves the Pokémon Musical lives in the house to the west of the fountain. Talk to him every day to get a Prop to use when you Dress Up your Pokémon. He will give you four different Props. Visit four days in a row to get all of the Props.

Would you like a new Prop to use in the musical?

Check how well you've raised your Pokémon

The girl in the first floor of a house will tell you how strong the first Pokémon in your party is. If she says, "It put in a great effort!" that's proof that your Pokémon has experienced many battles.

Step 4 — Experience Triple Battles in the Battle House

The Battle House is two buildings east of the Opelucid City Gym, and you can enjoy Triple Battles with two Pokémon Trainers here once a day. Also, if you ask the man on the first floor, he will teach you the detailed rules.

suggests, if you want to enjoy Triple Battles, you've come to the right spot. ▼

Step 5 — Show a Pokémon caught in *Pokémon Black Version*

A man on the second floor of the house on the north side of the Pokémon Center asks you to loan him a Pokémon that knows the move Charge. Trade with someone who has *Pokémon Black Version* for a Pokémon such as Blitzle, Zebstrika, or Klink. He will give you the Cell Battery as thanks.

If you're able, would you be willing to lend me a Pokémon like that?

▶ YES
   NO

Step 6 — You can't proceed to Route 11

The gate on the east side of the city is connected to Route 11. But you can't go to Route 11 until you complete the main story (p. 231). If you enter the gate and try to go east, a guard will block your way.

Rainy Lacunosa Town

There is something ahead, and the road is closed now. ▼

Visit everyone to get items

If you talk to the people on the second floor of Drayden's house, or the people on the first floor of the house directly to the west of the Battle House, they will give you items. Visit all of the homes, talk to people, and collect items.

Step 7 — Learn about the Legendary Pokémon from Drayden

Dark Stone, and Reshiram, who is already awake, were once the same Pokémon. ▼

Go to Drayden's house, and you will hear the story of the Legendary Pokémon. Reshiram and Zekrom, who were once a single Pokémon, became involved in a battle between the two heroes, and split its body into two. But even Drayden doesn't know how to awaken the Pokémon.

Step **8** **Take on the Opelucid City Gym**

After telling you about the Legendary Pokémon, Drayden asks Iris—who, it turns out, is the Opelucid City Gym Leader—to accept your challenge. Go west from Drayden's house, turn north at the fountain, and you will reach the Gym.

What's the price of Fresh Water?

Talk to Clyde at the entrance of the Opelucid City Gym after beating the Gym, and he will ask to be paid for all of the Fresh Water he has given you! (Luckily, he's joking.)

Gym battle 8 | *Opelucid City Gym Battle*

Gym Leader Iris

Ace Trainer Tom

Ace Trainer Dara

Ace Trainer Webster

Ace Trainer Jose

Ace Trainer Clara

Ace Trainer Olwen

Veteran Hugo

Veteran Kim

Entrance

Opelucid City Gym
Iris

● *Dragon-type Pokémon User*

Recommended Level for your Pokémon	Lv. 46

Hit their weak point with Ice- or Dragon-type moves

In this Gym, you proceed by changing the route with switches. Iris's Pokémon are all weak to Ice- and Dragon-type moves. If you don't have any of these moves, use a TM to teach your Pokémon Frost Breath or Blizzard. The move Dragon Dance raises Attack and Speed one level. If it is used several times, you could be in danger of taking big damage, so defeat the opposing Pokémon as quickly as you can.

Iris's Pokémon

◎ Fraxure ♀	Lv. 41	● Moves to watch out for:
Dragon		Dragon Dance — Dragon

◎ Druddigon ♀	Lv. 41	● Moves to watch out for:
Dragon		Revenge — Fighting

◎ Haxorus ♀	Lv. 43	● Moves to watch out for:
Dragon		Dragon Tail — Dragon

◎	
◎	
◎	

TM Received	TM **82** Dragon Tail

In a battle with a Trainer, this move forces another Pokémon to be switched in.

Legend Badge

All Pokémon, including those received in trades, will obey you.

After beating the Opelucid City Gym

Professor Juniper meets you outside the Gym

Professor Juniper is waiting for you when you leave the Gym after defeating Iris. She was planning to tell you how to reawaken Zekrom, but she hasn't figured out how to do it yet. The Professor guides you to the road to the Pokémon League.

Oh, I came to report on how to resurrect the legendary Zekrom.

After beating the Opelucid City Gym

Get the Master Ball from Professor Juniper

Just before the gate to Route 10, Professor Juniper asks if you regret going on your journey. When you answer, she gives you the Master Ball. It is the ultimate ball, the one that will surely catch any Pokémon.

Trainer obtained a Master Ball!

After beating the Opelucid City Gym

Hear about the storm on Route 7

At the entrance of the gate to Route 10, you hear about the storm striking Route 7 from the guide. What could be going on? Use Fly to get to Mistralton City and head for Route 7 (p. 134).

I just heard this on the Xtransceiver. There's a big storm on Route 7!

Meet the Pokémon that roams around Unova

When you visit the stormy Route 7, you'll meet Thundurus. It's a Pokémon that roams around the Unova region. Use the information displayed on the electric bulletin boards to chase it.

After visiting Route 7

Go north toward Route 10

Heal your Pokémon at the Pokémon Center, and once you are ready, head for Route 10 (p. 168). Route 10 is just beyond the gate in the north of Opelucid City. Beyond that are the Badge Check Gates and Victory Road.

Listen to the musician

There is a person playing a stringed instrument close to the Pokémon Center. Get close to hear the sound.

● Stringed Instrument

Route 10

Story

Route 10 is surrounded by green trees and a winding river. Lots of strong Pokémon Trainers also wait for you here. You can pass through the Badge Check Gates at the eastern end of the route if you have the necessary Gym Badges.

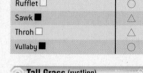

Field Moves Needed

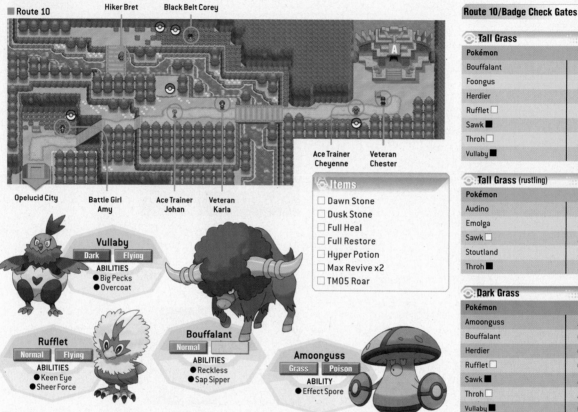

■ Route 10

Hiker Bret   Black Belt Corey

Opelucid City   Battle Girl Amy   Ace Trainer Johan   Veteran Karla

Ace Trainer Cheyenne   Veteran Chester

Vullaby
Dark   Flying
ABILITIES
● Big Pecks
● Overcoat

Rufflet
Normal   Flying
ABILITIES
● Keen Eye
● Sheer Force

Bouffalant
Normal
ABILITIES
● Reckless
● Sap Sipper

Amoonguss
Grass   Poison
ABILITY
● Effect Spore

Items
☐ Dawn Stone
☐ Dusk Stone
☐ Full Heal
☐ Full Restore
☐ Hyper Potion
☐ Max Revive x2
☐ TM05 Roar

Route 10/Badge Check Gates

Tall Grass

Pokémon	
Bouffalant	○
Foongus	△
Herdier	○
Rufflet ☐	○
Sawk ■	△
Throh ☐	△
Vullaby ■	○

Tall Grass (rustling)

Pokémon	
Audino	◎
Emolga	△
Sawk ☐	△
Stoutland	△
Throh ■	△

Dark Grass

Pokémon	
Amoonguss	△
Bouffalant	○
Herdier	○
Rufflet ☐	○
Sawk ■	△
Throh ☐	△
Vullaby ■	○

Step 1 Continue east while battling Trainers

Once you enter Route 10 from Opelucid City, go east. Strong Pokémon Trainers are waiting for you all along the way. This route can be challenging, so don't be reckless if your Pokémon get hurt—return to the Opelucid City Pokémon Center for some healing.

I'm the best around here. Can you possibly be a match for me?

Step 2 Cheren plants himself in your path

As you are about to finish crossing the bridge over the river, Cheren and Bianca come up from behind you. "You're heading for the Pokémon League, right?" asks Cheren. When you answer him, he says he wants to see how strong you are and challenges you to a battle. Accept the challenge and take him on.

to set the two Dragon-type Pokémon against each other in battle

Badge Check Gates

Badge needed
to pass

Bolt
Badge

Badge needed
to pass

Insect
Badge

Badge needed
to pass

Basic
Badge

Badge needed
to pass

Trio
Badge

A

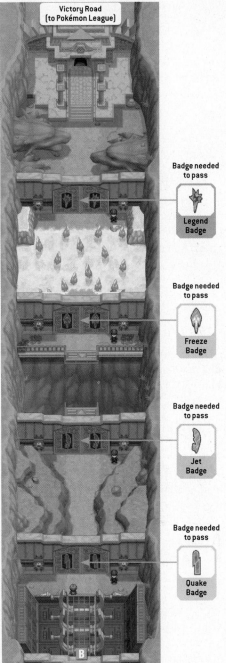

Victory Road
(to Pokémon League)

Badge needed
to pass

Legend
Badge

Badge needed
to pass

Freeze
Badge

Badge needed
to pass

Jet
Badge

Badge needed
to pass

Quake
Badge

B

UNOVA ADVENTURE WALKTHROUGH · ROUTE 10

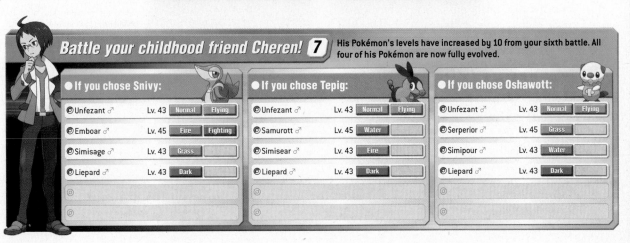

Battle your childhood friend Cheren! 7

His Pokémon's levels have increased by 10 from your sixth battle. All four of his Pokémon are now fully evolved.

● If you chose Snivy:

Unfezant ♂	Lv. 43	Normal	Flying
Emboar ♂	Lv. 45	Fire	Fighting
Simisage ♂	Lv. 43	Grass	
Liepard ♂	Lv. 43	Dark	

● If you chose Tepig:

Unfezant ♂	Lv. 43	Normal	Flying
Samurott ♂	Lv. 45	Water	
Simisear ♂	Lv. 43	Fire	
Liepard ♂	Lv. 43	Dark	

● If you chose Oshawott:

Unfezant ♂	Lv. 43	Normal	Flying
Serperior ♂	Lv. 45	Grass	
Simipour ♂	Lv. 43	Water	
Liepard ♂	Lv. 43	Dark	

ROUTE 10 · UNOVA ADVENTURE WALKTHROUGH

Step 3 — Cheren and Bianca cheer you up

After you defeat Cheren, he will acknowledge your strength and heal all of your Pokémon. Bianca gives you a Max Revive. A great trial stands before you, so the two of them give you some words of encouragement and leave.

Step 4 — Collect items in the northern side of the route

Just after you cross the bridge over the river, enter the small northward path covered in tall grass. You can continue to the north side of Route 10. Battle Pokémon Trainers and collect items. Continue over the bridge to the south and hop down the ledge to return to the main path.

A Foongus among us!

Sometimes, when you check items on the ground, a Foongus or Amoonguss will pop out and a battle will start. Both of them disguise themselves as items.

Step 5 — Battle Trainers as you head east

When you return from the north side of Route 10, head due east. You will see the Badge Check Gates at the end of the Route. Battle the two Pokémon Trainers in front of the gate and enter at last.

Step 6 — Pass through the Badge Check Gates

There is a door and gate for each of the eight Gym Badges at the Badge Check Gates. The guard at each gate checks your Gym Badge and opens the gate so you can continue.

No Badge, no gate

If you don't have the corresponding Badge for each of the eight gates, that gate won't open, and you can't go any further. Visit after you have collected all eight Gym Badges.

Step 7 — Head north to Victory Road

When your eighth Badge has been checked and the gate opens, you have reached the entrance to Victory Road. Victory Road is the greatest obstacle standing between you and the Pokémon League. Get pumped up, and make your charge!

A reminder of your Gym Battles

The area after each Badge Check Gate is designed to remind Trainers of each Gym they've faced and defeated. Take a moment to look around each area before you proceed to the next gate.

Victory Road

Story

Victory Road is carved into a steep cliff dotted with caves. You'll weave in and out of the caves as you climb toward the Pokémon League, and fearsome Pokémon Trainers stand in your way throughout your climb.

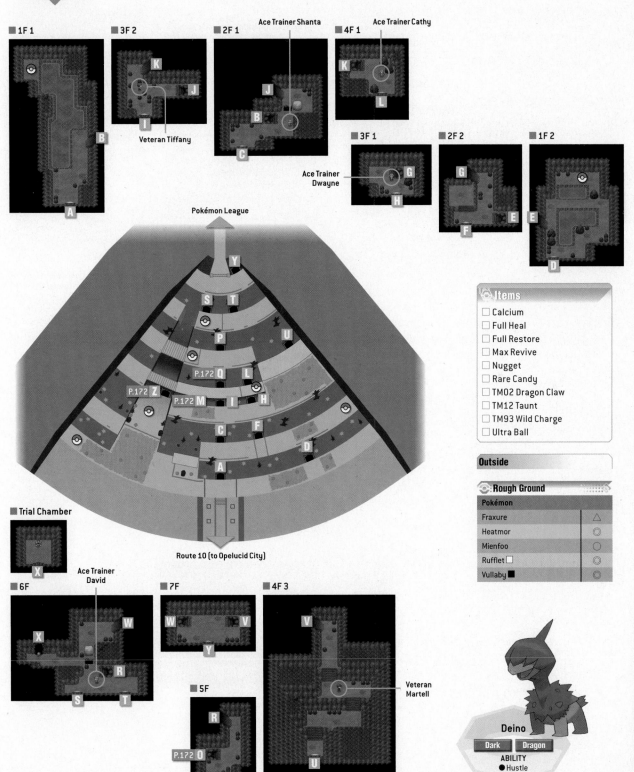

- **1F 1**
- **3F 2** — Veteran Tiffany
- **2F 1** — Ace Trainer Shanta
- **4F 1** — Ace Trainer Cathy
- **3F 1** — Ace Trainer Dwayne
- **2F 2**
- **1F 2**

Pokémon League

Route 10 (to Opelucid City)

- **Trial Chamber**
- **6F** — Ace Trainer David
- **7F**
- **4F 3** — Veteran Martell
- **5F**

Items
- [ ] Calcium
- [ ] Full Heal
- [ ] Full Restore
- [ ] Max Revive
- [ ] Nugget
- [ ] Rare Candy
- [ ] TM02 Dragon Claw
- [ ] TM12 Taunt
- [ ] TM93 Wild Charge
- [ ] Ultra Ball

Outside

Rough Ground

Pokémon	
Fraxure	△
Heatmor	◎
Mienfoo	○
Rufflet □	◎
Vullaby ■	◎

Deino

Dark   Dragon

ABILITY
● Hustle

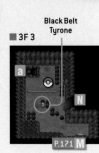

■ 3F 3

Black Belt Tyrone

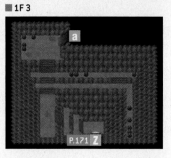

■ 4F 2

P. 171 **O**

N

Doctor Logan
◎ Restore your Pokémon's Health

P.171 **Q**

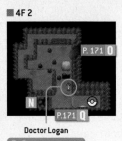

a

N

P.171 **M**

■ 1F 3

a

P. 171 **Z**

1F 1 • 2

Cave

Pokémon	
Boldore	◯
Deino	◯
Durant	◎
Mienfoo	△
Woobat	△

Cave (dust cloud)

Pokémon	
Excadrill	◎

Water Surface

Pokémon		
Basculin (Blue-Striped Form) ☐		◎
Basculin (Red-Striped Form) ■		◎

Water Surface (ripples)

Pokémon		
Basculin (Blue-Striped Form) ■		◎
Basculin (Red-Striped Form) ☐		◎

■ After finishing the main story

Fishing

Pokémon		
Basculin (Blue-Striped Form) ☐		◯
Basculin (Red-Striped Form) ■		◯
Poliwag		◎
Poliwhirl		△

Fishing (ripples)

Pokémon		
Basculin (Blue-Striped Form) ☐		◯
Basculin (Red-Striped Form) ■		◯
Poliwhirl		◎
Poliwrath		△

Other Places

Cave

Pokémon	
Boldore	◯
Durant	◎
Mienfoo	△
Woobat	◯

Cave (dust cloud)

Pokémon	
Excadrill	◎

Step 1 — Proceed while battling Trainers

Head north from the outside and go in to collect an item, and afterward continue into 2F 1. You'll immediately run into Ace Trainer Shanta. There's a rock you can move with Strength just north of her, but you can't push it from this side. After defeating Shanta, you can go outside from the south.

Before going to the Pokémon League, let me test my skills!

You can come back with Fly

If you use Fly, your Pokémon can take you to any city that has a Pokémon Center. Victory Road is an exception—it isn't a city, but you can use Fly to return to the entrance anyway.

Step 2 — You can slide down the cliff

Outside, you'll see the man on the first floor go sliding down the cliff wall through a gap in the fence. Now you know that you can move down by sliding down through gaps in the fence outside. You'll need to do some sliding to see every corner of Victory Road!

Find items with the Dowsing MCHN

Many items are hidden in Victory Road. Use the Dowsing MCHN to find them.

Step 3 — Make a shortcut with Strength

After sliding down from the gap in the fence, pass through 1F 2 and 2F 2 to reach 3F 1. From there you can reach 3F 2 and 3F 3 from the outside. Climb down the stairs from 3F 2, and push the rock in 2F 1 with Strength. This will make a shortcut from 2F 1 to 3F 2.

▶ YES
NO

Would you like to use Strength?

UNOVA ADVENTURE WALKTHROUGH — VICTORY ROAD ◎

Have Doctor Logan heal your Pokémon

Climb the stairs from 3F 3 to 4F 2 and you'll meet Doctor Logan. He will heal all of your Pokémon if you beat him in battle, and you can come back for more healing any time. Remember where Logan is so you can get his help if you need it.

Whether your Pokémon are healthy or not, I'll restore them to full health! ▾

Climb every mountain, battle every Trainer

At the end of Victory Road, the Elite Four are waiting in the Pokémon League. Rake in all the Experience Points you can now by battling all the Pokémon Trainers along your way!

 See everything and get all of the items

Climb the stairs and slide down the cliff from the Doctor on 4F 2 in order to see everything. At the top of the cliff is a man standing at the western edge. Slide down from either side of him to collect items in different places.

Trainers aren't your only source of Experience Points

The wild Pokémon in Victory Road are around Lv. 40. That means you'll get a good number of Experience Points for defeating them. Battle as many Pokémon as you can to make your Pokémon stronger.

 The northbound path goes to the Pokémon League

When you go outside from the seventh floor, head west. You will immediately come upon a path that extends straight north. If you go north on this road, you will reach the Pokémon League (p. 174). Defeat all of the Pokémon Trainers, collect all of the items, and head for the Pokémon League.

After capturing Cobalion **Capture Terrakion in the Trial Chamber**

After you've captured Cobalion in Mistralton Cave (p. 145), you can enter the Trial Chamber in the west part of the sixth floor. The Legendary Pokémon Terrakion is waiting for you inside. When you talk to it, the battle begins. Capture it so you can complete your Pokédex.

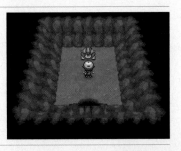

⬤ Capture Terrakion!

Terrakion Lv. 42

| Rock | Fighting |

ABILITY ⬤ Justified
MOVES ⬤ Helping Hand
⬤ Retaliate
⬤ Rock Slide
⬤ Sacred Sword

Terrakion's Ability, Justified, makes Terrakion's Attack rise one level when it is hit by a Dark-type move. When its Attack goes up, the move Sacred Sword becomes very powerful, so reduce its HP with Normal-, Fire-, or Bug-type moves.

Pokémon League

Story

The Pokémon League is a place to challenge the best Trainers in the region. Now that you've finally reached the Pokémon League, it's time to take on the Elite Four.

Field Moves Needed

■ Grimsley's Room

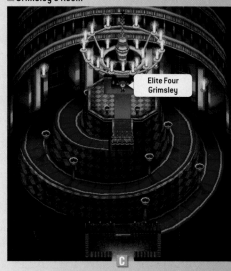

Elite Four Grimsley

C

■ Caitlin's Room

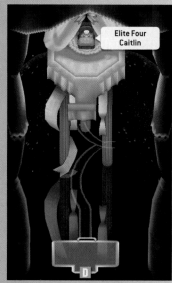

Elite Four Caitlin

D

■ Shauntal's Room

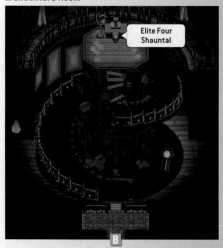

Elite Four Shauntal

B

■ The Elite Four's Plaza

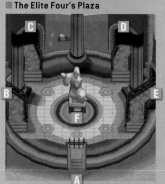

C   D

B   E

F

A

■ Marshal's Room

Elite Four Marshal

E

■ Entrance

Pokémon Center

A

Victory Road (to Opelucid City)

■ The Bridge to N's Castle   N's Castle

■ Champion's Room

■ Basement

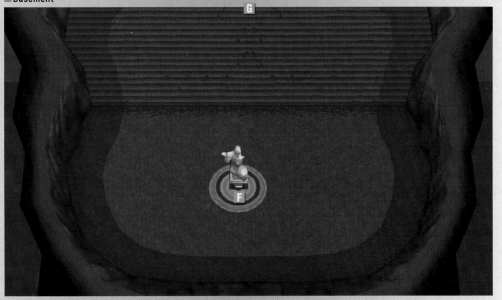

Poké Mart (Lower Clerk)	
Heal Ball	300
Dusk Ball	1,000
Luxury Ball	1,000
Nest Ball	1,000
Net Ball	1,000
Quick Ball	1,000
Repeat Ball	1,000
Timer Ball	1,000

Step 1 — Check your party Pokémon

Before taking on the Pokémon League, check the Pokémon in your party. Refer to pages 177 and 178 to check whether your Pokémon's moves will be effective against the Elite Four's Pokémon. And be sure to prepare your party in every way, such as by healing your Pokémon at the Pokémon Center.

Use items to heal your Pokémon

You can't return to the Pokémon Center once you start your battle with the Elite Four. Once you've ended your battle with one of them, use items to restore your Pokémon's health before you challenge the next member of the Elite Four. Check to make sure your Pokémon's PP hasn't gone down too much.

Step 2 — Prepare yourself for the Elite Four

Stock up on many different items so you are prepared if your Pokémon's HP gets low or if they are affected by a status condition during your battles with the Elite Four. In particular, it's a good idea to buy lots of Full Restores because they heal your Pokémon's HP and status problems at the same time.

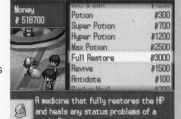

Challenge the Elite Four in any order

The Elite Four use Ghost-, Dark-, Psychic-, and Fighting-type Pokémon. Fight them in any order you like, based on the situation with your party. Then, you can take on the next Elite Four member after making your Pokémon even a little bit stronger.

Step 3 — Check the Pokémon League's rules

Once you enter the Elite Four's plaza in the Pokémon League, there's no going back. You can battle the Elite Four in any order you like, but if you are defeated, you will have to start the challenge over from the beginning even if you have defeated several of the Elite Four. Keep this special rule in the back of your mind.

Save, just to be sure

If you lose to any of the Elite Four, you have to start the whole Elite Four battle over again. Save after each victory. If you do, you can restart from where you saved last.

Step 4 — Take the Pokémon League challenge

Once you're prepared, approach the man at the entrance of the Elite Four's plaza. He will explain the rules of the Pokémon League. If you respond "Yes" at the end, he will open the way for you. The time for your battle with the Elite Four has finally come! Steel yourself and go inside.

The Elite Four's Caitlin appeared in the past

The Elite Four's Caitlin appeared in the Battle Frontier in *Pokémon Platinum*, *HeartGold*, and *SoulSilver Versions*. She must have risen to the Elite Four in this new region.

Elite Four Battle

Shauntal
● **Ghost-type Pokémon User**

| Recommended Level for your Pokémon | Lv. 53 |

Deal massive damage with Ghost- and Dark-type moves

Shauntal's Pokémon know more than Ghost-type moves—they use many powerful moves such as the Psychic-type move Psychic and the Ground-type move Earthquake. You are at a disadvantage if you battle with Pokémon that are weak against these types. Strike her Pokémon's weak points with Ghost-, Dark-, and Water-type moves to do big damage.

● Shauntal's Pokémon

			Effective Move Types	
◎ Cofagrigus ♀	Lv. 48	Ghost	Ghost	Dark
● Moves to watch out for:				
Shadow Ball	Ghost			

			Effective Move Types	
◎ Chandelure ♀	Lv. 50	Ghost / Fire	Water	Ground
			Rock	Ghost
● Moves to watch out for:			Dark	
Fire Blast	Fire			

			Effective Move Types	
◎ Golurk	Lv. 48	Ground / Ghost	Water	Grass
			Ice	Ghost
● Moves to watch out for:			Dark	
Earthquake	Ground			

			Effective Move Types	
◎ Jellicent ♀	Lv. 48	Water / Ghost	Grass	Electric
			Ghost	Dark
● Moves to watch out for:				
Surf	Water			

			Effective Move Types	
◎				
● Moves to watch out for:				

			Effective Move Types	
◎				
● Moves to watch out for:				

● Grimsley's Pokémon

			Effective Move Types	
◎ Scrafty ♂	Lv. 48	Dark / Fighting	Fighting	Flying
● Moves to watch out for:				
Brick Break	Fighting			

			Effective Move Types	
◎ Krookodile ♀	Lv. 48	Ground / Dark	Water	Grass
			Ice	Fighting
● Moves to watch out for:			Bug	
Earthquake	Ground			

			Effective Move Types	
◎ Bisharp ♀	Lv. 50	Dark / Steel	Fighting	Fire
			Ground	
● Moves to watch out for:				
Aerial Ace	Flying			

			Effective Move Types	
◎ Liepard ♀	Lv. 48	Dark	Fighting	Bug
● Moves to watch out for:				
Attract	Normal			

			Effective Move Types	
◎				
● Moves to watch out for:				

			Effective Move Types	
◎				
● Moves to watch out for:				

Elite Four Battle

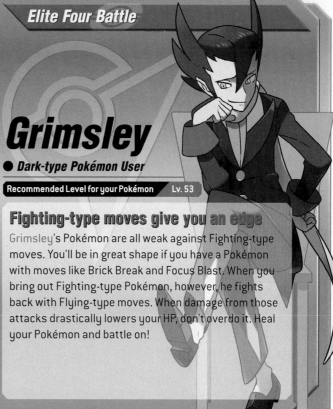

Grimsley
● **Dark-type Pokémon User**

| Recommended Level for your Pokémon | Lv. 53 |

Fighting-type moves give you an edge

Grimsley's Pokémon are all weak against Fighting-type moves. You'll be in great shape if you have a Pokémon with moves like Brick Break and Focus Blast. When you bring out Fighting-type Pokémon, however, he fights back with Flying-type moves. When damage from those attacks drastically lowers your HP, don't overdo it. Heal your Pokémon and battle on!

● Caitlin's Pokémon

			Effective Move Types	
Ⓟ **Reuniclus** ♀	Lv. 48		Bug	Ghost
Psychic			Dark	
● Moves to watch out for:				
Psychic	Psychic			

			Effective Move Types	
Ⓜ **Musharna** ♀	Lv. 48		Bug	Ghost
Psychic			Dark	
● Moves to watch out for:				
Charge Beam	Electric			

			Effective Move Types	
Ⓢ **Sigilyph** ♀	Lv. 48		Electric	Ice
Psychic	Flying		Rock	Ghost
● Moves to watch out for:			Dark	
Air Slash	Flying			

			Effective Move Types	
Ⓖ **Gothitelle** ♀	Lv. 50		Bug	Ghost
Psychic			Dark	
● Moves to watch out for:				
Shadow Ball	Ghost			

			Effective Move Types	
Ⓞ				
● Moves to watch out for:				

			Effective Move Types	
Ⓞ				
● Moves to watch out for:				

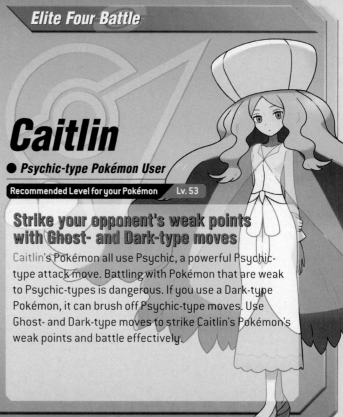

Elite Four Battle

Caitlin
● **Psychic-type Pokémon User**

Recommended Level for your Pokémon — Lv. 53

Strike your opponent's weak points with Ghost- and Dark-type moves

Caitlin's Pokémon all use Psychic, a powerful Psychic-type attack move. Battling with Pokémon that are weak to Psychic-types is dangerous. If you use a Dark-type Pokémon, it can brush off Psychic-type moves. Use Ghost- and Dark-type moves to strike Caitlin's Pokémon's weak points and battle effectively.

Elite Four Battle

Marshal
● **Fighting-type Pokémon User**

Recommended Level for your Pokémon — Lv. 53

Flying- and Psychic-type moves are the keys to victory

Marshal's Pokémon are weak to Flying- and Psychic-type moves. If you use a Flying-type Pokémon, however, he will attack with Rock-type moves. Use TM40 Aerial Ace to teach that move to your Pokémon. Aerial Ace is a move that many Pokémon can use, including Serperior and Samurott.

● Marshal's Pokémon

			Effective Move Types	
Ⓣ **Throh** ♂	Lv. 48		Flying	Psychic
Fighting				
● Moves to watch out for:				
Bulldoze	Ground			

			Effective Move Types	
Ⓢ **Sawk** ♂	Lv. 48		Flying	Psychic
Fighting				
● Moves to watch out for:				
Stone Edge	Rock			

			Effective Move Types	
Ⓜ **Mienshao** ♂	Lv. 50		Flying	Psychic
Fighting				
● Moves to watch out for:				
Jump Kick	Fighting			

			Effective Move Types	
Ⓒ **Conkeldurr** ♂	Lv. 48		Flying	Psychic
Fighting				
● Moves to watch out for:				
Hammer Arm	Fighting			

			Effective Move Types	
Ⓞ				
● Moves to watch out for:				

			Effective Move Types	
Ⓞ				
● Moves to watch out for:				

After defeating the Elite Four — Check the shining statue

After you defeat all four of the Elite Four, visit the statue in the center of the Elite Four's plaza. Check the plaque on the shining statue, and go underground. Go underground and head north. Soon, you will see a building on top of the plateau. This is the Champion's Room. Go inside.

Until you beat the Elite Four, you can't proceed

You can't go to the Champion's room, where Alder is, until you've beaten all of the Elite Four. The statue in the Elite Four's Plaza will not shine, and it won't move, even if you check it.

After defeating the Elite Four — N has defeated Alder

N and Alder are facing each other in the Champion's Room. The battle is already over, and amazingly, Alder has lost to N. Alder begs N not to separate Pokémon and people, but N will hear none of it.

After defeating the Elite Four — A giant castle appears

N realizes you have obtained the Light Stone (Dark Stone) and is pleased about that. But he declares this place isn't suitable for the Legendary Pokémon. Moments later, a giant castle rises out of the ground, as if it's surrounding the Pokémon League.

After defeating the Elite Four — Go into N's Castle to defend peace

N tells you to come inside, and he goes into N's Castle. Alder and Cheren give you their thoughts on the situation. To settle everything with N and Team Plasma, climb the stairs to N's Castle (p. 180).

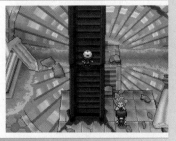

N's Castle

Story

N's Castle was constructed in secret over many years, and it was hidden in the land around the Pokémon League. You enter the stronghold alone to prevent N and Team Plasma from separating people from Pokémon.

Field Moves Needed

■ 3F

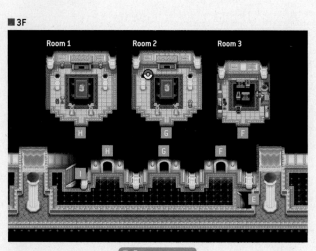

■ Throne Room

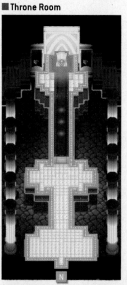

Items
- ☐ Full Restore
- ☐ Max Potion
- ☐ Max Revive
- ☐ Rare Candy
- ☐ Ultra Ball

■ 2F

Restore your Pokémon's Health

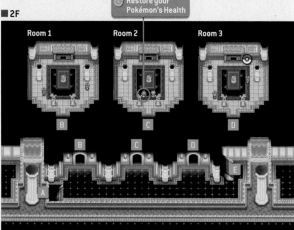

■ 5F

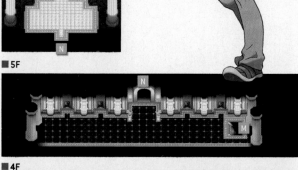

■ 4F

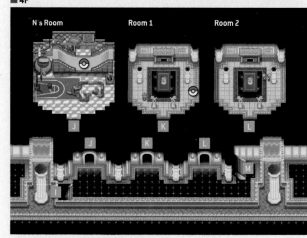

■ 1F

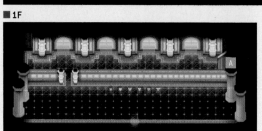

Step 1 — **The Gym Leaders to the rescue**

When you go inside, six of the Seven Sages are waiting on the first floor. When they are about to attack you, the Gym Leaders jump into the fray and take them on for you. Leave this battle to the Gym Leaders and go on ahead.

Not only are we stronger than you, but there are a lot of us!

What happened to Striaton City's Gym Leaders?

Striaton City's Gym Leaders, Chili, Cress, and Cilan, aren't among the Gym Leaders that stand up to the Seven Sages. The truth is, Bianca went to get them, but she didn't make it in time.

Step 2 | The Shadow Triad helps you

When you reach the second floor, one of the Shadow Triad appears. The Shadow Triad member tells you not to fear, because you can heal your Pokémon and access your PC even inside N's Castle. It's a nice thing to hear from a surprising place.

In this castle, you may rest your Pokémon and access your PC.

Step 3 | Anthea heals your Pokémon

Two women are standing in Room 2 on the second floor: Anthea on the left and Concordia to the right. If you talk to Anthea, she will restore your Pokémon's health. Your Pokémon are probably hurt after the battle with the Elite Four, so talk to her and get their health restored.

Trainer. Before you go to confront my lord N, please take a moment to rest...

Listen to Concordia's story

In Room 2 on the second floor, talk to Concordia to hear a story about N's past. Because of the strange way Ghetsis raised him, he doesn't trust people—only Pokémon.

Step 4 | Use the room with the PC

The room to your right when you reach the third floor is Room 3. It's a laboratory. You'll find a PC next to the entrance, so you can change your party Pokémon here. Any time you want to change your party Pokémon around while in the castle, use this PC.

Step 5 | Talk to the Grunt to return to the Pokémon League

When you talk to the Grunt in Room 1 on the third floor, he will send you back to the Pokémon Center at the Pokémon League. When you need more items, briefly return to the Pokémon League. Talk to the Team Plasma Grunt in the Pokémon Center to return to N's Castle.

YES
NO

Will you go to the Pokémon League?

Team Plasma's plans for the PC

In Room 3 on the third floor, the researcher tells you Team Plasma managed to break into the Pokémon Storage System. On N's command, they plan to release all of the Pokémon stored in PC Boxes.

Step 6 | Peek inside N's room

Another member of the Shadow Triad appears when you reach the fourth floor and tells you that the room to your left is N's room. Why is he living in a room full of toys?

It's a set of trains and tracks. Has it been played with recently?

Step 7 | Ghetsis comes out of the room

Climb to the fifth floor and go north to reach the throne room. When you try to enter, Ghetsis comes out from inside. He is excited because his ambitions are about to be realized. He tells you that you should see if you have what it takes to be the hero, and he invites you into the throne room.

We can bring into being the world that I—no, that Team Plasma—desires

Step 8 — N approaches you from the throne

N is sitting on the throne when you enter the room. He tells you to show him the depth of your determination and calls the Legendary Pokémon Zekrom (Reshiram). The Legendary Pokémon breaks through the far wall and floats down to N.

If that's so, prove it to me!
Show me the depth of your determination! ▾

Step 9 — The stone turns into Reshiram (Zekrom)

When Zekrom (Reshiram) comes to N, the Light Stone (Dark Stone) suddenly jumps out of your Bag. Floating in the air, the stone slowly absorbs the surrounding aura, and reawakens Reshiram (Zekrom).

Pokémon Black Version

Pokémon White Version

Pokémon Black Version — *Catch Reshiram!*

First, use Ground-, Rock-, or Dragon-type moves to lower its HP quickly. After that, lower its HP gradually with Fire- or Grass-type moves. Even if you accidentally knock it out, as long as your party and Boxes are not full, you can keep challenging it until you catch it.

Reshiram Lv. 50
Dragon | Fire

ABILITY ● Turboblaze
MOVES ● DragonBreath
Slash
Extrasensory
Fusion Flare

Pokémon White Version — *Catch Zekrom!*

First, use Ice-, Ground-, or Dragon-type moves to lower its HP quickly. After that, lower its HP gradually with Fire-, Grass, or Electric-type moves. Even if you accidentally knock it out, as long as your party and Boxes are not full, you can keep challenging it until you catch it.

Zekrom Lv. 50
Dragon | Electric

ABILITY ● Teravolt
MOVES ● DragonBreath
Slash
Zen Headbutt
Fusion Bolt

Step 10 — Put Reshiram (Zekrom) in your party

When you catch Reshiram (Zekrom), select whether you want to add it to your party. Your battle with N is up next, and he sends out Zekrom (Reshiram). Put this Pokémon in your party and have the two Legendary Pokémon battle.

► YES
  NO

Add Reshiram to your party from the Box?

The first Pokémon in your party changes

When you add the caught Reshiram (Zekrom) to your party, it will always become the first Pokémon in your party no matter what position Pokémon you swapped out for it was in. That way it will be the first Pokémon that appears when you battle with N.

Pokémon Black Version

Battle Team Plasma's King, N

● User of many Pokémon types

Recommended Level for your Pokémon	Lv. 55

Battle N's Zekrom with Reshiram

When you catch Reshiram and put in your party, you begin a direct battle with Zekrom. If you use Reshiram's move Fusion Flare directly after Zekrom uses Fusion Bolt, it will do double its normal damage. Strike his other Pokémon's weak points by swapping in Pokémon that are strong against his Pokémon.

● N's Pokémon

Zekrom — Lv. 52
Type: Dragon / Electric
Effective Move Types: Ice, Ground, Dragon
Moves to watch out for: Fusion Bolt (Electric)

Carracosta♂ — Lv. 50
Type: Water / Rock
Effective Move Types: Grass, Electric, Fighting, Ground
Moves to watch out for: Stone Edge (Rock)

Vanilluxe♂ — Lv. 50
Type: Ice
Effective Move Types: Fire, Fighting, Rock, Steel
Moves to watch out for: Blizzard (Ice)

Klinklang — Lv. 50
Type: Steel
Effective Move Types: Fire, Fighting, Ground
Moves to watch out for: Hyper Beam (Normal)

Zoroark♂ — Lv. 50
Type: Dark
Effective Move Types: Fighting, Bug
Moves to watch out for: Focus Blast (Fighting)

Archeops♂ — Lv. 50
Type: Rock / Flying
Effective Move Types: Water, Electric, Ice, Rock, Steel
Moves to watch out for: Acrobatics (Flying)

● N's Pokémon

Reshiram — Lv. 52
Type: Dragon / Fire
Effective Move Types: Ground, Rock, Dragon
Moves to watch out for: Fusion Flare (Fire)

Carracosta♂ — Lv. 50
Type: Water / Rock
Effective Move Types: Grass, Electric, Fighting, Ground
Moves to watch out for: Stone Edge (Rock)

Vanilluxe♂ — Lv. 50
Type: Ice
Effective Move Types: Fire, Fighting, Rock, Steel
Moves to watch out for: Blizzard (Ice)

Klinklang — Lv. 50
Type: Steel
Effective Move Types: Fire, Fighting, Ground
Moves to watch out for: Hyper Beam (Normal)

Zoroark♂ — Lv. 50
Type: Dark
Effective Move Types: Fighting, Bug
Moves to watch out for: Focus Blast (Fighting)

Archeops♂ — Lv. 50
Type: Rock / Flying
Effective Move Types: Water, Electric, Ice, Rock, Steel
Moves to watch out for: Acrobatics (Flying)

Pokémon White Version

Battle Team Plasma's King, N

● User of many Pokémon types

Recommended Level for your Pokémon	Lv. 55

Battle N's Reshiram with Zekrom

When you catch Zekrom and put it in your party, you begin a direct battle with Reshiram. If you use Zekrom's move Fusion Bolt directly after Reshiram uses Fusion Flare, it will do double its normal damage. Strike his other Pokémon's weak points by swapping in Pokémon that are strong against N's Pokémon.

Step 11

The final foe, Ghetsis, stands in your way

After you defeat N, Ghetsis appears. Even though N has been defeated, he hasn't given up on his ambitions. Ghetsis says that those who get in the way must be eliminated before challenging you to battle. It's time for the final battle. Prepare yourself and accept the challenge.

Ghetsis: I won't allow anyone to stop me! No matter who does what!

N is Ghetsis's son?!

After you defeat N in battle, Ghetsis's words imply that N is Ghetsis's son. Apparently, they are father and son who share the same last name: Harmonia.

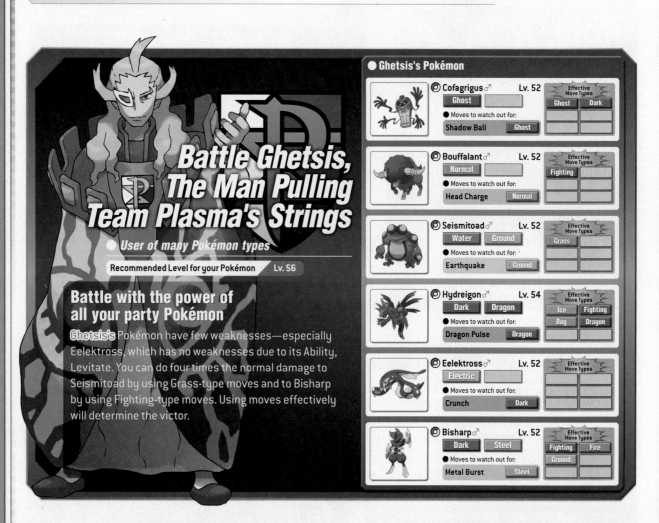

Battle Ghetsis, The Man Pulling Team Plasma's Strings

● *User of many Pokémon types*

Recommended Level for your Pokémon　Lv. 56

Battle with the power of all your party Pokémon

Ghetsis's Pokémon have few weaknesses—especially Eelektross, which has no weaknesses due to its Ability, Levitate. You can do four times the normal damage to Seismitoad by using Grass-type moves and to Bisharp by using Fighting-type moves. Using moves effectively will determine the victor.

● Ghetsis's Pokémon

	Pokémon	Level	Type		Moves to watch out for		Effective Move Types			
	Cofagrigus ♂	Lv. 52	Ghost		Shadow Ball	Ghost	Ghost	Dark		
	Bouffalant ♂	Lv. 52	Normal		Head Charge	Normal	Fighting			
	Seismitoad ♂	Lv. 52	Water	Ground	Earthquake	Ground	Grass			
	Hydreigon ♂	Lv. 54	Dark	Dragon	Dragon Pulse	Dragon	Ice	Fighting	Bug	Dragon
	Eelektross ♂	Lv. 52	Electric		Crunch	Dark				
	Bisharp ♂	Lv. 52	Dark	Steel	Metal Burst	Steel	Fighting	Fire	Ground	

◎ Defeat Ghetsis to see the ending!

Defeating Ghetsis in the Pokémon battle will mean the end of your fight with Team Plasma, and the story comes to a close. The adventure, however, is not over yet. Even after the end of the main story, there are new areas to explore. Unknown adventures await! After the end credits, you will set out for Nuvema Town again on a new journey and adventure (p. 186).

You are challenged by Team Plasma Ghetsis!

184

Keep Training Your Pokémon for the Tough Battles Ahead

Newly accessible areas are full of tough Trainers

In the areas you can access after completing the main story, the Pokémon Trainers and the wild Pokémon are very strong. Even if you were good enough to beat Ghetsis, you'll find yourself in tough battles. Look around after finishing the main story, and strengthen your Pokémon so you can defeat the Champion.

● **Examples of strong Pokémon**

 Use TMs to teach your Pokémon powerful moves

The easiest way to make your Pokémon more powerful is to teach them strong moves with TMs. Some recommended moves are TM02 Dragon Claw, which is found on the third floor of Victory Road, and TM29 Psychic, which you can get on Route 13.

2 Level up your Pokémon in Victory Road

Before you finish the main story, the area with the highest-level wild Pokémon is Victory Road. Go back there to check out every corner, and level up the Pokémon you want to make stronger. Give the Pokémon you are leveling up the Lucky Egg to hold, so they gain increased Experience Points from battle.

 Bring powerful Pokémon over with Poké Transfer

If you have a strong Pokémon in *Pokémon Diamond, Pearl, Platinum, HeartGold,* or *SoulSilver Version,* go to the Poké Transfer Lab on Route 15 and use Poké Transfer to bring your high-level Pokémon into your game. Put your old friends in your new party.

Take your first steps into a new area

Once you defeat N and Ghetsis, the main story comes to a close. Your adventure, however, is not over yet. You become able to visit new areas, discover Pokémon from other regions, and take on new challenges and exciting events.

A New World of Adventure

Nuvema Town — Your mom's twin downstairs

When you come downstairs from your room, there are two of your mom! Actually, one of them is Looker, a member of the International Police. Looker changes out of his disguise and asks you to look for Team Plasma's Seven Sages. Ghetsis is gone, so look for the whereabouts of the other six (p. 233).

"Mom": Oh!
I still wear my disguise! Pardon!

Look at your Trainer Card

When you meet certain conditions, your Trainer Card's color changes. One of these conditions is finishing the main story with the battle in N's Castle. Check your card and see whether it has changed from green to purple.

Nuvema Town — Get the Super Rod from Looker

When you agree to search for the Seven Sages, Looker gives you the Super Rod. When you use it in the water you can catch even-stronger Pokémon that live in the water. Give the rod a try! When you see an exclamation mark (!) press the A Button to reel in the Pokémon.

Trainer obtained the Super Rod!

Super Rod

Nuvema Town — Reunite with Cheren and Bianca

When you leave your house, Cheren and Bianca are waiting. When Cheren asks what everyone is going to do, Bianca says she plans to go to Black City (White Forest). You can now visit Black City (White Forest).

Cheren: Hey, Trainer.
Is Looker through talking to you?

Nuvema Town — Upgrade your Pokédex

Cedric Juniper walks up to you while you are talking with Bianca and Cheren. Apparently, he has received the National Pokédex data from a colleague. Cedric Juniper upgrades everyone's Pokédex.

Trainer's Pokédex was upgraded with the National Mode!

Show your Pokédex to the two professors

After you complete the main story, Professor Juniper will tell you how many Pokémon you've seen at her lab in Nuvema Town. After you've seen all of the Pokémon in the Pokédex, she will evaluate the Pokédex based on how many Pokémon you've obtained. Cedric Juniper evaluates how many Pokémon you've obtained, including those from other regions.

Nuvema Town — Head for newly accessible areas

After you complete the main story, you can visit new areas in addition to the places you've already been. Use Fly to go to Nimbasa City and head east to go to Route 16. Look around the new areas from the Marvelous Bridge (p. 201).

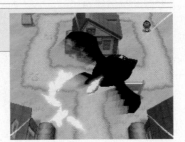

Use Surf from Route 1

Route 18 is connected to Route 17. When you leave for Route 1 from Nuvema Town, use Surf and head to the gate to the west. Once you pass through the gate, you're on Route 17.

Route 18 — Search for Rood of the Seven Sages

Go to Route 18 from Route 17. Continue west, and you will find Rood, one of the Seven Sages, on the beach. Talk to him, and he will give you TM32 Double Team after telling you about N and Ghetsis. After that, Looker comes to arrest him.

Rood: It smells of the sea here.

Dreamyard Map

Field Moves Needed

Strength

■ Outside

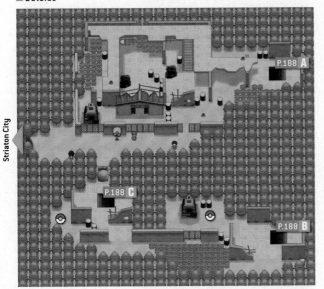

Striaton City

P.188 A

P.188 C

P.188 B

Outside

Tall Grass

Pokémon	
Munna	◎
Patrat	◎
Purrloin	◎

Tall Grass (rustling)

Pokémon	
Audino	◎
Musharna	△

Dark Grass

Pokémon	
Ariados	△
Kricketune	△
Ledian	△
Liepard	◯
Munna	△
Raticate	△
Venomoth	△
Watchog	◯

Items

- ☐ Hyper Potion
- ☐ Revive
- ☐ TM75 Swords Dance
- ☐ TM85 Dream Eater
- ☐ TwistedSpoon

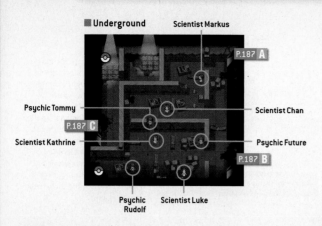

■ Underground

Scientist Markus

P.187 A

Psychic Tommy

P.187 C

Scientist Chan

Scientist Kathrine

Psychic Future

P.187 B

Psychic Rudolf

Scientist Luke

Underground	
✿: Dark Grass	⋯⋯⋯
Pokémon	
Ariados	△
Kricketune	◎
Ledian	△
Munna	○
Raticate	◎

Dreamyard — Battle the Trainers underground

In the Dreamyard, the obstacles are gone, and you can enter the underground room. Some Pokémon Trainers in the underground room will run when you approach them. Wait around the corner from them and talk to them from the side when they approach to make it easier to battle them.

To research strange Pokémon, having a battle is a good approach.

On Fridays Musharna appears

On Fridays, Musharna appears in the tall grass north of the underground room. The Musharna you meet here have the Hidden Ability Telepathy. Musharna with this Ability don't appear elsewhere, so make sure to catch it!

Dreamyard — Search for Gorm of the Seven Sages

When you climb the stairs to the south of the underground room in the Dreamyard, Gorm of the Seven Sages pops out from behind a wall. After he tells you about N's Castle and Team Plasma, Gorm gives you TM75 Swords Dance. After that, he is arrested by Looker.

Gorm: Boo!

New wallpaper is added

After you complete the main story, check your PC. There will be new wallpaper for your PC Boxes. Check out the newly added wallpaper, such as the Reshiram and Zekrom designs.

Nacrene City — Battle the girl you traded with

If you trade Pokémon with the girl in the house in Nacrene City, you can battle her after you finish the main story. The girl uses the evolved form of the Pokémon you traded to her. In *Pokémon Black Version*, it's Whimsicott, and in *Pokémon White Version*, it's Lilligant.

Let's have a battle!

Trade and battle even after finishing the main story

Even if you wait to make this trade after you finish the main story, you can battle right after you're done. After trading, leave the house, and then come back in and talk to the girl.

Castelia City — Talk to the Sound Designer at GAME FREAK

Visit the GAME FREAK building in Castelia City and take the elevator to the 22nd floor. If you talk to the Sound Designer, the background music will change to the music of Team Rocket, the villains of *Pokémon HeartGold* and *SoulSilver Versions*.

What do you think about this dramatic sound?

UNOVA ADVENTURE WALKTHROUGH

NEW ADVENTURES AWAIT

Castelia City

Enjoy a Pokémon battle at GAME FREAK

Visit the 22nd floor of the GAME FREAK building in Castelia City. You can battle Morimoto, across from the Sound Designer, once a day. Morimoto's Pokémon are very strong, around level 75 to 77. Take him on after raising your Pokémon's levels enough.

Visit again once your Pokédex is complete

When you complete the Unova Pokédex, visit the 22nd floor of GAME FREAK's building. Talk to the Game Director, and he will give you an award certificate. After that, the award certificate will be hung on the wall in your bedroom in Nuvema Town.

Royal Unova Map

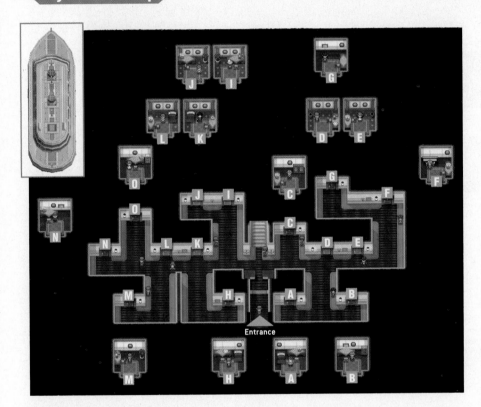

Entrance

Castelia City

Ride the *Royal Unova* in the evening

You can board the *Royal Unova* at Castelia City in the evening. If you defeat a certain number of Trainers in the ship, you can get a prize. The challenge is different on different days of the week. Whistles blow several times in the ship, and eventually the ship will return to port. Defeat the Trainers within the time limit.

Enjoy the scenery from the deck

Climb the stairs in the center of the ship, and you can see the sunset from the deck. Take a break from battling Trainers to gaze at the beautiful sight of the Unova region changing from twilight to night.

● Number of Trainers per day and prizes

Day	Number of Trainers	Price
Monday	Four people	Lava Cookie
Tuesday	Three people	Berry Juice
Wednesday	Four people	Lava Cookie
Thursday	Five people	Old Gateau
Friday	Four people	Lava Cookie
Saturday	Six people	RageCandyBar
Sunday	Seven people	Rare Candy

Talk to the crew to get hints

Talk to the crew inside to learn how many Trainers you need to beat and to get hints on whether the Trainers are on the left side or right side of the ship.

Relic Castle Map

■ **Tower 1F**

a

Desert Resort (p. 100)

Items
- ☐ TM04 Calm Mind
- ☐ TM26 Earthquake

Tower 1F/Tower B1F

Inside

Pokémon	
Sandile	◎
Yamask	◎

B5F/Tower B2 to B6

Inside

Pokémon	
Cofagrigus	◎
Krokorok	◎

Passageway 6/Lowest Floor—Deepest Part

Inside

Pokémon	
Claydol	◎

Other places

Inside

Pokémon	
Cofagrigus	◎
Krokorok	◎
Onix	◎
Sandslash	◎

■ **Tower B1F**

a
z

■ **Tower B2F**

Z
Y

■ **Tower B3F**

Y
X

■ **Tower B4F**

X
W

■ **Tower B5F**

W
V

■ **Tower B6F**

V
U

■ Passage ⑫

T P
O

■ Passage ⑬

P
Q

■ Passage ⑭

Q
R R

■ Passage ⑮

R
S S

■ Passage ①

S
B
C
— Team Plasma Grunt

■ Passage ⑪

O
N N

■ Passage ⑨

N
L L
K

■ Passage ⑩

L
M M
E

■ Passage ③

M
D D

■ Passage ②

C
D

■ **Lowest Floor—Deepest Part**

H

■ Passage ⑧

K
J J

■ Passage ⑦

J
I

■ Passage ⑥

I H
G G

■ Passage ⑤

G
F F

■ Passage ④

E
F

■ **Hallway leading to the lowest floor (tower side)**
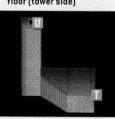
U
T

■ **B5F**

Relic Castle (p. 103)
A

Relic Castle (p. 103)

■ **Hallway leading to the lowest floor (castle side)**

B
A

Desert Resort

Get a RageCandyBar

When you try to enter the Relic Castle, Professor Juniper comes out from inside. The professor is checking the Pokémon statues, which she says are actually Darmanitan in a sleeping state. She gives you a RageCandyBar to wake up one of the Darmanitan.

Trainer obtained a RageCandyBar!

NEW ADVENTURES AWAIT

UNOVA ADVENTURE WALKTHROUGH

Desert Resort — Catch Darmanitan!

Check the Pokémon statues while you are holding a RageCandyBar and Darmanitan will wake up and attack you. The Darmanitan here have the Hidden Ability Zen Mode. These Darmanitan don't appear anywhere else, so make sure to catch them and use them in battle.

The Pokémon was a sleeping Darmanitan!

RageCandyBars can be found elsewhere

You can only use a RageCandyBar once. If you want to wake up Darmanitan again, battle six Trainers on the *Royal Unova* on Saturday (p. 189). If you beat all of them, you get a RageCandyBar.

Relic Castle — New areas of the Relic Castle

After entering the Relic Castle, continue until you reach B5F, which you've visited before. Sand has piled up so you can reach the door on the east side of the room. Go inside and meet some remnants of Team Plasma. They are protecting one of the Seven Sages. Accept the challenge for a Pokémon battle.

Sand falls down to B5F

Fall through the flowing sands to B5F. Refer to p. 102 to 103, and head for the hallway connected to the lowest floor.

Relic Castle — Go from the maze to the tower

The lowest floor of the Relic Castle is a maze. Use Passage 1, where a Team Plasma member is standing, as a guide. Head directly west from Passage 1, and you can go to the tower. Climb the stairs and continue to Tower 1F. Get the item, but don't cross the ledge. Go back down to Passage 1.

Relic Castle — Return to the maze and go to the deepest room

After getting the item in Tower 1F, return to the underground and go directly east. Return to Passage 1, where a member of Team Plasma is standing. Following the map to the left, from there go south, west, and then south. Then, go west two rooms, and you will reach Passage 6.

Relic Castle — Search for Ryoku of the Seven Sages

Ryoku of the Seven Sages is standing in front of the north exit of Passage 6, as if he were blocking it. Talk to him to learn about the Sun Pokémon Volcarona, and then he gives you TM04 Calm Mind. After that, Looker arrives to arrest Ryoku.

Ryoku: I was planning to catch the Pokémon called Volcarona that lives

Relic Castle — Volcarona appears in the deepest room

Go north from where Ryoku was, and head for the deepest room on the lowest floor. Volcarona is at the end of the room. Ryoku planned to give this Pokémon to Ghetsis. Talk to it, and it will attack. This Pokémon doesn't appear in the wild, so make sure to catch it.

Volcarona is Larvesta's evolution

The Egg you get from the prefab house on Route 18 will hatch into a Larvesta. If you raise Larvesta to Lv. 59, it will evolve into Volcarona. If you can't catch Volcarona here, you can get its entry in the Pokédex by evolving Larvesta.

Capture Volcarona!

First, use moves that do double damage such as Water- and Flying-type moves. After that, lower its HP gradually with Bug- or Grass-type moves. Watch out for the move Quiver Dance, which raises its stats. Dusk Balls are effective when you are trying to catch Volcarona.

Volcarona Lv. 70

Bug	Fire

ABILITY ● Flame Body

MOVES ● Silver Wind
● Quiver Dance
● Heat Wave
● Bug Buzz

Nimbasa City — Take the Battle Test at the Battle Institute

You can now take the Battle Test at Nimbasa City's Battle Institute. The Battle Test assigns ranks based on the results of battling five Trainers (p. 203). Aim for a high rank by challenging it with your best-trained Pokémon.

Please bear in mind that once you start the challenge, you will face five battles ▾

The Judge appears in the Battle Subway

The Judge will appear in the Battle Subway's Gear Station. He will size up the potential of a Pokémon in your party. Have him help you when you're deciding which Pokémon to train.

Nimbasa City — Visit Big Stadium and Small Court

At the practice areas in Big Stadium and Small Court, you can enjoy battles with Trainers every day. After you finish the main story, the number of Trainers in the practice areas increases, and the level of your opponents' Pokémon is dramatically higher. Enjoy challenging battles daily.

and become a great player!
Now, let's play ball! ▾

Some Trainers give you items

The Trainers you fight at Big Stadium and Small Court change every day (except for the Backers and athletes). Some of them will give you valuable items, such as Max Revive and PP Max, after you defeat them. Visit and battle every day to get lots of items!

Route 5 — Cheren leaves for Victory Road

When you go to Route 5, you'll find Cheren standing there. Approach him, and he'll start talking to you. After he announces his plan to evaluate himself at Victory Road, he leaves. After this, you can battle with him once a day on the seventh floor of Victory Road (p. 196).

Visit me sometime, if you want.
He'll have a battle like old times. ▾

Driftveil City — Battle the boy you traded with

If you trade Pokémon with the boy in the house in Driftveil City, you can battle him after you finish the main story. The boy will use the Minccino you traded him, but it has evolved into a Cinccino. Have a serious match with Cinccino.

Hey, hey! Let's jump on this! My Minccino and your Pokémon battle!

Trade and battle even after finishing the main story

Even if you wait to make this trade after you finish the main story, you can battle right after you're done. After trading, leave the house, and then come back in and talk to the boy.

Driftveil City — Buy Incense at the Driftveil Market

When you go to the Driftveil Market, there is a new salesperson. You can buy nine types of incense, such as Odd Incense or Lax Incense. They all sell for an expensive 9,600 in prize money, but many of them are useful in battle. Save money and make sure to buy some.

Money
₽1465300

Odd Incense	₽9600
Sea Incense	₽9600
Rose Incense	₽9600
Wave Incense	₽9600
Rock Incense	₽9600
Pure Incense	₽9600
Luck Incense	₽9600

An item to be held by a Pokémon. It is an exotic-smelling incense that boosts the power of Psychic-type moves.

● Incense can be bought after you complete the main story

Item	Effect	Price
Full Incense	When held by a Pokémon, this item makes it slower in battle.	9,600
Lax Incense	When held by a Pokémon, this item raises evasion.	9,600
Luck Incense	It doubles a battle's prize money if the holding Pokémon joins in.	9,600
Odd Incense	When held by a Pokémon, it boosts the power of Psychic-type moves.	9,600
Pure Incense	It helps keep wild Pokémon away if the holder is the first one in the party.	9,600
Rock Incense	When held by a Pokémon, it boosts the power of Rock-type moves.	9,600
Rose Incense	When held by a Pokémon, it boosts the power of Grass-type moves.	9,600
Sea Incense	When held by a Pokémon, it boosts the power of Water-type moves.	9,600
Wave Incense	When held by a Pokémon, it boosts the power of Water-type moves.	9,600

Cold Storage — Search for Zinzolin of the Seven Sages

When you enter the Cold Storage, check the refrigerated containers and you'll find Zinzolin of the Seven Sages. Zinzolin talks about how working with Ghetsis made him feel alive, and then he gives you TM01 Hone Claws. After that, he is arrested by Looker.

Zinzolin: So, you returned? You're an odd Trainer.

Chargestone Cave — Search for Bronius of the Seven Sages

Head to B2F in Chargestone Cave, and go south. Bronius of the Seven Sages is standing where the path comes to a dead end. After you defeat the Team Plasma Grunt standing with him, Bronius gives you TM69 Rock Polish. After that, he is arrested by Looker.

Bronius: Those who left Team Plasma and are behaving with respect and

Celestial Tower

Listen to Alder's story on the roof

Climb to the fifth floor of the Celestial Tower to find Alder. When you approach him, he tells you about his former partner, who is resting here, and the reason he left on his journey. After that, Alder tells you he will be waiting for you in the Pokémon League and leaves.

My old partner is resting here in the Celestial Tower.

Twist Mountain

Get Fossils from the Worker

Talk to the Worker in Lower Level 1 in Twist Mountain, and you can get a Pokémon Fossil once a day. The Fossil you get is random, so you might get a Fossil you've received before. Talk to him every day and get all seven Fossils so you can register them to your Pokédex.

Like this Fossil I just found! Take this!

Restore the Fossils at the museum

Visit Nacrene City after obtaining the Pokémon Fossils. Make space in your party, enter the Nacrene Museum, and talk to the woman on the right in the reception area. She will restore the Pokémon from the Fossil.

● **Pokémon you can restore from Fossils obtained at Twist Mountain**

Armor Fossil	→ Shieldon		Old Amber	→	Aerodactyl
Claw Fossil	→ Anorith		Root Fossil	→	Lileep
Dome Fossil	→ Kabuto		Skull Fossil	→	Cranidos
Helix Fossil	→ Omanyte				

Dragonspiral Tower

Battle Reshiram (Zekrom) again

If your party and Boxes are full when you meet Reshiram in *Pokémon Black Version* or Zekrom in *Pokémon White Version* in N's Castle, you can't catch it. If you go to Dragonspiral Tower after completing the main story, you will have another chance to catch Reshiram (Zekrom) on the seventh floor.

Reshiram

Zekrom

UNOVA ADVENTURE WALKTHROUGH

NEW ADVENTURES AWAIT

Field Moves Needed

Flash   Surf

Challenger's Cave Map

1F

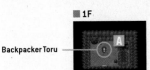

Backpacker Toru — A

Route 9 (to Opelucid City)

B1F

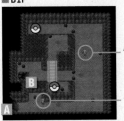

B

A

Ace Trainer Beverly

Ace Trainer Terry

B2F

Veteran Julia   Veteran Shaun

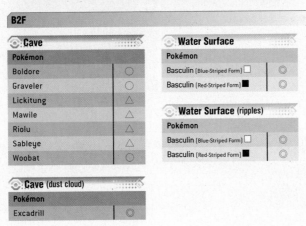

B

Items

- ☐ Black Belt
- ☐ Nugget
- ☐ Oval Stone
- ☐ PP Up
- ☐ Protein
- ☐ Timer Ball
- ☐ TM71 Stone Edge

1F

Cave

Pokémon	
Boldore	○
Graveler	○
Lickitung	○
Mawile	△
Sableye	△
Woobat	○

Cave (dust cloud)

Pokémon	
Excadrill	◎

B1F

Cave

Pokémon	
Boldore	○
Graveler	○
Lickitung	○
Mawile	△
Riolu	△
Sableye	△
Woobat	○

Cave (dust cloud)

Pokémon	
Excadrill	◎

B2F

Cave

Pokémon	
Boldore	○
Graveler	○
Lickitung	△
Mawile	△
Riolu	△
Sableye	△
Woobat	○

Cave (dust cloud)

Pokémon	
Excadrill	◎

Water Surface

Pokémon	
Basculin (Blue-Striped Form) ☐	◎
Basculin (Red-Striped Form) ■	◎

Water Surface (ripples)

Pokémon	
Basculin (Blue-Striped Form) ☐	◎
Basculin (Red-Striped Form) ■	◎

■ After finishing the main story

Fishing

Pokémon	
Basculin (Blue-Striped Form) ☐	○
Basculin (Red-Striped Form) ■	○
Poliwag	◎
Poliwhirl	△

Fishing (ripples)

Pokémon	
Basculin (Blue-Striped Form) ☐	○
Basculin (Red-Striped Form) ■	○
Poliwhirl	◎
Poliwrath	△

Challenger's Cave

See everything and battle Trainers

Challenger's Cave, which you can access from Route 9, is a sprawling cave with three floors. Inside, five Pokémon Trainers are waiting. Use Flash to light up the cave. Collect items and battle the Trainers.

Oh, are you the legendary Pokémon that is said to live here?

Opelucid City
Teach your Pokémon the strongest Dragon-type move

In Drayden's house in Opelucid City, you can have Iris (in *Pokémon Black Version*) or Drayden (in *Pokémon White Version*) teach your Pokémon the strongest Dragon-type move—Draco Meteor. Teach this move to a Dragon-type Pokémon with high friendship.

I can teach you the strongest Dragon-type move!

Victory Road
Have a Pokémon battle with Cheren

Go to Victory Road from the Pokémon League and continue to the seventh floor. If you've talked to him on Route 5, Cheren will be there. You can battle Cheren once a day. Enjoy battles with his toughened-up Pokémon.

OK, Trainer! Accept this Pokémon battle!

Battle every day to strengthen your Pokémon

Cheren's Pokémon are at a very high level, so you get a lot of Experience Points for defeating them. To prepare for the tough battle ahead at the Pokémon League, come here every day to make your Pokémon stronger.

Battle your childhood friend Cheren! 8
His Pokémon are 22 levels higher than they were in your seventh battle, and he has added Gigalith and Haxorus to his party.

If you chose Snivy:

Liepard ♂	Lv. 65	Dark	
Emboar ♂	Lv. 67	Fire	Fighting
Haxorus ♂	Lv. 65	Dragon	
Unfezant ♂	Lv. 65	Normal	Flying
Gigalith ♂	Lv. 65	Rock	
Simisage ♂	Lv. 65	Grass	

If you chose Tepig:

Liepard ♂	Lv. 65	Dark	
Samurott ♂	Lv. 67	Water	
Haxorus ♂	Lv. 65	Dragon	
Unfezant ♂	Lv. 65	Normal	Flying
Gigalith ♂	Lv. 65	Rock	
Simisear ♂	Lv. 65	Fire	

If you chose Oshawott:

Liepard ♂	Lv. 65	Dark	
Serperior ♂	Lv. 67	Grass	
Haxorus ♂	Lv. 65	Dragon	
Unfezant ♂	Lv. 65	Normal	Flying
Gigalith ♂	Lv. 65	Rock	
Simipour ♂	Lv. 65	Water	

Pokémon League
Take on the Elite Four and the Champion

After you have seen all of the areas that open up after finishing the main story, it's time to take on the Pokémon League. The Elite Four and the Champion are tough—their Pokémon are around levels 71 through 77. Make sure to raise your party Pokémon well and stock up on healing items before challenging them.

Could I use you and your Pokémon as a subject?

Check the statue after defeating the Elite Four

Even though you defeated the Elite Four during the main story, you must battle them again to challenge the Champion. After you've emerged victorious from your battle with the Elite Four, check the statue, and proceed to the underground.

Elite Four Battle

Shauntal
● **Ghost-type Pokémon User**

| Recommended Level for your Pokémon | Lv. 78 |

Deal massive damage with Ghost- and Dark-type moves

Shauntal's Pokémon team now includes Froslass and Drifblim. They are both weak to Ghost- and Dark-type moves. If you have Pokémon that can use these moves, you may feel reassured, but remember that Shauntal's team also attacks these weaknesses. You need to be clever. Try a strategy like teaching the Ghost-type move Shadow Ball to a Normal-type Pokémon.

● Shauntal's Pokémon

Cofagrius ♀ — Lv. 71
Ghost
● Moves to watch out for:
Shadow Ball — Ghost

Effective Move Types:
Ghost	Dark

Jellicent ♀ — Lv. 71
Water / Ghost
● Moves to watch out for:
Hydro Pump Ball — Water

Effective Move Types:
Grass	Electric
Ghost	Dark

Froslass ♀ — Lv. 71
Ice / Ghost
● Moves to watch out for:
Psychic — Psychic

Effective Move Types:
Fire	Rock
Ghost	Dark
Steel	

Golurk — Lv. 71
Ground / Ghost
● Moves to watch out for:
Hammer Arm — Fighting

Effective Move Types:
Water	Grass
Ice	Ghost
Dark	

Drifblim ♀ — Lv. 71
Ghost / Flying
● Moves to watch out for:
Thunder — Electric

Effective Move Types:
Electric	Ice
Rock	Ghost
Dark	

Chandelure ♀ — Lv. 73
Ghost / Fire
● Moves to watch out for:
Payback — Dark

Effective Move Types:
Water	Ground
Rock	Ghost
Dark	

● Grimsley's Pokémon

Sharpedo ♂ — Lv. 71
Water / Dark
● Moves to watch out for:
Night Slash — Dark

Effective Move Types:
Grass	Electric
Fighting	Bug

Krookodile ♀ — Lv. 71
Ground / Dark
● Moves to watch out for:
Foul Play — Dark

Effective Move Types:
Water	Grass
Ice	Fighting
Bug	

Scrafty ♀ — Lv. 71
Dark / Fighting
● Moves to watch out for:
Head Smash — Rock

Effective Move Types:
Fighting	Flying

Liepard ♀ — Lv. 71
Dark
● Moves to watch out for:
Sucker Punch — Dark

Effective Move Types:
Fighting	Bug

Bisharp ♀ — Lv. 73
Dark / Steel
● Moves to watch out for:
Aerial Ace — Flying

Effective Move Types:
Fighting	Fire
Ground	

Drapion ♀ — Lv. 71
Poison / Dark
● Moves to watch out for:
Poison Fang — Poison

Effective Move Types:
Ground	

Elite Four Battle

Grimsley
● **Dark-type Pokémon User**

| Recommended Level for your Pokémon | Lv. 78 |

Use Fighting- and Ground-type moves to gain an advantage

Grimsley has added Sharpedo and Drapion to his party. All of his Pokémon, other than Drapion, are weak to Fighting-type moves. You'll be in great shape if you have a Pokémon with the moves Brick Break and Focus Blast. Deal with Drapion by teaching a Pokémon in your party a powerful Ground-type move such as Earthquake.

● Caitlin's Pokémon

● Musharna ♀	Lv. 71	Effective Move Types	
Psychic		Bug	Ghost
		Dark	
● Moves to watch out for:			
Dream Eater	Psychic		

● Sigilyph ♀	Lv. 71	Effective Move Types	
Psychic	Flying	Electric	Ice
		Rock	Ghost
● Moves to watch out for:		Dark	
Flash Cannon	Steel		

● Metagross	Lv. 73	Effective Move Types	
Steel	Psychic	Fire	Ground
● Moves to watch out for:			
Earthquake	Ground		

● Bronzong	Lv. 71	Effective Move Types	
Steel	Psychic	Fire	
● Moves to watch out for:			
Psychic	Psychic		

● Reuniclus ♀	Lv. 71	Effective Move Types	
Psychic		Bug	Ghost
		Dark	
● Moves to watch out for:			
Thunder	Electric		

● Gothitelle ♀	Lv. 71	Effective Move Types	
Psychic		Bug	Ghost
		Dark	
● Moves to watch out for:			
Flatter	Dark		

Elite Four Battle

Caitlin
● Psychic-type Pokémon User

Recommended Level for your Pokémon	Lv. 78

Utilize Ghost-, Dark-, and Fire-type moves

Caitlin has added Metagross and Bronzong to her party. Both of these Pokémon are weak to Fire-type moves. TM35 Flamethrower is a good choice for a powerful Fire-type move that can be used by many types of Pokémon. Watch out for the move Flatter—it'll leave your Pokémon confused.

Elite Four Battle

Marshal
● Fighting-type Pokémon User

Recommended Level for your Pokémon	Lv. 78

Psychic-type moves give you an advantage

Marshal has added Breloom and Toxicroak to his party. All of his Pokémon are weak to Psychic-type moves—especially Toxicroak, who takes four times the normal damage. Use TM29 Psychic to teach this move to a Pokémon in your party. If you have Flying-type moves, you can strike all of his weak points as well.

● Marshal's Pokémon

● Breloom ♂	Lv. 71	Effective Move Types	
Grass	Fighting	Flying	Fire
		Ice	Poison
● Moves to watch out for:		Psychic	
Spore	Grass		

● Throh ♂	Lv. 71	Effective Move Types	
Fighting		Flying	Psychic
● Moves to watch out for:			
Earthquake	Ground		

● Toxicroak ♂	Lv. 71	Effective Move Types	
Fighting	Poison	Psychic	Ground
		Flying	
● Moves to watch out for:			
Toxic	Poison		

● Conkeldurr ♂	Lv. 73	Effective Move Types	
Fighting		Flying	Psychic
● Moves to watch out for:			
Hammer Arm	Fighting		

● Mienshao ♂	Lv. 71	Effective Move Types	
Fighting		Flying	Psychic
● Moves to watch out for:			
Hi Jump Kick	Fighting		

● Sawk ♂	Lv. 71	Effective Move Types	
Fighting		Flying	Psychic
● Moves to watch out for:			
Close Combat	Fighting		

Champion Battle

Alder

● **User of many Pokémon types**

Recommended Level for your Pokémon **Lv. 82**

Keep switching your Pokémon to respond to the situation

Alder's Pokémon have a variety of types, but some of them do share a weak spot—Fire-type moves are effective on Accelgor, Escavalier, and Vanilluxe. For the others, you may have to keep switching to find effective moves. Alder's Pokémon all attack with powerful moves, so taking too much time is dangerous. Strike weak points and defeat them quickly.

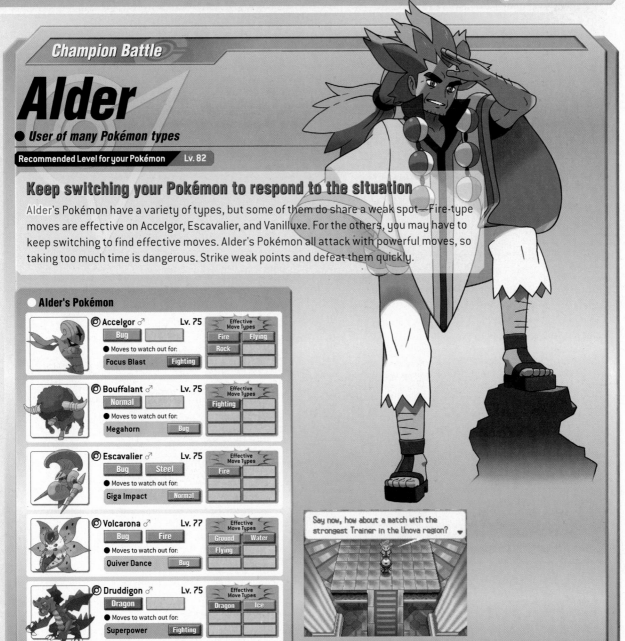

● Alder's Pokémon

⊘ Accelgor ♂   **Lv. 75**

Bug		Effective Move Types	
● Moves to watch out for:		Fire	Flying
Focus Blast	Fighting	Rock	

⊘ Bouffalant ♂   **Lv. 75**

Normal		Effective Move Types	
● Moves to watch out for:		Fighting	
Megahorn	Bug		

⊘ Escavalier ♂   **Lv. 75**

Bug	Steel	Effective Move Types	
● Moves to watch out for:		Fire	
Giga Impact	Normal		

⊘ Volcarona ♂   **Lv. 77**

Bug	Fire	Effective Move Types	
● Moves to watch out for:		Ground	Water
Quiver Dance	Bug	Flying	

⊘ Druddigon ♂   **Lv. 75**

Dragon		Effective Move Types	
● Moves to watch out for:		Dragon	Ice
Superpower	Fighting		

⊘ Vanilluxe ♂   **Lv. 75**

Ice		Effective Move Types	
● Moves to watch out for:		Fire	Fighting
Flash Cannon	Steel	Rock	Steel

Say now, how about a match with the strongest Trainer in the Unova region?

When you just can't win, rethink the Pokémon you have in your party. Use TMs to teach them powerful moves and fight effectively.

Defeat the Champion and Enter the Hall of Fame!

When you defeat Alder, you'll enter the Hall of Fame, and you and your party Pokémon will be recorded for posterity by the device deep in the Pokémon League. Here, you will see the ending credits again. Now, it's time to set out on a journey to complete your Pokédex.

You are challenged by Champion Alder!

Various items and the people who buy them

Some people in the Unova region will buy only certain items, but they will pay handsomely for them. If you sell these items to them, they will pay more than the Poké Mart would. There are also some special items that the Poké Mart won't buy.

Sell the items you get for a lot

If you've got food, she'll buy it

Where: Trailer on Route 5

In addition to all types of Berries, she will buy items that have names related to food, such as Lucky Egg and Casteliacone. You can't sell BalmMushrooms to the Poké Mart, so sell them to the Maid.

Head west from Nimbasa City. Right after you enter Route 5, you'll see the trailer where the Maid lives.

Do you have a wonderful ingredient in your Bag?

 (p. 112)

If you've got gems, he'll buy them

Where: Icirrus City Pokémon Center

He will buy the gems you can find in dust clouds, plus the stones related to Pokémon evolution. The Poké Mart won't buy Pearl Strings, Big Nuggets, or Comet Shards, but you can sell them to him.

Don't you have an adorable ore that shakes my core?

The old gentleman who will buy stones is in the Icirrus City Pokémon Center.

 (p. 146)

If you have something cool, he'll buy it

Where: Prefab house on Route 18

The guy in sunglasses says he'll buy "something cool" from you, but doesn't specify that what he wants is the Rare Bone. Rarely, if you catch a wild Crustle in the dark grass, it will be holding this item. If you happen to catch a Crustle holding a Rare Bone, be sure to sell the item to this guy!

What's up?
Did you find something cool for me?

Head for Route 18 from Route 17, and enter the prefab house on the plateau. A man in sunglasses is at the north wall.

(p. 142)

If you have artifacts and old relics, he'll buy them

Where: The big villa in Undella Town

He'll buy the five types of flutes you can get from the sunglasses-wearing man on Route 13, plus rare items such as Relic Gold and Relic Vase, which are found somewhere in the Unova region. They will fetch an astounding price.

Do you have such a rare item?
Do you?

Enter the big villa in Undella Town. At the back of the room to the west is a rich man who buys items.

(p. 216)

VARIOUS ITEMS AND THE PEOPLE WHO BUY THEM

Marvelous Bridge

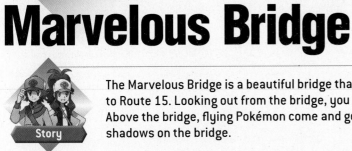

Story

The Marvelous Bridge is a beautiful bridge that connects Route 16 to Route 15. Looking out from the bridge, you only see the ocean. Above the bridge, flying Pokémon come and go, casting their shadows on the bridge.

Field Moves Needed

Route 16 (to Driftveil City)

A

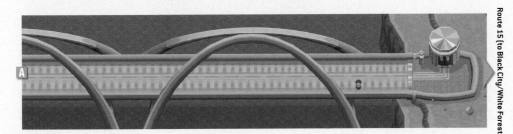

A

Route 15 (to Black City/White Forest)

Items

- [ ] Adamant Orb
- [ ] Lustrous Orb
- [ ] Griseous Orb

Pokémon Shadows

Pokémon	
Swanna	◎

Swanna

`Water` `Flying`

ABILITIES
- Keen Eye
- Big Pecks

500 gets you a Magikarp

Talk to the man on the bridge, and he'll sell you a Magikarp for 500 in prize money. You can't buy it if your party is full, so if you're interested, make space in your party before you talk to him.

Step 1 — **Enter the Marvelous Bridge from Route 16**

Go east from Nimbasa City to Route 16. Keep going east and you'll arrive at the Marvelous Bridge. Ride the elevator and you can walk on top of the bridge. Continue east from there.

UNOVA ADVENTURE WALKTHROUGH

MARVELOUS BRIDGE ◎

Step 2 ▶ Get items from the Shadow Triad

When you go east, the Shadow Triad suddenly appears. Saying it is at Ghetsis's request, they hand you the Adamant Orb, the Lustrous Orb, and the Griseous Orb. After they give you the items, they suddenly disappear.

Also, Ghetsis said to give you this...

The Griseous Orb is related to a Pokémon

The Griseous Orb you receive from the Shadow Triad has something to do with the Forme change of Giratina, a Legendary Pokémon who lives in another region (p. 249).

Step 3 ▶ Cross the bridge to reach Route 15

At the eastern end of the bridge, there's an elevator. Ride the elevator down, and keep going east. Once you get through the gate, you're at Route 15. You can encounter Pokémon from other regions in the tall grass of Route 15 (p. 204).

The mysteriously vanishing girl

Sometimes a girl stands next to the man on the east side of the bridge. When you approach, she disappears. When you talk to the lady at the base of the elevator, she says there used to be a girl who always played with Abra before the bridge was built...

After visiting Village Bridge ▶ Watch the famous Patrat show

If you talk to the lady with the Patrat in the house on Village Bridge, you can watch the Patrat show on the Marvelous Bridge. If you correctly guess which Patrat is holding the Big Mushroom, she'll give you the item.

It's holding a Big Mushroom! Ready, set, go!

Battle the Trainer in front of the elevator

Ace Trainer Glinda, who stands just a little past where you get off the east-side elevator, will challenge you to a Triple Battle in *Pokémon Black Version* or a Rotation Battle in *Pokémon White Version*.

Take the Battle Test at the Battle Institute

After you defeat Ghetsis in N's Castle and see the ending credits, you can take the Battle Test in the Battle Institute in Nimbasa City. Use well-trained Pokémon to take the test, and aim for the highest rank, Master Rank.

 ## The results of your battle with five Trainers are ranked

In the Battle Test you receive points depending on the results of your battles with five Trainers, and you're given a rank based on those points. Depending on how you fought and which Pokémon you used, your score changes. Test yourself often for a high score!

Check your results on the computer

Check the black PC next to the usual PC to see your results so far.

1 Choose your Pokémon

Choose three Pokémon from your party or Battle Box when taking the Single Battle test, and four when taking the Double Battle test. You may not use duplicate Pokémon or duplicate held items.

● Ranks are based on the number of points

	Rank	Points Received
★★★★★★	Master Rank	Over 6,000 points
★★★★★☆	Elite Rank	Over 5,000 points
★★★★☆☆	Hyper Rank	Over 4,000 points
★★★☆☆☆	Super Rank	Over 3,000 points
★★☆☆☆☆	Normal Rank	Over 2,000 points
★☆☆☆☆☆	Novice Rank	Over 1,000 points
★☆☆☆☆☆	Beginner Rank	Less than 1,000

 ### 2 Battle five Trainers

After each battle, your Pokémon will be healed. Even if you lose a battle, the Battle Test will continue until you've battled all five Trainers.

I think I am a Pokéfan, therefore I am a Pokéfan.

You can download opponents to battle!

Battle Test data will be distributed at Pokémon-related events, and you can download it and take the test. You can even enjoy distributed tests before finishing the main game.

Check the official site at www.pokemon.com for details.

▶ YES
NO

Would you like to download a special Battle Test?

 ### 3 See the results

Your results are calculated based on the number of Trainers you defeated, the number of your Pokémon your opponent defeated, etc. Your results are displayed as points and ranks.

SINGLE BATTLE TEST RESULT

1068 POINTS

NOVICE RANK

Route 15

Route 15 has bridges and stairs carved into a sheer cliff so people can come and go. On top of the cliff is the Poké Transfer Lab, a facility with a device for bringing over Pokémon from other regions.

Field Moves Needed

Strength

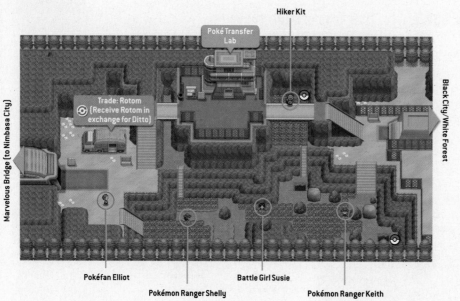

Hiker Kit

Poké Transfer Lab

Trade: Rotom (Receive Rotom in exchange for Ditto)

Marvelous Bridge (to Nimbasa City)

Black City/White Forest

Pokéfan Elliot

Pokémon Ranger Shelly

Battle Girl Susie

Pokémon Ranger Keith

Items

- First visit
- ☐ TM09 Venoshock
- ☐ Up-Grade
- After defeating Pokémon Ranger Shelly
- ☐ Sitrus Berry
- After defeating Pokémon Ranger Keith
- ☐ Sitrus Berry

Tall Grass

Pokémon	
Fearow	○
Gligar	○
Kangaskhan	△
Marowak	○
Pupitar	△
Sawk ■	○
Throh ☐	○

Tall Grass (rustling)

Pokémon	
Audino	◎
Emolga	△
Gliscor	△
Sawk ☐	△
Throh ■	△
Tyranitar	△

Dark Grass

Pokémon	
Fearow	○
Gligar	△
Kangaskhan	△
Marowak	○
Pupitar	△
Sawk ■	○
Throh ☐	○
Watchog	△

Step 1 — Trade Pokémon with the person in the camper

Near the west entrance, you will see a woman in a parked camper. If you talk to her, she will trade you a Rotom for a Ditto. You can catch a Ditto in Giant Chasm, which you will visit later (p. 225). When you capture one, trade it for Rotom.

I would be very happy if you would trade my Rotom for your Ditto.

Take Rotom to the mall

Once you have a Rotom, put it in your party and take it to Shopping Mall Nine on Route 9. If you check the cardboard boxes in the warehouse on the first floor, you can change its form (p. 249).

2 Use Poké Transfer in the Poké Transfer Lab

In the Poké Transfer Lab, you can bring Pokémon over from *Pokémon Diamond, Pearl, Platinum, HeartGold,* and *SoulSilver Versions* using Poké Transfer. Bring over well-trained Pokémon to have them help you in your adventure.

device, you may be able to bring Pokémon here from other regions.

Pokémon can't be returned

Pokémon brought over from a different region using Poké Transfer can't be returned to the region they came from. Also, you can't transfer Pokémon that know HMs.

 3 Use Strength to get items

On the east side of Route 15, you'll find two rocks that can be moved with Strength. If you push each of those rocks into the hole, you can get items. If you move them incorrectly, leave using the eastern gate and come right back. The rock will have moved back to where it started.

▶ YES
　 NO

Would you like to use Strength?

Get Berries by defeating Trainers

Defeat Pokémon Rangers Shelly and Keith in battle to get Sitrus Berries. Shelly and Keith are in the tall grass below the stairs. Be sure to battle them for their Berries.

Step 4 Black City/White Forest

Once you've battled the Pokémon Trainers and gathered items, continue to the eastern end of the route. Pass through the gate to reach Black City in *Pokémon Black Version* (p. 208), or White Forest in *Pokémon White Version* (p. 210).

Changes in the Weather

Most areas in the Unova region are always sunny. In certain areas, however, the weather changes depending on the date and season.

See the changes in weather that depend on the date and season.

The area along the mountains from Driftveil City to Icirrus City is prone to changes in the weather. In spring, summer, and autumn, it often rains, and in winter, snow and hail will fall. Depending on the date, it may also be sunny. When you visit the mountain areas, be sure to watch the weather.

● Where the weather changes

Driftveil City | Rain, snow, or hail falls

Rain sometimes falls from spring to autumn in Driftveil City. When it's winter, sometimes you'll see snow or hail.

Mistralton City | Rain, snow, or hail falls

Rain often falls from spring to autumn in Mistralton City. When it's winter, the city sometimes gets snow or hail.

Icirrus City | Rain, snow, or blizzards

Rain often falls from spring to autumn in Icirrus City. During winter, everything is covered in snow, and there may even be blizzards.

Route 8 | In winter, the marshes ice over

Rain often falls from spring to autumn on Route 8. During winter, the marsh is covered in ice. Snow may fall during winter.

Some places change on your birthday

Routes 14 and 15 are always covered in mist. If you set your birthday in your Nintendo DS and visit on that day, the fog will clear and you can enjoy the beautiful scenery.

Route 14

Route 15

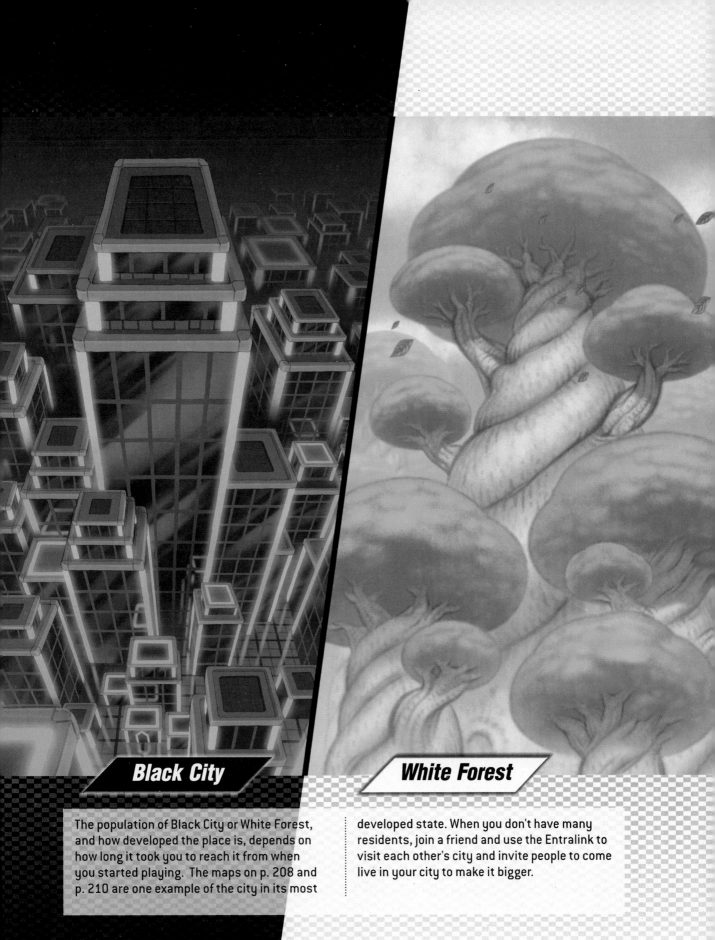

Black City

White Forest

The population of Black City or White Forest, and how developed the place is, depends on how long it took you to reach it from when you started playing. The maps on p. 208 and p. 210 are one example of the city in its most developed state. When you don't have many residents, join a friend and use the Entralink to visit each other's city and invite people to come live in your city to make it bigger.

Black City

Pokémon Black Version

Story

Black City is a sprawling metropolis that exists only in *Pokémon Black Version*. When the population increases, the buildings become bigger, and become smaller as the population decreases. When the city develops and the population increases, you can battle many different Trainers.

Field Moves Needed

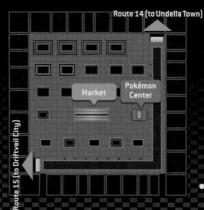

Route 14 (to Undella Town)

Market

Pokémon Center

Route 15 (to Driftveil City)

● City's development is at maximum in this example

Poké Mart
(Lower Clerk)

Item	Price
BridgeMail M	50
Favored Mail	50
Greet Mail	50
Inquiry Mail	50
Like Mail	50
Reply Mail	50
RSVP Mail	50
Thanks Mail	50

● Residents and purchasable items

Resident	Item Sold	Price	Likelihood of Leaving		Resident	Item Sold	Price	Likelihood of Leaving
Grace	Dawn Stone	10,000	Very High		Vincent	Fire Stone	10,000	High
Lena	Sun Stone	10,000	Very High		Carlos	Oval Stone	10,000	Low
Molly	Shiny Stone	10,000	Very High		Dave	TinyMushroom	3,000	Low
Britney	Rare Bone	30,000	High		Doug	Red Shard	3,000	Low
Collin	Yellow Shard	3,000	High		Eliza	Blue Shard	3,000	Low
Emi	Fluffy Tail	15,000	High		Ken	Thunderstone	10,000	Low
Frederic	Luxury Ball	50,000	High		Leo	Stardust	10,000	Low
Gene	Big Mushroom	20,000	High		Lynette	Heart Scale	10,000	Low
Jacques	Poké Doll	18,000	High		Marie	Green Shard	3,000	Low
Karenna	Leaf Stone	10,000	High		Miho	Big Pearl	38,000	Low
Miki	Max Repel	5,500	High		Piper	Star Piece	48,000	Low
Pierce	Poké Ball	10,000	High		Robbie	Fresh Water	1,000	Low
Ralph	Water Stone	10,000	High		Ryder	Nugget	50,000	Low
Shane	Berry Juice	1,500	High		Herman	Dusk Stone	10,000	Very Low
Silvia	Pearl	6,000	High		Rosa	Moon Stone	10,000	Very Low

Step 1 — Black City develops

The number of people living here is determined by the number of days it took you to reach the city from starting *Pokémon Black Version*. The number of buildings also depends on the number of residents. The number of residents (see the list above) can be as few as zero and as many as ten.

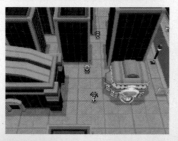

High level of development

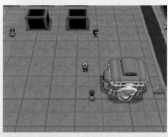

Low level of development

Step 2 — Bring people over with Entralink when your city is small

If you don't talk to the people living in Black City for awhile, they will disappear. Use the Entralink to visit another player's White Forest and bring people over to replace the residents who left. Depending on the number of people living in the city, how quickly a person leaves the city changes.

Leo: Check me out! The excitement of the big city has made me stronger!

Why can't you invite certain residents?

Sometimes you can't invite people to come live in your city even if you go to White Forest via the Entralink. This means either you already have ten people living in your Black City, or a person with the same name is already living in your city.

Step 3 — Buy many items at the market

The market has five counters and the number of people selling items will increase as the city's level of development increases. All of the items sold at the market are expensive, but sometimes valuable items related to evolution are sold. Here's your chance to pick up items such as the Oval Stone and the Sun Stone.

Money
₽ 575900

Rare Bone	₽30000
Poké Ball	₽10000
Cancel	

A bone that is extremely valuable for Pokémon archeology. It can be sold for a high price to shops.

The items you can buy depend on the residents

The goods sold at the market change depending on the people living in the city. If the population goes up, you can buy more items. Invite people corresponding to the items you want.

Step 4 — Get a reward for battling Trainers

Talk to the boss in the market, and he will give you a reward for the number of residents you've defeated in Pokémon battles. If you talk to him after you defeat ten people, he will give you 10,000 in prize money. Keep battling and making more money for each time you defeat ten. There is, however, a limit to the number of people you can defeat.

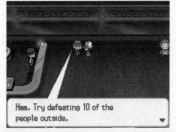

Hmm. Try defeating 10 of the people outside.

Step 5 — Head north to Route 14

Pass through the gate to the north once you've finished looking around the town. The gate goes to Route 14 (p. 212). Wild Pokémon and Pokémon Trainers are waiting to battle you, so heal your Pokémon and get any items you may need before continuing.

White Forest

Pokémon White Version

Field Moves Needed

Surf

Story

White Forest is a verdant woodland that only exists in *Pokémon White Version*. As the number of residents increases, the forest becomes more lush. If the number decreases, the trees become smaller. As the forest grows, you will also see more tall grass, and hard-to-find Pokémon will appear.

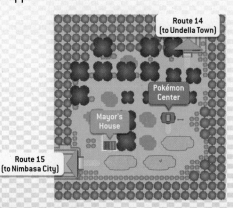

Route 14 (to Undella Town)

Pokémon Center

Mayor's House

Route 15 (to Nimbasa City)

- The forest's development is at maximum in this example
- Depending on the map, there may or may not be water surfaces.

Poké Mart (Lower Clerk)

BridgeMail M	50
Favored Mail	50
Greet Mail	50
Inquiry Mail	50
Like Mail	50
Reply Mail	50
RSVP Mail	50
Thanks Mail	50

● Pokémon that appear with a resident

Resident	Pokémon Grass	Pokémon Water	Item Dropped	Likelihood of Leaving
Frederic	Budew	Wooper	Honey	Very High
Herman	Porygon	Wooper	Dusk Stone	Very High
Rosa	Whismur	Lotad	Moon Stone	Very High
Carlos	Starly	Corphish	Oval Stone	High
Dave	Gastly	Surskit	TinyMushroom	High
Doug	Shinx	Lotad	Red Shard	High
Eliza	Trapinch	Lotad	Blue Shard	High
Grace	Bagon	Wooper	Dawn Stone	High
Ken	Nidoran♂	Corphish	Thunderstone	High
Leo	Pidgey	Surskit	Stardust	High
Lynette	Oddish	Surskit	Heart Scale	High
Marie	Magnemite	Lotad	Green Shard	High
Miho	Seedot	Surskit	Ultra Ball	High
Piper	Bellsprout	Surskit	Nest Ball	High
Robbie	Elekid	Surskit	Great Ball	High

Resident	Pokémon Grass	Pokémon Water	Item Dropped	Likelihood of Leaving
Ryder	Machop	Lotad	Quick Ball	High
Britney	Hoppip	Surskit	Rare Bone	Low
Collin	Abra	Lotad	Yellow Shard	Low
Emi	Happiny	Corphish	Timer Ball	Low
Gene	Aron	Surskit	Big Mushroom	Low
Jacques	Nidoran♀	Lotad	Dive Ball	Low
Karenna	Slakoth	Lotad	Leaf Stone	Low
Miki	Togepi	Surskit	Repeat Ball	Low
Pierce	Mareep	Surskit	Poké Ball	Low
Ralph	Lotad	Surskit	Water Stone	Low
Shane	Rhyhorn	Surskit	Net Ball	Low
Silvia	Wurmple	Surskit	Poké Ball	Low
Vincent	Magby	Corphish	Fire Stone	Low
Lena	Ralts	Wooper	Sun Stone	Very Low
Molly	Azurill	Lotad	Shiny Stone	Very Low

Step 1 White Forest grows larger

The number of people living here is determined by the number of days it took you to reach this forest from starting *Pokémon White Version*. The amount of tall grass or water varies depending on the number of residents. The number of residents can be as few as zero and as many as ten.

High level of development

Low level of development

Step 2 — Bring people over with Entralink when the forest is small

If you don't talk to the people living in White Forest for awhile, they will disappear. Use the Entralink to visit another player's Black City and bring people over to replace the residents who left. How quickly a person leaves depends on how many people are living in the forest.

Shane: Here both Pokémon and people can just be themselves.

Why can't you invite certain residents?

Sometimes you can't invite people to come live in your forest even if you go to Black City via the Entralink. This means either you already have ten people living in your White Forest or a person with the same name is already living in your forest.

Step 3 — Get Berries by showing Pokémon

Show the mayor the Pokémon he wants to see and you'll receive one of the following Berries a day: Pecha Berry, Bluk Berry, Lum Berry, Chesto Berry, or Leppa Berry. The Pokémon the mayor wants to see changes daily. Talk to him once each day and get Berries.

If you see Corphish in this forest, please let me know.

Step 4 — Catch Pokémon from other regions

Wild Pokémon can be found in the tall grass or on the water. The Pokémon that appear here are from other regions. They are all Lv. 5 and don't appear in other areas. Different Pokémon appear depending on who is living in your White Forest. Talk to the residents of the forest, and they will tell you which kinds of Pokémon you will meet in the tall grass.

A wild Bagon appeared!

Pick up dropped items

Sometimes people drop items in White Forest. The types of items vary according to the people living there. They are not always dropped, and the number of items and places where they're dropped differ from day to day.

Step 5 — Head north to Route 14

Pass through the gate to the north once you've finished looking around the town. The gate goes to Route 14 (p. 212). Wild Pokémon and Pokémon Trainers are waiting to battle you, so heal your Pokémon and get any items you may need before continuing.

Route 14

A majestic river with waterfalls flows from west to east in Route 14. The Abundant Shrine is to the west, and the route continues to Undella Town in the north. The spray from the river's water turns into mist, so the entire road is often enveloped in fog.

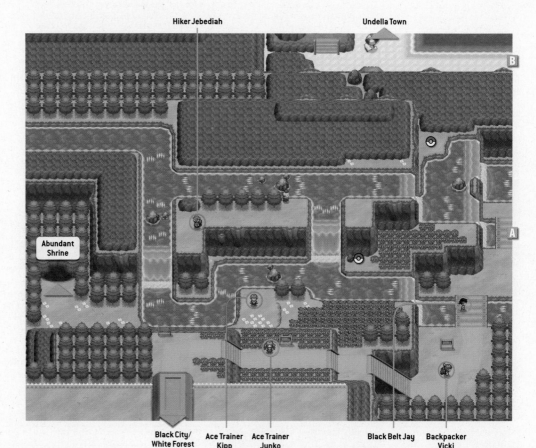

Hiker Jebediah · Undella Town · Abundant Shrine · Black City/White Forest · Ace Trainer Kipp · Ace Trainer Junko · Black Belt Jay · Backpacker Vicki

Fog makes it hard to see

Route 14 is often enveloped in a thick fog. A white haze covers everything so it's hard to see what's around you. Be careful not to overlook any items and check every corner as you go through the route.

Step 1   Use HMs to continue

Route 14 is bisected by a large river, and there are waterfalls due to the many hills. To see everything, you need the HMs Surf and Waterfall. Put a Pokémon in your party that knows these moves and look at every corner of the route.

It's a large waterfall.
Would you like to use Waterfall?

Step 2   Search for Giallo of the Seven Sages

If you use Waterfall to climb the river to the west, you will find Giallo of the Seven Sages on a plateau. After Giallo tells you about N and the Legendary Dragon-type Pokémon, he gives you HM08 Bulk Up. After that, he is arrested by Looker (p. 233).

Giallo: Greetings to you, strong Pokémon Trainer who came to Dragonspiral Tower.

Items

☐ Reaper Cloth
☐ TM08 Bulk Up
☐ Ultra Ball

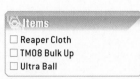

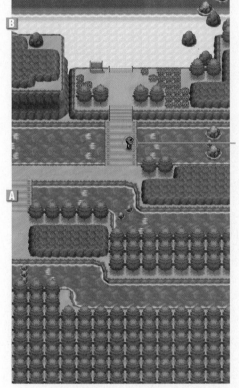

Fisherman Sid

Tall Grass

Pokémon	
Altaria	△
Beheeyem	△
Drifblim	△
Golduck	○
Jigglypuff	○
Mienfoo	△
Shuckle	△
Tropius	○

Tall Grass (rustling)

Pokémon	
Audino	◎
Emolga	△
Wigglytuff	△

Dark Grass

Pokémon	
Altaria	△
Beheeyem	△
Drifblim	△
Golduck	○
Jigglypuff	○
Mienshao	△
Shuckle	△
Tropius	○

Water Surface

Pokémon		
Basculin (Blue-Striped Form) ☐		◎
Basculin (Red-Striped Form) ■		◎
Buizel		○

Water Surface (ripples)

Pokémon		
Basculin (Blue-Striped Form) ■		○
Basculin (Red-Striped Form) ☐		○
Buizel		◎
Floatzel		△

Fishing

Pokémon		
Basculin (Blue-Striped Form) ☐		○
Basculin (Red-Striped Form) ■		○
Goldeen		◎

Fishing (ripples)

Pokémon		
Basculin (Blue-Striped Form) ■		○
Basculin (Red-Striped Form) ☐		○
Goldeen		◎
Seaking		△

---

 3 ### A passage to the Abundant Shrine

Continue west from where Giallo was, then use Surf and go down the waterfall. When you land on the west side, you will find the entrance to the Abundant Shrine at the dead end. Go inside and have a look around the Abundant Shrine (p. 214).

Step 4 ### Head north to Undella Town

When you return to Route 14 from the Abundant Shrine, continue east. Go north when you can't go any further east, and after you cross the bridge with the Fisherman, you will be in Undella Town. Use Surf to cross the ocean and enter Undella Town (p. 216).

Abundant Shrine

Story

The Abundant Shrine is a place where people used to live—if you look closely, you can still see remnants from that time. There is a small shrine at the north end of this area, and legend has it that a Pokémon called Landorus protects this land.

Field Moves Needed

Surf

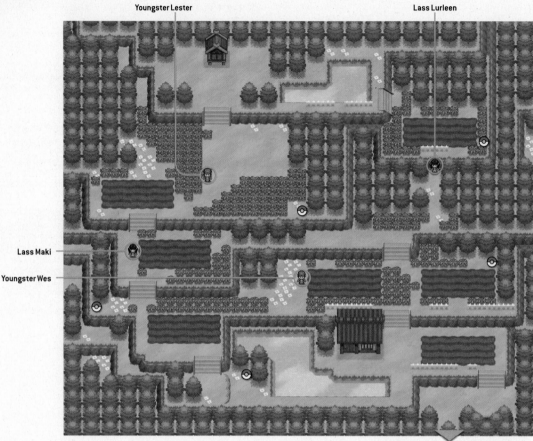

Youngster Lester

Lass Lurleen

Lass Maki

Youngster Wes

Route 14 (to Black City/White Forest)

Tall Grass

Pokémon	
Bronzong	△
Chimecho	○
Cottonee ■	△
Misdreavus □	△
Murkrow ■	△
Noctowl	○
Petilil □	△
Stantler	△
Vulpix	○

Tall Grass (rustling)

Pokémon	
Audino	◎
Emolga	△
Honchkrow ■	△
Lilligant □	△
Mismagius □	△
Ninetales	△
Whimsicott ■	△

Dark Grass

Pokémon	
Bronzong	△
Chimecho	○
Cottonee ■	△
Misdreavus □	△
Murkrow ■	△
Noctowl	○
Petilil □	△
Stantler	△
Vulpix	○

Items

- □ Hyper Potion
- □ Rare Candy
- □ Razor Fang
- □ TM35 Flamethrower
- □ TM92 Trick Room

Water Surface

Pokémon	
Basculin (Blue-Striped Form) □	◎
Basculin (Red-Striped Form) ■	◎
Slowpoke	○

Water Surface (ripples)

Pokémon	
Basculin (Blue-Striped Form) ■	○
Basculin (Red-Striped Form) □	○
Slowbro	△
Slowking	△
Slowpoke	◎

Fishing

Pokémon	
Basculin (Blue-Striped Form) □	○
Basculin (Red-Striped Form) ■	○
Goldeen	◎

Fishing (ripples)

Pokémon	
Basculin (Blue-Striped Form) ■	○
Basculin (Red-Striped Form) □	○
Goldeen	◎
Seaking	△

1 Continue north and find the shrine

Head north to the shrine. If you've caught Tornadus (Thundurus), continue to the shrine at the northern end of the area and you will find some kids arguing about Landorus.

This is a shrine for Great Landorus. It punished a Pokémon that did a bad thing! ▼

This used to be a village

Abundant Shrine used to be a village where people lived, and the fields are exactly as they were at the time. It must have been a village with fruitful fields spreading throughout the entire place.

 2 Bring Tornadus and Thundurus

Landorus is the Pokémon that punished Tornadus and Thundurus when they were flying about the Unova region wrecking homes and fields. When you approach the shrine with both Tornadus and Thundurus, Landorus will appear.

Tornadus and Thundurus are struggling inside their Poké Balls! ▼

Cooperate with friends and family

In *Pokémon Black Version*, Tornadus appears, and in *Pokémon White Version*, Thundurus appears. To meet Landorus, you have to exchange with your friends and family. Lend Tornadus and Thundurus to each other so you can all meet Landorus.

⊙ Catch Landorus!

First, use Water-type moves to do double damage and lower its HP quickly. After that, use Fighting-, Poison-, or Bug-type moves to lower its HP gradually. Bring many Ultra Balls, and keep trying until you catch it.

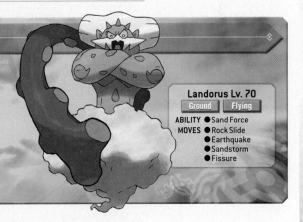

Landorus Lv. 70

| Ground | Flying |

ABILITY ● Sand Force
MOVES ● Rock Slide
● Earthquake
● Sandstorm
● Fissure

 3 Return to Route 14 and continue your journey

Battle Pokémon Trainers and gather items, having a look around as you do. While surfing, you can catch Slowpoke, Slowbro, and Slowking, which can only be encountered here. After you've had a good look around, return to Route 14 (p. 213).

UNOVA ADVENTURE WALKTHROUGH ◎ ABUNDANT SHRINE

Undella Town

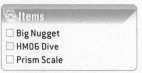

Story

Undella Town is an elegant place to beat the heat, and many manors line the beach. During summer, lots of people visit on vacation. A large villa sits at the western edge of town. It's visited by members of the very wealthy family known as The Riches.

Field Moves Needed

Surf

Items
- [ ] Big Nugget
- [ ] HM06 Dive
- [ ] Prism Scale

Poké Mart
(Lower Clerk)

Item	Price
Favored Mail	50
Greet Mail	50
Inquiry Mail	50
Like Mail	50
Reply Mail	50
RSVP Mail	50
Thanks Mail	50
Dive Ball	1,000
Luxury Ball	1,000

Route 13
(to Lacunosa Town)

Large Villa

Trade: Munchlax
(Trade Cinccino)
*Summer only

Cynthia's Villa

Pokémon Center

Undella Bay

The Riches' Draco

Route 14
(to Black City/White Forest)

Water Surface

Pokémon	
Mantyke	○
Pelipper	△
Wingull	◎

Water Surface (ripples)

Pokémon	
Corsola	○
Mantine	△
Wailmer	◎

Fishing

Pokémon	
Luvdisc	△
Remoraid	◎
Shellder	◎

Fishing (ripples)

Pokémon	
Cloyster	△
Luvdisc	○
Octillery	△
Shellder	◎

● Items the billionaire in the large villa will buy

Item	Price	Item	Price
Blue Flute	7,000	Relic Band	???
Red Flute	7,500	Relic Copper	???
Yellow Flute	7,500	Relic Crown	???
Black Flute	8,000	Relic Gold	???
White Flute	8,000	Relic Silver	???
		Relic Statue	???
		Relic Vase	???

Step 1 ▶ ### Get HM06 Dive from a girl

Talk to the girl on the plateau to the west of the Pokémon Center, and get HM06 Dive. If you use this where the water is dark, you can dive underwater. You can find areas of dark water in Undella Bay to the east of Undella Town, so try using it there.

Trainer obtained an HM06 Dive!

A trade that can only happen during summer

During summer, a man comes to the manor to the east of the large villa. If you give him a Cinccino, he'll give you a Munchlax. The man only visits during summer, so once the summer is gone, so is he.

Step 2 ▶ ### Meet the Sinnoh region's Champion, Cynthia

You can meet the Sinnoh region's Champion, Cynthia, in the manor west of the Pokémon Center. The first time you meet her, you can enjoy a Pokémon battle with her regardless of the season. After that, you can only battle her during spring once a day. If you meet her in spring, challenge her every day.

I have an insatiable curiosity for researching Pokémon myths.

The Gym Leaders come to play

The female Gym Leaders and Elite Four members come to hang out in the villa where Cynthia stays. If you talk to the Elite Four's Caitlin, you will learn it's her villa.

Sinnoh League Champion

Battle Cynthia

● *User of many Pokémon types*

Recommended Level for your Pokémon — Lv. 82

Battle while switching in response to your foe's Pokémon

Cynthia's Pokémon will attack your Pokémon's weaknesses. Before you take big damage, turn the tide of battle and do the same to them. Note, however, her Spiritomb and Eelektross have no weaknesses. Fight back with moves that do the biggest damage. Don't forget that Normal-, Fighting-, and Psychic-type moves have no effect on Spiritomb and Ground-type moves don't work on Eelektross.

● Cynthia's Pokémon

Pokémon	Lv.	Type		Effective Move Types	
◎ Spiritomb ♀	Lv. 75	Ghost	Dark		
● Moves to watch out for: Shadow Ball — Ghost					
◎ Milotic ♀	Lv. 75	Water		Grass	Electric
● Moves to watch out for: Blizzard — Ice					
◎ Braviary ♂	Lv. 75	Normal	Flying	Electric / Ice / Rock	
● Moves to watch out for: Brave Bird — Flying					
◎ Lucario ♂	Lv. 75	Fighting	Steel	Fire / Fighting / Ground	
● Moves to watch out for: ExtremeSpeed — Normal					
◎ Garchomp ♀	Lv. 77	Dragon	Ground	Ice	Dragon
● Moves to watch out for: Dragon Rush — Dragon					
◎ Eelektross ♀	Lv. 75	Electric			
● Moves to watch out for: Wild Charge — Electric					

Step 3 — ### A Pokémon battle with The Riches

Talk to The Riches' Draco in front of the big mansion, and he will challenge you to a Pokémon battle. If you talk to him again on another day in the large villa, the number of people you can battle will increase every time, up to six. When you defeat Miles, the head of the family, the challenge is over.

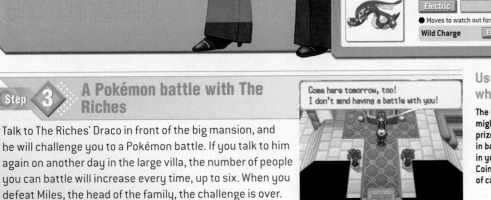

Come here tomorrow, too!
I don't mind having a battle with you!

Use the Amulet Coin when you battle

The Riches are wealthy, as you might expect, so you win a lot of prize money for defeating them in battle. Have the first Pokémon in your party hold an Amulet Coin and you'll end up with a ton of cash!

Step 4 — ### Sell your rare items to this collector

The billionaire in the west room of the large villa buys rare items from you. He will buy the flutes you get from the sunglasses-wearing man on Route 13 and the ancient items you get from somewhere. After you get these items, talk to the billionaire.

Do you have such a rare item?
Do you?

Step 5 — ### Head east to Undella Bay

Have a look around town, then continue east over the water to Undella Bay (p. 218). Undella Bay is a small bay surrounded by rocks, and rumors abound that mysterious ruins lie on the seafloor. Pokémon Trainer battles also wait, so heal your Pokémon before you head out.

Teach Dive to your Pokémon

There are a few places in Undella Bay where you can dive to the seafloor. Put a Pokémon that can learn Dive in your party, and use the HM to teach it the move.

Step 6 Head north to Route 13

When you return from Undella Bay, go through the gate to the left of the Pokémon Center to Route 13 (p. 221). Route 13 is packed with Pokémon Trainers, so make sure to take lots of healing items with you.

A world-famous sea of shining waves

Undella Bay • Abyssal Ruins

Story

Visitors to Undella Town come to swim in beautiful Undella Bay. It's surrounded by rocks and small islands, so the area you can swim in is small—but if you explore below the surface, you'll find the mysterious Abyssal Ruins spread out over the seafloor.

Field Moves Needed

Surf   Dive

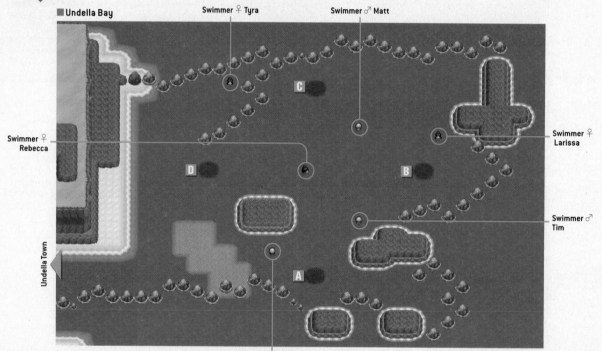

Undella Bay

Swimmer ♀ Tyra   Swimmer ♂ Matt

Swimmer ♀ Rebecca

Swimmer ♀ Larissa

Swimmer ♂ Tim

Swimmer ♂ Bart

Undella Town

Spring Summer Autumn		Winter		All Seasons	
Water Surface		**Water Surface**		**Fishing**	
Pokémon		Pokémon		Pokémon	
Mantyke	○	Pelipper	△	Luvdisc	△
Pelipper	△	Spheal	○	Remoraid	◎
Wingull	◎	Wingull	◎	Shellder	○
Water Surface (ripples)		**Water Surface** (ripples)		**Fishing** (ripples)	
Pokémon		Pokémon		Pokémon	
Mantine	△	Sealeo	○	Cloyster	△
Wailmer	◎	Wailmer	◎	Luvdisc	○
Wailord	△	Wailord	△	Octillery	△
		Walrein	△	Shellder	◎

UNDELLA TOWN • UNDELLA BAY • ABYSSAL RUINS

UNOVA ADVENTURE WALKTHROUGH

■ **Abyssal Ruins**

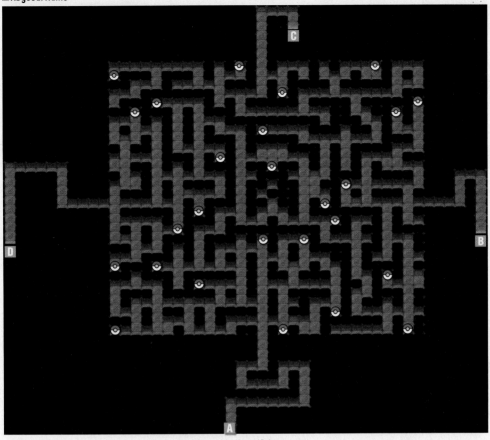

● Only the first floor is mapped in this book, but there are more floors in the Abyssal Ruins.
The items you get here will be a surprise.
Solve the mystery on your own, and find the way through the maze.

 Step 1   **Battle Trainers swimming in the water**

Six Trainers are swimming in Undella Bay. Battle with them as you surf around. All of the Swimmers will use Water-type Pokémon against you.

I just love swimming, so I have only fought against wild Pokémon.

Cynthia, the secret swimmer

In Undella Bay, Swimmer ♀ Tyra tells you a rumor that Cynthia likes to go swimming when no one is around. Maybe she's shy about her bathing suit.

 Step 2   **Use Dive to explore underwater**

Press the A Button when you're in a patch of darker water, and you can go underwater with Dive. While underwater, continue to press the Control Pad, and you can enter the building on the seafloor. If you release the Control Pad, you will be returned to the surface.

It's a deep part of the sea. Would you like to use Dive?

▶ YES
   NO

Get Dive in Undella Town

You need the HM Dive to go to the Abyssal Ruins. If you don't have it yet, talk to the woman in front of Cynthia's villa in Undella Town (p. 216).

Step 3 The Abyssal Ruins are a giant maze

When you enter the Abyssal Ruins, you'll hear the sound of a switch being pushed. If you travel a certain number of steps from this point, you'll automatically return to the water's surface. In other words, the time you have to search through the Abyssal Ruins is limited.

The sound reverberates.

Step 4 Mysterious letters are carved in the stones

Purple stones are set in various places in the Abyssal Ruins. Check these stones, and you will see they are covered in mysterious letters. These letters have not been deciphered. What could be written here?

Step 5 Proceed while collecting items

Many items have been dropped in the first floor of the Abyssal Ruins. The inside is a maze, however, and it's easy to lose track of where you are. Refer to the map on p. 219 and pick up every item.

How do you use the items you find here?

The items found in the Abyssal Ruins can be roughly divided into two types: Items that are useful in battle, and items you can sell for a lot of money. After you get them, think about how to use them.

Step 6 Go in through all four entrances

The Abyssal Ruins has four entrances, and although you can see everything from each entrance, you can't explore the whole place in a single trip because of the time limit. If you're sent back to the surface, try a different entrance on your next dive.

It's a deep part of the sea. Would you like to use Dive?
▶ YES
   NO

Step 7 The Abyssal Ruins might hide a secret

The Abyssal Ruins still hide many mysteries. By solving these mysteries, you might be able to get to the other floors. See if you can unlock the mystery by yourself and try to make the entire image of the Abyssal Ruins clear.

Step 8 Return to Undella Town when you're finished exploring

Undella Bay is surrounded by rocks and small islands, so the only exit is back to Undella Town. When you're done exploring Undella Bay and the Abyssal Ruins, return to Undella Town to go to Route 13 (p. 218).

Route 13

Route 13 is a picturesque route lined with ocean beaches and trees. You'll meet a person who will give you a precious item every day, and a person who can teach your Pokémon an ultimate move.

Field Moves Needed

Cut Surf Strength

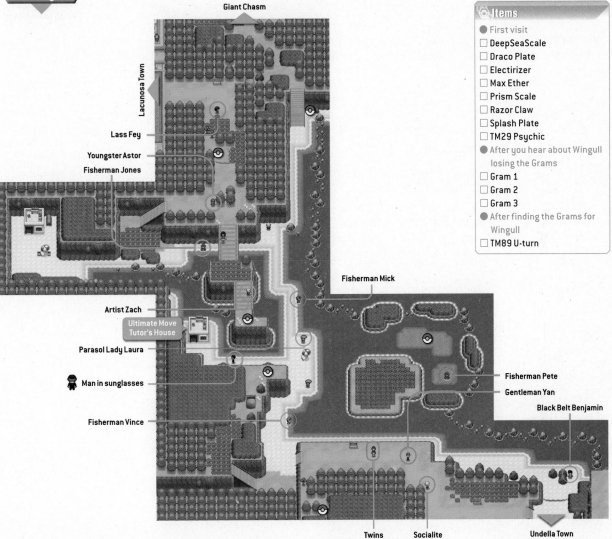

Giant Chasm

Lacunosa Town

Lass Fey

Youngster Astor

Fisherman Jones

Fisherman Mick

Artist Zach

Ultimate Move Tutor's House

Parasol Lady Laura

Man in sunglasses

Fisherman Vince

Fisherman Pete

Gentleman Yan

Black Belt Benjamin

Twins
Emy & Lin

Socialite
Marian

Undella Town

Items

- ● First visit
- ☐ DeepSeaScale
- ☐ Draco Plate
- ☐ Electirizer
- ☐ Max Ether
- ☐ Prism Scale
- ☐ Razor Claw
- ☐ Splash Plate
- ☐ TM29 Psychic
- ● After you hear about Wingull losing the Grams
- ☐ Gram 1
- ☐ Gram 2
- ☐ Gram 3
- ● After finding the Grams for Wingull
- ☐ TM89 U-turn

● Items you can get from the man in sunglasses

Item	Item
Big Pearl	Metal Powder
Black Flute	Protector
Blue Flute	Razor Claw
DeepSeaScale	Razor Fang
DeepSeaTooth	Reaper Cloth
Dragon Scale	Red Flute
Dubious Disc	Shoal Salt
Electirizer	Shoal Shell
Heart Scale	Stick
King's Rock	Thick Club
Lucky Egg	Up-Grade
Lucky Punch	White Flute
Magmarizer	Yellow Flute
Metal Coat	

Tall Grass

Pokémon	
Absol	△
Drifblim	△
Golbat	○
Lunatone	△
Solrock	△
Swellow	○
Tangela	○

Tall Grass (rustling)

Pokémon	
Audino	◎
Emolga	△
Crobat	△
Tangrowth	△

Dark Grass

Pokémon	
Absol	△
Drifblim	△
Golbat	○
Lunatone	△
Solrock	△
Swellow	○
Tangela	△

Water Surface			Water Surface (ripples)			🎣 Fishing			🎣 Fishing (ripples)	
Pokémon			**Pokémon**			**Pokémon**			**Pokémon**	
Pelipper	△		Corsola	○		Krabby	◎		Cloyster	△
Staryu	○		Starmie	△		Luvdisc	△		Kingler	△
Wingull	◎		Staryu	◎		Shellder	○		Luvdisc	○
									Shellder	◎

Step 1 — Go north while battling Trainers

When you go on Route 13, follow the road west. Continue while battling Pokémon Trainers and you will reach a plateau. Climb the stairs and use Strength to move a rock out of the way and get items. When you're done, go north on the beach.

Hey! Please show me what kinds of great Pokémon you have caught!

Find Items with the Dowsing MCHN

Many items are hidden in the beaches that span Route 13. Use the Dowsing MCHN to find them.

Step 2 — Get precious items from the man in sunglasses

At the fork in the road, go west. Talk to the man in sunglasses along the way, and you can get a different item every day. The items you get are valuable items you can't obtain anywhere else. Come by every day and get items (p. 221).

But it's the same one as I found before, so I will give this to you.

The Prism Scale is related to evolution

On the north side of Route 13, you can get a Prism Scale. This item is related to the evolution of a Pokémon that lives in a different region (p. 252).

Step 3 — Learn the ultimate move from the Move Tutor

Keep going west past the man in sunglasses, and you'll reach the ultimate Move Tutor's house. Talk to the old man inside, and he will teach Serperior, Emboar, or Samurott the ultimate move—but only if you have a very strong bond with your Pokémon.

YES
NO

Shall I teach them to your Pokémon?

● Unova Pokémon that can learn the ultimate moves

Move	Type	Effect	Pokémon that can learn it
Frenzy Plant	Grass	A move with a power of 150. The user can't move during the next turn.	Serperior
Hydro Cannon	Water	A move with a power of 150. The user can't move during the next turn.	Samurott
Blast Burn	Fire	A move with a power of 150. The user can't move during the next turn. If the target is Frozen, it will be thawed.	Emboar

Serperior   Samurott   Emboar

ROUTE 13 — UNOVA ADVENTURE WALKTHROUGH

Step 4 — Help Wingull by finding the dropped Grams

Go north on the beach, and climb the stairs up to the high area. A girl with a Wingull is on a bridge to the south. Talk to the girl, and she will tell you that Wingull is in trouble because it dropped the Grams it was going to deliver. Collect all of the Grams that Wingull dropped.

This Wingull looks like it lost three Grams on Route 13. I wish I could help it...

Grams

Step 5 — Give the three Grams to Wingull

Gram 2 is just south of that bridge. Get Gram 1 from the old man to the east when you go down to the beach, and Gram 3 from the Parasol Lady to the south. Give them all to Wingull, and you'll get TM89 U-turn as thanks.

Trainer obtained the Gram 1!

Step 6 — The Giant Chasm is just past the stairs.

Go north over the water from the old man who gave you Gram 1. The Giant Chasm is just past the stairs (p. 225). Before going any further, however, head west toward Lacunosa Town. If you use Strength to push the boulder, it will be easy to get there and back.

Push the boulder with Strength

If you push the boulder aside with Strength as you pass, it will be easier to reach the Giant Chasm from Lacunosa Town. Push the boulder into the hole to create a shortcut.

Step 7 — Go west to Lacunosa Town

Your Pokémon are probably tired from all the battling on Route 13. Before going to the Giant Chasm, it would be best to heal them. Head west to Lacunosa Town (p. 224).

Lacunosa Town

Story

Lacunosa Town is a tiny town with little more than a Pokémon Center. The people who live here believe in a legend that a monster attacks at night, so they stay indoors after dark.

Field Moves Needed

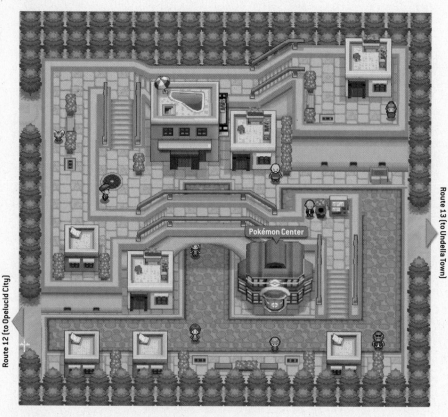

Pokémon Center

Route 12 (to Opelucid City)

Route 13 (to Undella Town)

Items
- When you talk to the woman when Shaymin is in your party
- ☐ Gracidea

Poké Mart (Lower Clerk)

BridgeMail V	50
Favored Mail	50
Greet Mail	50
Inquiry Mail	50
Like Mail	50
Reply Mail	50
RSVP Mail	50
Thanks Mail	50

Step 1 — Learn about the Gracidea from the woman

Talk to the woman in the Pokémon Center, and she will tell you about the Gracidea. If Shaymin is in your party, and you don't have the Gracidea yet, she will give it to you. This item can change Shaymin's Forme (p. 250).

Do you know about Gracidea flowers?

Gracidea

Step 2 — Listen to the old woman's folktale

Talk to an old woman in front of a house in the north of town and she will tell you about the town's folktale, which influences their customs. If you talk to the old woman in her house at night, she will talk to you...but she's half-asleep, and it's hard to understand what she's saying.

There's a great big hole at the back of this town.

How to bring Shaymin over

If you've already received Shaymin in another Pokémon game, you can go to the Poké Transfer Lab on Route 15 and bring it to this game via Poké Transfer.

Step 3 — Go to the Giant Chasm

Heal your Pokémon in the Pokémon Center, and once you're ready, head to the Giant Chasm. If you used Strength to push the rock, you can reach it by heading east from the city.

Step 4 — Head west towards Route 12

When you return from the Giant Chasm, first rest your Pokémon at the Pokémon Center. After that, head west from the town, and go to Route 12 (p. 228). Route 12 is a short route that connects Lacunosa Town and Village Bridge.

The difference between day and night

The people of the town still follow old customs, so they all stay inside all night (p. 49). If you walk around town at night, you'll find that the streets are empty.

Get Berries on Sunday nights

Go into a house in the north of the city on Sundays, anytime at night, and you'll meet a Clerk ♂. Talk to him, and he will give you a Pecha Berry, Bluk Berry, Lum Berry, or Leppa Berry. You can visit him every Sunday to get a Berry.

Legend says if you approach this big chasm, disasters surely follow

Giant Chasm

Story — The Giant Chasm is a crater-shaped cave, with a verdant forest covering the floor of the crater. The deepest part is where the Legendary Pokémon Kyurem lives. The residents of Lacunosa Town fear that it is a monster and avoid it.

Field Moves Needed: Surf, Strength

Entrance

Tall Grass

Pokémon	
Absol	△
Drifblim	△
Golbat	○
Lunatone	△
Solrock	△
Swellow	○
Tangela	○

Tall Grass (Rustling Grass)

Pokémon	
Audino	◎
Crobat	△
Emolga	△
Tangrowth	△

Dark Grass

Pokémon	
Absol	△
Drifblim	△
Golbat	○
Lunatone	△
Solrock	△
Swellow	○
Tangela	○

Entrance — Route 13 (to Undella Town)

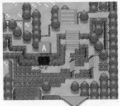
Cave

Items

- ☐ Carbos
- ☐ Comet Shard
- ☐ Full Heal
- ☐ Max Elixir
- ☐ Max Potion
- ☐ Max Revive
- ☐ Revive
- ☐ Star Piece x2
- ☐ TM03 Psyshock
- ☐ TM13 Ice Beam

Cave/Cave's deepest part

👁 Cave

Pokémon	
Boldore	△
Delibird	△
Golbat	○
Jynx	△
Lunatone	△
Piloswine	○
Sneasel	△
Solrock	△

👁 Cave (dust cloud)

Pokémon	
Excadrill	◎

👁 Water Surface

Pokémon	
Basculin (Blue-Striped Form) ☐	◎
Basculin (Red-Striped Form) ■	◎
Seel	○

👁 Water Surface (ripples)

Pokémon	
Basculin (Blue-Striped Form) ■	○
Basculin (Red-Striped Form) ☐	○
Dewgong	△
Seel	◎

👁 Fishing

Pokémon	
Basculin (Blue-Striped Form) ☐	○
Basculin (Red-Striped Form) ■	○
Poliwag	◎
Poliwhirl	△

👁 Fishing (ripples)

Pokémon	
Basculin (Blue-Striped Form) ■	○
Basculin (Red-Striped Form) ☐	○
Poliwhirl	◎
Poliwrath	△

Crater Forest

👁 Tall Grass

Pokémon	
Clefairy	○
Ditto	○
Lunatone	△
Metang	△
Piloswine	○
Solrock	△

👁 Tall Grass (rustling)

Pokémon	
Audino	◎
Clefable	△
Mamoswine	△
Metagross	△

👁 Dark Grass

Pokémon	
Clefairy	○
Ditto	○
Lunatone	△
Metang	△
Piloswine	○
Solrock	△

■ Crater Forest

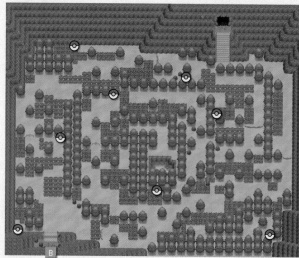

■ Cave's Deepest Part

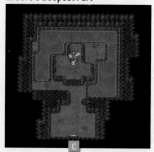

■ Crater Forest (after approaching the pit in the center)

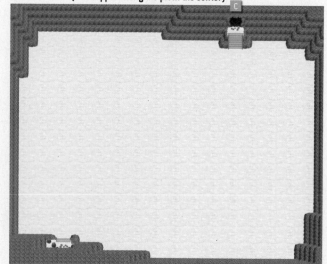

Step 1 Collect items

Enter the cave and go around the walls while collecting items. Once you've made a lap, go north and you will reach the Crater Forest. The trees and ledges make it hard to move around freely. The easiest way to get around is to go clockwise and collect items.

Not a Trainer in sight

There isn't a single Pokémon Trainer in Giant Chasm, but many different wild Pokémon appear. Battle and catch them as you head deeper into the chasm.

Step 2 Approach the pit, and everything is covered by snow

When you approach the pit in the center of the Crater Forest, a Pokémon cry sounds out of nowhere, and in an instant, everything is covered with snow. The snow covers up all the trees and other obstacles so you can proceed directly to the deepest part of the cave. When you go inside, Kyurem is waiting for you in the cave's center.

Leave Ditto at the Day Care

When you leave two Pokémon at the Pokémon Day Care on Route 3, an Egg will sometimes be found. If one of those two Pokémon is Ditto, you will find Eggs with many combinations of Pokémon.

Catch Kyurem!

First, use moves that do double damage such as Fighting-, Rock-, and Dragon-type moves. After that, lower its HP gradually with Water-, Grass-, or Electric-type moves. The battle takes place inside a cave, so Dusk Balls are effective.

Kyurem Lv. 75

Dragon   Ice

ABILITY ●Pressure
MOVES ●Glaciate
Dragon Pulse
Imprison
Endeavor

Step 3 Use a shortcut to return to Lacunosa Town

Return to the Crater Forest from the deepest chamber, and climb down the ledges while heading south to the exit. In the cave, climb the stairs and go south. Hop down the ledge for a shortcut to the exit. Once you've left the Giant Chasm, return to Lacunosa Town (p. 225).

Catch Kyurem and the snow disappears

The moment you approach the pit in the center of Crater Forest, everything becomes covered in snow. After you catch Kyurem, however, the snow disappears entirely. If you missed any items on the way to the pit, you can pick them up on the way out.

Route 12

Story

Route 12 is a short route with gentle hills and large expanses of tall grass. Go east to reach Lacunosa Town. The western exit goes to Village Bridge. Many Bug-type Pokémon live in the tall grass.

Field Moves Needed

Items

- ● First visit
- ☐ Full Heal
- ☐ Revive
- ☐ TM53 Energy Ball
- ● After defeating
  Pokémon Breeder Eustace
- ☐ Sitrus Berry
- ● After defeating
  Pokémon Breeder Ethel
- ☐ Sitrus Berry

Tall Grass

Pokémon	
Cherrim	△
Combee	○
Dunsparce	△
Heracross	△
Kakuna ■	△
Metapod ☐	△
Pinsir	△
Rapidash	△
Sunkern	○
Tranquill	○

Tall Grass (rustling)

Pokémon	
Audino	◎
Beedrill ■	△
Butterfree ☐	△
Emolga	△
Sunflora	△
Unfezant	△
Vespiquen	△

Dark Grass

Pokémon	
Cherrim	△
Combee	○
Dunsparce	△
Heracross	△
Kakuna ■	△
Metapod ☐	△
Pinsir	△
Rapidash	△
Sunkern	○
Tranquill	○

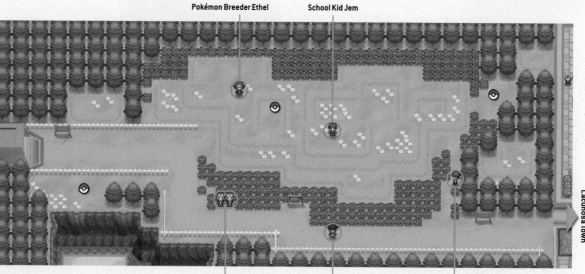

Pokémon Breeder Ethel

School Kid Jem

Village Bridge (to Opelucid City)

Lacunosa Town

Backers Fey & Sue

School Kid Ann

Pokémon Breeder Eustace

Step 1 Go west while battling Trainers

Even though it's short, six Pokémon Trainers are waiting for you on Route 12. Battle with them, gather items, and catch Pokémon in the tall grass. On the other side of the gate to the west is Village Bridge.

It's OK to have a battle during a picnic. Right?

Get Berries by defeating Breeders

Pokémon Breeders Eustace and Ethel give you Sitrus Berries after you defeat them in battle. Eustace is next to the east gate, and Ethel is on the west side. Be sure to challenge them and get the Berries.

Village Bridge

Story

Village Bridge is a bridge with houses on top, as the name implies. The bridge has a long history—it's said to have been built while the Unova region was being developed 200 years ago.

Field Moves Needed

Surf

Items
- ☐ Calcium
- ☐ Ultra Ball

Tall Grass

Pokémon	
Bibarel	○
Golduck	○
Rufflet ☐	○
Seviper	○
Vullaby ■	○
Zangoose	○

Tall Grass (rustling)

Pokémon	
Audino	◎
Emolga	△

Dark Grass

Pokémon	
Bibarel	○
Braviary ☐	○
Golduck	○
Mandibuzz ■	○
Seviper	○
Zangoose	○

Water Surface

Pokémon		
Basculin (Blue-Striped Form) ☐	◎	
Basculin (Red-Striped Form) ■	◎	

Water Surface (ripples)

Pokémon		
Basculin (Blue-Striped Form) ■	◎	
Basculin (Red-Striped Form) ☐	◎	
Lapras	△	

Fishing

Pokémon		
Basculin (Blue-Striped Form) ☐	○	
Basculin (Red-Striped Form) ■	○	
Carvanha	◎	

Fishing (ripples)

Pokémon		
Basculin (Blue-Striped Form) ■	○	
Basculin (Red-Striped Form) ☐	○	
Carvanha	◎	
Sharpedo	△	

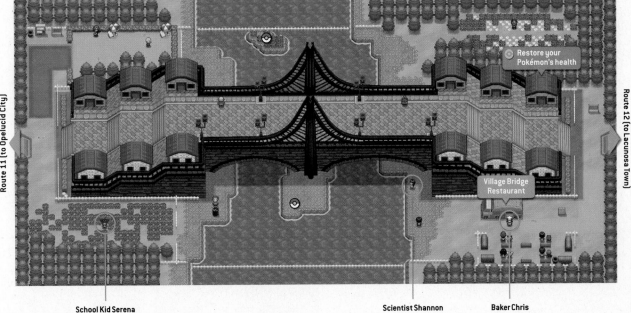

Restore your Pokémon's health

Village Bridge Restaurant

Route 11 (to Opelucid City)

Route 12 (to Lacunosa Town)

School Kid Serena

Scientist Shannon

Baker Chris

A part-time job at the Village Bridge Restaurant

Village Bridge Restaurant is housed in a camper below the east side of the bridge. If you defeat Baker Chris, you can work here part-time. Talk to Chris and listen to the customers' orders. Tell Chris the orders and give each customer the correct sandwich, and you get a Lum Berry as a reward.

Heal your Pokémon in the house

Talk to the girl in the house to the east and she will heal your Pokémon. There's no Pokémon Center here, so let this girl take care of your Pokémon after battling.

 Talk to the woman with four Patrat

A woman and four Patrat live in the second house from the east. Talk to the woman, and she explains she is aiming for new heights, and she will depart with her Patrat. Now you can see the Patrat Show on Marvelous Bridge (p. 202).

Find Leftovers

Use the Dowsing MCHN around Village Bridge and you can find Leftovers. When a Pokémon holds Leftovers, it recovers a little HP at the end of every turn. Check every corner to find it.

 Show the Fisherman Pokémon you've caught

A Fisherman lives in the third house from the east. If you talk to him, he invites you to join the Hip Waders. Select "Yes" to become a member. If you join and show him the Pokémon he wants to see, he will give you a Dive Ball.

Village Bridge has a storied history

A stonecutter lives in the westernmost house. By talking to him, you learn that Village Bridge was built during his great-great-great-great-grandfather's time. That was a long time ago.

 Head west toward Route 11

Look at everything around Village Bridge and then go west. You'll find the start of Route 11 on the other side of the western gate. Travel along Route 11 to the west, and you will return to Opelucid City.

Talk to the musicians and make the music richer

Four musicians play on and around Village Bridge. Talk to them and they will add their instrument to the music. Enjoy a unique song with vocals.

•Guitar •Flute •Drums •Vocals

Route 11

Route 11 crosses over a flowing river with a giant waterfall. A camper is parked next to the waterfall. You can battle Pokémon Trainers who came from abroad and are here to marvel at the striking natural scenery.

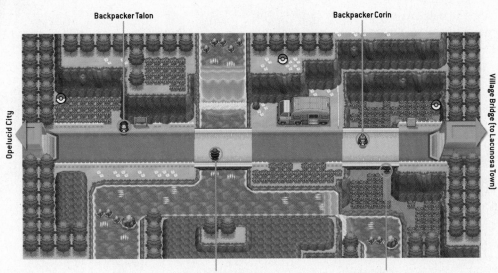

Backpacker Talon

Backpacker Corin

Opelucid City

Village Bridge (to Lacunosa Town)

Pokémon Ranger Thalia

Pokémon Ranger Crofton

Items

- ● First visit
- ☐ Hyper Potion
- ☐ Protector
- ☐ TM50 Overheat
- ● After defeating Pokémon Ranger Crofton
- ☐ Leppa Berry
- ● After defeating Pokémon Ranger Thalia
- ☐ Leppa Berry

Tall Grass

Pokémon	
Amoonguss	△
Gligar	○
Golduck	○
Karrablast	△
Pawniard	△
Rufflet ☐	○
Seviper	△
Vullaby ■	○
Zangoose	△

Tall Grass (rustling)

Pokémon	
Audino	◎
Emolga	△
Gliscor	△

Dark Grass

Pokémon	
Amoonguss	△
Bisharp	△
Braviary ☐	○
Gligar	○
Golduck	○
Karrablast	△
Mandibuzz ■	○
Seviper	△
Zangoose	△

Water Surface

Pokémon	
Basculin (Blue-Striped Form) ☐	◎
Basculin (Red-Striped Form) ■	◎
Buizel	○

Water Surface (ripples)

Pokémon	
Basculin (Blue-Striped Form) ■	○
Basculin (Red-Striped Form) ☐	○
Buizel	◎
Floatzel	△

Fishing

Pokémon	
Basculin (Blue-Striped Form) ☐	○
Basculin (Red-Striped Form) ■	○
Goldeen	◎

Fishing (ripples)

Pokémon	
Basculin (Blue-Striped Form) ■	○
Basculin (Red-Striped Form) ☐	○
Goldeen	◎
Seaking	△

Step 1 Go west while battling Trainers

Go west while battling Pokémon Trainers. When you pass through the gate, you're in Opelucid City. Now, you've seen the whole Unova region! Check out the areas you've already seen, and aim for the Pokémon League (p. 196).

Do you think you can win against us?

Get Berries by defeating Trainers

Defeat Pokémon Rangers Crofton and Thalia to get Leppa Berries. Crofton is in the tall grass below the paved road, and Thalia is on the road. Make sure to fight them, and gather Berries.

The adventure continues even after seeing the credits twice

When you defeat the Elite Four and the Champion at the Pokémon League, the story comes to a close for a second time. After that, the goal of your adventure becomes completing the Pokédex. First, complete the Unova Pokédex, and then set off on another journey with the big dream of completing the National Pokédex.

Your Adventure after the Hall of Fame

Nuvema Town	**Have a Pokémon battle with Bianca on the weekend**

When you enter the Hall of Fame, you will return to your room in Nuvema Town. Talk to Bianca in the Pokémon Lab, and you can hear about mass outbreaks of Pokémon. After that, you can enjoy Pokémon battles with Bianca every Saturday and Sunday.

Would you have a Pokémon battle with me today?

New wallpaper is added

After you enter the Hall of Fame, check your PC. You will find new wallpaper for your Pokémon Box, such as the Munna and Zoroark designs.

Battle your childhood friend Bianca! **6**

Her Pokémon are 25 levels higher than they were in your fifth battle, and she has added Chandelure and Mienshao to her party.

● If you chose Snivy:

◎ Stoutland ♀	Lv. 63	Normal	
◎ Chandelure ♀	Lv. 63	Ghost	Fire
◎ Samurott ♂	Lv. 65	Water	
◎ Musharna ♀	Lv. 63	Psychic	
◎ Simisear ♂	Lv. 63	Fire	
◎ Mienshao ♀	Lv. 63	Fighting	

● If you chose Tepig:

◎ Stoutland ♀	Lv. 63	Normal	
◎ Chandelure ♀	Lv. 63	Ghost	Fire
◎ Serperior ♂	Lv. 65	Grass	
◎ Musharna ♀	Lv. 63	Psychic	
◎ Simipour ♂	Lv. 63	Water	
◎ Mienshao ♀	Lv. 63	Fighting	

● If you chose Oshawott:

◎ Stoutland ♀	Lv. 63	Normal	
◎ Chandelure ♀	Lv. 63	Ghost	Fire
◎ Emboar ♂	Lv. 65	Fire	Fighting
◎ Musharna ♀	Lv. 63	Psychic	
◎ Simisage ♂	Lv. 63	Grass	
◎ Mienshao ♀	Lv. 63	Fighting	

Search for the Remaining Seven Sages

Special Feature

Stop Team Plasma by having Looker arrest the remaining Seven Sages

After you finish the main story, you may want to set off to defeat the Champion and enter the Hall of Fame, but there is something you should do first. Cooperate with Looker from the International Police and look for the remaining members of the Seven Sages (except for Ghetsis). Their locations are listed here.

● **Where the remaining Seven Sages are hidden**

Giallo — Where Route 14

Go to Route 14 from Undella Town. Use the HM Waterfall to climb the waterfall. He's just past the top.

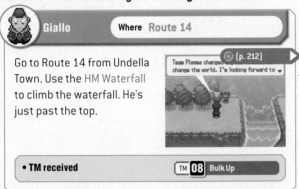
(p. 212)
Team Plasma changed... change the world. I'm looking forward to

• TM received — TM **08** Bulk Up

Rood — Where Route 18

Use the HM Surf to go west from Nuvema Town, and you'll find him at the southwesternmost point when you are coming from Route 17 and 18.

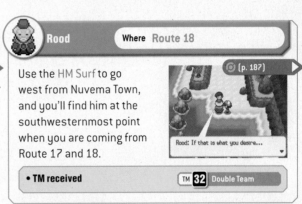
(p. 187)
Rood: If that is what you desire...

• TM received — TM **32** Double Team

Gorm — Where The Dreamyard

Go to the Dreamyard from Striaton City. Go downstairs, then climb the next set of stairs. He's hiding behind a wall on the east side when you come out.

(p. 188)
The dreams you realize with your own abilities are the real dreams.

• TM received — TM **75** Swords Dance

Ryoku — Where The Relic Castle

Go to the Relic Castle in the Desert Resort, and aim for the deepest chamber of the lowest floor where Volcarona is. He is just before that room.

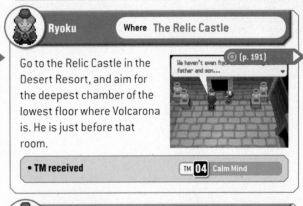
(p. 191)
He haven't even fig... father and son...

• TM received — TM **04** Calm Mind

Zinzolin — Where The Cold Storage

Deep within the Cold Storage, you'll find a container with Zinzolin hidden in it.

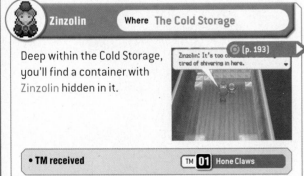
(p. 193)
Zinzolin: It's too co... tired of shivering in here.

• TM received — TM **01** Hone Claws

Bronius — Where Chargestone Cave

He's in the southernmost point of Chargestone Cave's B2F. When you talk to him, he will call two former Team Plasma Grunts, and they will battle you.

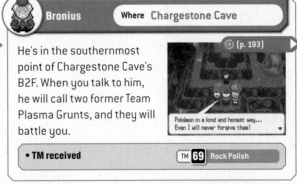
(p. 193)
Pokémon in a kind and honest way... Even I will never forgive them!

• TM received — TM **69** Rock Polish

Capture all of the Seven Sages to hear about N

There is no particular order to finding the Seven Sages. When Looker captures the sixth sage, he thanks you by telling you that he heard an eyewitness report of a person who matched N's description with a dragon Pokémon somewhere far away.

Go on a new adventure
and fantastic journey

You've defeated the Pokémon League's Champion
and are the new Pokémon Champion!
It's proof positive that your hard work paid off! Congratulations!
It's not over yet, though—there's still so much to do
in *Pokémon Black* and *Pokémon White*!
Try tons of fun-filled activities such as completing your Unova Pokédex,
Pokémon Musicals, the Battle Subway,
wireless battles with friends both near and far,
the Pokémon Global Link,
and so much more!
Take advantage of everything *Pokémon Black* and *Pokémon White* have to offer.

Trainer List

A Look Back at the Trainers You Battle in the Unova region

Make your Pokémon stronger by battling all of the Trainers

In every part of the Unova region, Pokémon Trainers are waiting to challenge you to battle. Here, we've organized all of the Pokémon Trainers by where they appear. When you defeat a Trainer, sometimes you'll get items or Gym Badges. This also shows which Trainers will heal your Pokémon after you defeat them.

| Before Finishing the Main Story | Nuvema Town (p. 58) ▶ | Pokémon Trainer Bianca  | Pokémon Trainer Cheren  | Route 1 (p. 61) ▶ | Fisherman Sean  | Pokémon Ranger Claude  ITEM ● Persim Berry |

| Pokémon Ranger Brenda  ITEM ● Persim Berry | Accumula Town (p. 63) ▶ | Pokémon Trainer N  | Route 2 (p. 66) ▶ | Youngster Jimmy  | Youngster Roland  | Lass Mali  |

| Pokémon Trainer Bianca  | Striaton City (p. 68) ▶ | Pokémon Trainer Cheren  ITEM ● Oran Berry ×3 | Waiter Maxwell  | Waitress Tia  | Gym Leader Chili  BADGE ● Trio Badge | Gym Leader Cress  BADGE ● Trio Badge |

| Gym Leader Cilan  BADGE ● Trio Badge | Dreamyard (p. 73) ▶ | Lass Eri  | Youngster Joey  | Team Plasma Grunt  | Team Plasma Grunt  | |

| Route 3 (p. 75) ▶ | Preschooler Doyle  | Preschooler Wendy  | Preschooler Tully  | Nursery Aide Autumn  | Twins Kumi & Amy  | Pokémon Trainer Cheren  |

| Pokémon Breeder Adelaide  ITEM ● Oran Berry | School Kid Al  | School Kid Marsha  | School Kid Edgar  | School Kid Gina  | Pokémon Breeder Galen  ITEM ● Lum Berry | |

Wellspring Cave (p. 78)	Team Plasma Grunt	Team Plasma Grunt	Team Plasma Grunt	Black Belt Edward	Battle Girl Xiao	Battle Girl Maggie
Nacrene City (p. 82)	Pokémon Trainer N	Scientist Satomi	School Kid Lydia	School Kid Carter	Gym Leader Lenora BADGE ● Basic Badge	
Pinwheel Forest (p. 87)	Nurse Shery ● Heals All Pokémon	Preschooler Homer	Preschooler Juliet	Black Belt Kentaro	Youngster Keita	Youngster Zachary
Battle Girl Lee	School Kid Sammy	School Kid Millie	Youngster Nicholas	Twins Mayo & May	Team Plasma Grunt	Team Plasma Grunt
Team Plasma Grunt	Team Plasma Grunt	Pokémon Ranger Audra ITEM ● Chesto Berry	Pokémon Ranger Miguel ITEM ● Pecha Berry	Pokémon Ranger Forrest ITEM ● Chesto Berry	Pokémon Ranger Irene ITEM ● Pecha Berry	Lass Eva
Castelia City (p. 92)	Clerk ♀ Ingrid	Clerk ♀ Alberta	Scientist Randall	Clerk ♂ Clemens	Clerk ♂ Warren	Scientist Samantha
Scientist Steve	Clerk ♂ Ivan	Clerk ♂ Wade	Janitor Geoff ITEM ● Exp. Share	Dancer Mickey	Dancer Edmond	Dancer Raymond
Team Plasma Grunt	Harlequin Kerry	Harlequin Jack	Harlequin Louis	Harlequin Rick	Gym Leader Burgh BADGE ● Insect Badge	Pokémon Trainer Bianca

Route 4

(p. 100) ▶

Pokémon Trainer Cheren	Worker Gus

Worker Gus

Worker Zack

Worker Scott

Worker Shelby

Fisherman Hubert

Fisherman Andrew

Backpacker Jill

Backpacker Anna

Backpacker Keane

Backpacker Waylon

Backpacker Jerome

Parasol Lady April

Desert Resort

(p. 100) ▶

Psychic Gaven

Psychic Cybil

Psychic Low

Doctor Jerry
● Heals All Pokémon

Backpacker Liz

Backpacker Nate

Backpacker Kelsey

Backpacker Elaine

Pokémon Ranger Jaden
ITEM
● Rawst Berry

Pokémon Ranger Mylene
ITEM
● Rawst Berry

Relic Castle

(p. 102) ▶

Psychic Dua

Psychic Perry

Team Plasma Grunt

Team Plasma Grunt

Team Plasma Grunt

Team Plasma Grunt

Team Plasma Grunt

Team Plasma Grunt

Team Plasma Grunt

Nimbasa City

(p. 105) ▶

Team Plasma Grunt

Team Plasma N

Lady Magnolia

Lady Colette

Rich Boy Cody

Rich Boy Rolan

Gym Leader Elesa
BADGE
● Bolt Badge

Lass Maya

Hiker Andy

Clerk ♀ Trisha

Preschooler Winter

Dancer Dirk

Ace Trainer Austin

Waitress Aurora

Rich Boy Martin

Infielder Alex

Backers Ami & Eira

Infielder Connor

Striker Tony

Backers Kay & Ali

Striker Roberto 	Linebacker Dan 	Backers Hawk & Dar 	Linebacker Bob 	Smasher Elena 	Backers Joe & Ross 	Smasher Aspen

Striker Roberto	Linebacker Dan	Backers Hawk & Dar	Linebacker Bob	Smasher Elena	Backers Joe & Ross	Smasher Aspen

Hoopster Bobby	Backers Masa & Yas	Hoopster John	**Route 16** [p. 110] ▷	Policeman Daniel	Cyclist Hector	Cyclist Krissa

Backpacker Stephen	Backpacker Peter	Backpacker Lora	**Route 5** [p. 112] ▷	Pokémon Trainer Cheren	Preschooler Billy	Preschooler Sarah

Harlequin Paul	Artist Horton	Dancer Brian	Backpacker Lois	Backpacker Michael	Baker Jenn	Musician Preston

Driftveil City [p. 116] ▷	Motorcyclist Charles	Clerk ♀ Katie	Worker Felix	Worker Sterling	Worker Don	Clerk ♂ Isaac

Gym Leader Clay BADGE ● Quake Badge	Pokémon Trainer Bianca ITEM ● HM02 Fly	**Cold Storage** [p. 121] ▷	Worker Eddie	Youngster Kenneth	Youngster Albert	Worker Glenn

Worker Victor	Worker Filipe	Worker Patton	Worker Ryan	Team Plasma Grunt	Team Plasma Grunt	Team Plasma Grunt

Team Plasma Grunt	**Route 6** [p. 124] ▷	Scientist William	Scientist Maria	Scientist Ron	Parasol Lady Tihana	Parasol Lady Nicole

Pokémon Ranger Shanti — ITEM ● Cheri Berry	Pokémon Ranger Richard — ITEM ● Cheri Berry	Chargestone Cave [p. 126] ▶	Ace Trainer Allison	Ace Trainer Stella	Ace Trainer Jared	Ace Trainer Corky
Scientist Orville	Scientist Naoko	Scientist Ronald	Doctor Wayne ● Heals All Pokémon	Team Plasma Grunt	Team Plasma Grunt	Team Plasma Grunt
Team Plasma Grunt	Team Plasma Grunt	Team Plasma Grunt	Team Plasma Grunt	Hiker Hardy	Team Plasma N	
Mistralton City [p. 129] ▶	Worker Cliff	Worker Arnold	Worker Brady	Pilot Ted	Pilot Chase	Gym Leader Skyla — BADGE ● Jet Badge
Route 7 [p. 132] ▶	Harlequin Ian	Harlequin Pat	Youngster Mikey	Youngster Parker	Backpacker Ruth	Backpacker Terrance
Pokémon Ranger Mary — ITEM ● Aspear Berry	Pokémon Ranger Pedro — ITEM ● Aspear Berry	Ace Trainer Elmer	Celestial Tower [p. 135] ▶	Psychic Micki	Psychic Bryce	Ace Trainer Beckett
Ace Trainer Kassandra	Psychic Doreen	Psychic Belle	Psychic Lin	Pokéfan Jude	Pokéfan Georgia	Nurse Sachiko ● Heals All Pokémon
Lass Kara	Twist Mountain [p. 136] ▶	Pokémon Trainer Cheren	Hiker Terrell	Ace Trainer Caroll	Ace Trainer Jordan	Black Belt Teppei

240

Worker Cairn 	Worker Heath	Worker Brand 	Worker Rich 	Worker Rob 	Doctor Hank  ● Heals All Pokémon	Battle Girl Sharon 
Hiker Darrell 	Hiker Neil 	Route 17 P2 Laboratory ◎ (p. 140) ▶	Swimmer ♂ Wright 	Swimmer ♂ Berke	Fisherman Lydon 	Swimmer ♀ Caroline 
Swimmer ♀ Joyce 	Scientist Nathan 	Route 18 ◎ (p. 140) ▶	Hiker Jeremiah 	Backpacker Kumiko 	Backpacker Sam 	Battle Girl Hillary 
Veteran Ray 	Mistralton Cave ◎ (p. 143) ▶	Hiker Clarke 	Hiker Hugh 	Icirrus City ◎ (p. 146) ▶	Black Belt Kendrew 	Black Belt Grant 
Black Belt Thomas 	Battle Girl Miriam	Battle Girl Chandra 	Battle Girl Mikiko 	Gym Leader Brycen  BADGE ● Freeze Badge	Dragonspiral Tower ◎ (p. 151) ▶	Ace Trainer Jamie 
Ace Trainer Jesse 	Team Plasma Grunt 	Team Plasma Grunt 	Team Plasma Grunt 	Team Plasma Grunt 	Team Plasma Grunt 	Team Plasma Grunt 
Team Plasma Grunt	Team Plasma Grunt 	Team Plasma Grunt 	Route 8 ◎ (p. 154) ▶	Fisherman Bruce 	Parasol Lady Melita 	Parasol Lady Lumi 
Pokémon Ranger Lewis  ITEM ● Pecha Berry	Pokémon Ranger Annie  ITEM ● Pecha Berry	Pokémon Trainer Bianca  ITEM ● Full Restore	Moor of Icirrus ◎ (p. 154) ▶	Fisherman Damon 	Parasol Lady Mariah 	Pokémon Ranger Harry  ITEM ● Sitrus Berry

Pokémon Ranger Chloris — ITEM ● Sitrus Berry	**Tubeline Bridge** (p. 156) ▷	**Biker Jeremy**	**Biker Morgann**	**Route 9** (p. 157) ▷	**Roughneck Chance**	**Roughneck Reese**
Hooligans Jim & Cas	**Biker Zeke**	**Biker Phillip**	**Waiter Bert**	**Waitress Flo**	**Lady Isabel**	**Rich Boy Manuel**
Opelucid City (p. 160) ▷ (p. 164) ▷	**Ace Trainer Eileen**	**Ace Trainer Lou**	**Ace Trainer Jose**	**Ace Trainer Clara**	**Ace Trainer Tom**	**Ace Trainer Olwen**
Ace Trainer Dara	**Ace Trainer Webster**	**Veteran Hugo**	**Veteran Kim**	**Gym Leader Drayden** — *Pokémon Black Version* BADGE ● Legend Badge	**Gym Leader Iris** — *Pokémon White Version* BADGE ● Legend Badge	
Route 10 (p. 168) ▷	**Pokémon Trainer Cheren**	**Ace Trainer Cheyenne**	**Ace Trainer Johan**	**Black Belt Corey**	**Battle Girl Amy**	**Veteran Karla**
Veteran Chester	**Hiker Bret**	**Victory Road** (p. 171) ▷	**Ace Trainer Cathy**	**Ace Trainer Dwayne**	**Ace Trainer Shanta**	**Ace Trainer David**
Black Belt Tyrone	**Doctor Logan** — ● Heals All Pokémon	**Veteran Martell**	**Veteran Tiffany**	**Pokémon League** (p. 174) ▷	**Elite Four Shauntal**	**Elite Four Grimsley**
Elite Four Caitlin	**Elite Four Marshal**	**N's Castle** (p. 180) ▷	**Team Plasma N**	**Team Plasma Ghetsis**		

After Finishing the Main Story

Marvelous Bridge
(p. 201) ▶

Ace Trainer Glinda

Route 15
(p. 204) ▶

Pokéfan Elliot

Battle Girl Susie

Pokémon Ranger Shelly

ITEM
● Sitrus Berry

Pokémon Ranger Keith

ITEM
● Sitrus Berry

Hiker Kit

Black City (Pokémon Black Version)
(p. 208) ▶

Clerk ♀ Britney

Clerk ♀ Piper

Ace Trainer Vincent

Ace Trainer Lena

Lady Lynette

Rich Boy Pierce

Black Belt Ryder

Scientist Marie

Scientist Jacques

Gentleman Frederic

School Kid Leo

School Kid Shane

School Kid Silvia

Roughneck Johnny

Roughneck Dave

Youngster Robbie

Backpacker Emi

Backpacker Carlos

Backpacker Kiyo

Backpacker Herman

Backpacker Molly

Battle Girl Karenna

Clerk ♂ Doug

Clerk ♂ Collin

Veteran Ken

Veteran Rosa

Nursery Aide Miho

Pokémon Ranger Eliza

Pokémon Ranger Ralph

Socialite Grace

Lass Miki

Hiker Gene

White Forest (Pokémon White Version)
(p. 210) ▶

School Kid Shaye

Nursery Aide Briana

Route 14
(p. 212) ▶

Ace Trainer Junko

Ace Trainer Kipp

Black Belt Jay

Fisherman Sid

Backpacker Vicki

Hiker Jebediah

Abundant Shrine
(p. 214) ▶

Youngster Wes

Youngster Lester

Lass Lurleen

Lass Maki	Undella Town (p. 216) ▷	Pokémon Trainer Cynthia	The Riches Draco	The Riches Susan	The Riches Clairdonna	The Riches Zillion

The Riches Trish	The Riches Miles	Undella Bay (p. 218) ▷	Swimmer ♂ Bart	Swimmer ♂ Matt	Swimmer ♂ Tim	Swimmer ♀ Rebecca

Swimmer ♀ Larissa	Swimmer ♀ Tyra	Route 13 (p. 221) ▷	Black Belt Benjamin	Artist Zach	Gentleman Yan	Youngster Astor

Fisherman Mick	Fisherman Vince	Fisherman Jones	Fisherman Pete	Parasol Lady Laura	Socialite Marian	Lass Fey

Twins Emy & Lin	Route 12 (p. 228) ▷	School Kid Ann	School Kid Jem	Backers Fey & Sue	Pokémon Breeder Eustace	Pokémon Breeder Ethel

					ITEM ● Sitrus Berry	ITEM ● Sitrus Berry

Village Bridge (p. 229) ▷	Scientist Shannon	School Kid Serena	Baker Chris	Route 11 (p. 231) ▷	Backpacker Corin	Backpacker Talon

Pokémon Ranger Crofton	Pokémon Ranger Thalia	Dreamyard (p. 188) ▷	Scientist Markus	Scientist Kathrine	Scientist Luke	Scientist Chan

ITEM ● Leppa Berry	ITEM ● Leppa Berry					

Psychic Rudolf	Psychic Tommy	Psychic Future	Royal Unova (p. 189) ▷	Ace Trainer Henry	Ace Trainer Mariana	Lady Elizandra

Rich Boy Brad 	Gentleman Robert 	Youngster Abe 	Clerk ♂ Chaz 	Socialite Cassandra 	Lass Sibyl 	Maid Tanya 

Relic Castle ⊙ [p. 190] ▷	Team Plasma Grunt 	**Nimbasa City** ⊙ [p. 192] ▷	Infielder Alex 	Infielder Connor 	Infielder Todd 	Backers Ami & Eira 

Backers Alf & Fred 	Striker Tony 	Striker Roberto 	Striker Marco 	Backers Kay & Ali 	Backers Les & Web 	Linebacker Dan 

Linebacker Bob 	Linebacker Jonah 	Backers Hawk & Dar 	Backers Cam & Abby 	Smasher Elena 	Smasher Aspen 	Smasher Mari

Backers Joe & Ross 	Backers Ai & Ciel 	Hoopster Bobby 	Hoopster John 	Hoopster Lamarcus 	Backers Masa & Yas 	Backers Kat & Phae 

Clerk ♀ Wren 	Waiter Clint  ITEM ● Fresh Water	Waitress Bonita  ITEM ● Fresh Water	Ace Trainer Charlie  ITEM ● PP Up	Ace Trainer Lucille  ITEM ● PP Up	Preschooler Mia 	Preschooler Evan 

Lady Sophie 	Rich Boy Anthony 	Policeman Jeff 	Black Belt Lao 	Harlequin Charley 	Artist Pierre 	Scientist Blythe  ITEM ● Ether

Scientist Simon  ITEM ● Ether	Psychic Gerard 	Psychic Madhu 	Worker Tyler 	Worker Matthew 	Gentleman Renaud  ITEM ● Nugget	School Kid Sally 

School Kid Alan	Roughneck Fletcher	Janitor Caleb	Pokéfan Darcy	Pokéfan Colin	Dancer Davey	Youngster Kevin
						ITEM ● Ultra Ball

Fisherman Devon	Depot Agent Josh	Doctor Jules	Nurse Kirsten	Pilot Leonard	Backpacker Patty	Backpacker Alexander
		ITEM ● Max Revive	ITEM ● Full Restore		ITEM ● Max Repel	ITEM ● Max Repel

Battle Girl Janie	Parasol Lady Gwyneth	Clerk ♂ Fredric	Clerk ♂ Nelson	Baker Lilly	Veteran Arlen	Veteran Sayuri
				ITEM ● Moomoo Milk	ITEM ● PP Max	ITEM ● PP Max

Nursery Aide Leah	Pokémon Breeder Brooke	Pokémon Breeder Owen	Pokémon Ranger Alain	Pokémon Ranger Heidi	Socialite Emilia	Lass Dana
ITEM ● Rare Candy					ITEM ● Big Pearl	ITEM ● Ultra Ball

Musician Boris	Maid Alica	Hiker Russel	Chargestone Cave (p. 193) ▶	Team Plasma Grunt	Team Plasma Grunt	

Challenger's Cave (p. 195) ▶	Ace Trainer Terry	Ace Trainer Beverly	Backpacker Toru	Veteran Shaun	Veteran Julia	

Victory Road (p. 196) ▶	Pokémon Trainer Cheren	Pokémon League (p. 197) ▶	Elite Four Shauntal	Elite Four Grimsley	Elite Four Caitlin	Elite Four Marshal

Champion Alder	Nuvema Town (p. 232) ▶	Pokémon Trainer Bianca				

Pokémon Form Changes and Special Evolutions

Form or Forme Changes and Special Conditions for Evolution in the Unova Region

Form or Forme changes

In the Unova region, how do Pokémon like Giratina and Shaymin change Forme? What about Pokémon with special evolutions, like Magnezone and Milotic? This section shines a light on those mysteries. It should help you with Pokémon battles or completing your Pokédex.

Deerling/Sawsbuck — Changes its form depending on the season

Deerling and Sawsbuck change their form depending on the season in the Unova region. Deerling's fur changes color, and Sawsbuck's horns change dramatically. The Unova region's season changes every month in real-world time. For example, March is autumn, April is winter, May is spring, and June is summer. You can see all of Sawsbuck's fantastic form changes over four months.

● **Deerling's Seasonal Changes**

Deerling (Spring Form)   Deerling (Summer Form)   Deerling (Autumn Form)   Deerling (Winter Form)

● **Sawsbuck's Seasonal Changes**

Sawsbuck (Spring Form)

Sawsbuck (Summer Form)

Sawsbuck (Autumn Form)

Sawsbuck (Winter Form)

Darmanitan | When half its HP is lost, it changes form

A Darmanitan with the Hidden Ability called Zen Mode can change its form during battle. If its HP falls to half or less than half during a battle, it will automatically change into Zen Mode at the end of the turn. This change only happens during battle—once the battle is over, Darmanitan goes back to Standard Mode.

● Darmanitan's Form Changes

Standard Mode

Zen Mode

Darmanitan

Rotom | Check the cardboard boxes in Shopping Mall Nine

Rotom has several alternate forms, all with different types: Heat Rotom, Wash Rotom, Frost Rotom, Fan Rotom, and Mow Rotom. To change its form, go through the door on the first floor of Shopping Mall Nine and check the cardboard boxes while Rotom is in your party. The boxes hold appliances that can change Rotom's form.

● Rotom's Form Changes

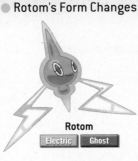

Rotom

Electric | Ghost

Heat Rotom

Electric | Fire

Wash Rotom

Electric | Water

Frost Rotom

Electric | Ice

Fan Rotom

Electric | Flying

Mow Rotom

Electric | Grass

Giratina | Give Giratina the Griseous Orb to change it into Origin Forme

Giratina is normally in its Altered Forme. When you have it hold the Griseous Orb, it changes into Origin Forme. You'll get the Griseous Orb from the Shadow Triad on the Marvelous Bridge.

● Giratina's Forme Changes

Giratina
(Altered Forme)

Giratina
(Origin Forme)

Shaymin | Use the Gracidea to change to Sky Forme

Use the Gracidea on Shaymin and it will turn into its Sky Forme. Talk to the woman in Lacunosa Town's Pokémon Center while Shaymin is in your party, and she will give you the Gracidea.

Trainer obtained the Gracidea!

● Shaymin's Forme Changes

Shaymin
(Sky Forme)

Shaymin
(Land Forme)

Conditions that revert Shaymin to Land Forme	● At night and late night	● When left at the Day Care
	● When Frozen	● When Link Traded
	● When put in the PC	● When put on the GTS

● Shaymin can be obtained during special distribution periods. Check www.pokemonblackwhite.com to find out if any Pokémon are currently being distributed.

Deoxys | Examine the meteor in the Nacrene Museum

Deoxys changes into Normal Forme, Attack Forme, Defense Forme, or Speed Forme. Change its Forme by putting Deoxys in your party and examining the meteor in the Nacrene Museum. Every time you examine the meteor, Deoxys will change into another Forme.

Deoxys has changed to have superior stats for attacking!

● Deoxys can be obtained during special distribution periods. Check www.pokemonblackwhite.com to find out if any Pokémon are currently being distributed.

● Deoxys's Forme Changes

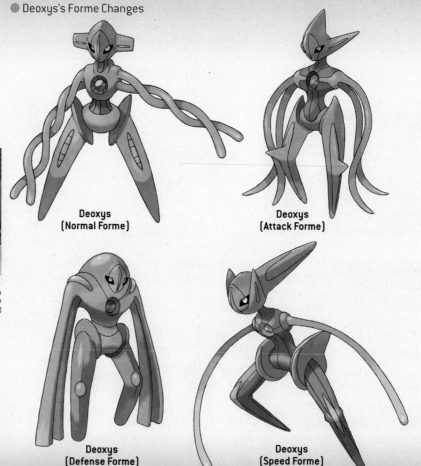

Deoxys
(Normal Forme)

Deoxys
(Attack Forme)

Deoxys
(Defense Forme)

Deoxys
(Speed Forme)

Arceus | Holding a plate shifts Arceus's type

Give Arceus a plate to hold, such as the Draco Plate or the Splash Plate, and its type and appearance will shift. There are many mysteries surrounding the location of the plates. Try to find them all!

Trainer obtained a Draco Plate!

Arceus

● Arceus's Type Shift

Normal

When it's not holding a plate, Arceus is a Normal type.

Fire

Holding the Flame Plate makes it a Fire type. Its location is unknown.

Water

Holding the Splash Plate makes it a Water type. Get the plate on Route 13.

Grass

Holding the Meadow Plate makes it a Grass type. Its location is unknown.

Electric

Holding the Zap Plate makes it an Electric type. Its location is unknown.

Ice

Holding the Icicle Plate makes it an Ice type. Its location is unknown.

Fighting

Holding the Fist Plate makes it a Fighting type. Its location is unknown.

Poison

Holding the Toxic Plate makes it a Poison type. Its location is unknown.

Ground

Holding the Earth Plate makes it a Ground type. Its location is unknown.

Flying

Holding the Sky Plate makes it a Flying type. Its location is unknown.

Psychic

Holding the Mind Plate makes it a Psychic type. Its location is unknown.

Bug

Holding the Insect Plate makes it a Bug type. Its location is unknown.

Rock

Holding the Stone Plate makes it a Rock type. Its location is unknown.

Ghost

Holding the Spooky Plate makes it a Ghost type. Its location is unknown.

Dragon

Holding the Draco Plate makes it a Dragon type. Get the plate on Route 13.

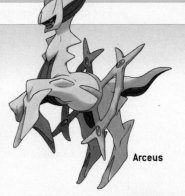

Dark

Holding the Dread Plate makes it a Dark type. Its location is unknown.

Steel

Holding the Iron Plate makes it a Steel type. Its location is unknown.

● Arceus can be obtained during special distribution periods. Check www.pokemonblackwhite.com to find out if any Pokémon are currently being distributed.

These five Pokémon have special evolutions

Magnezone | **Level up in Chargestone Cave**

In the Unova region, you evolve Magneton into Magnezone by leveling it up in Chargestone Cave.

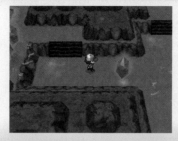

Magneton → Magnezone

Probopass | **Level up in Chargestone Cave**

In the Unova region, you evolve Nosepass into Probopass by leveling it up in Chargestone Cave.

Nosepass → Probopass

Leafeon | **Level up in Pinwheel Forest**

In the Unova region, you evolve Eevee into Leafeon by leveling it up near the moss-covered rock in Pinwheel Forest.

The surface is covered with moss. Touching it feels good somehow.

 Eevee → Leafeon

Glaceon | **Level up in Twist Mountain**

In the Unova region, you evolve Eevee into Glaceon by leveling it up near the ice-covered rock in Twist Mountain.

It's a rock covered with ice. Touching it could make you freeze.

Eevee → Glaceon

Milotic | **Link Trade while it is holding a Prism Scale**

In the Unova region, trade Feebas while it is holding a Prism Scale to evolve Feebas into Milotic. You can get a Prism Scale on Route 13.

Samurott Lv.85 262/262	Watchog Lv.62 165/165
Musharna Lv.86 322/322	Galvantula Lv.41 119/119
Feebas Lv.36 67/67	Tranquill

Feebas was given the Prism Scale to hold.

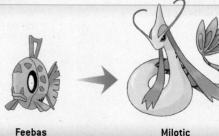

Feebas → Milotic

Items and Gym Badges

● This index lists the names of things and people that will be useful during your adventure. Please make use of it while you are playing.

● TMs/HMs

● Main Characters

● Red page numbers indicate this is a Pokémon Battle, Gym Battle, or a match with a special Trainer.

Type Matchup Chart

Types are assigned both to moves and to the Pokémon themselves. These types can greatly affect the amount of damage dealt or received in battle, so learn how they line up against one another and give yourself the edge in battle.

Attacking Pokémon's Move Type / **Defending Pokémon's Type**

	Normal	Fire	Water	Grass	Electric	Ice	Fighting	Poison	Ground	Flying	Psychic	Bug	Rock	Ghost	Dragon	Dark	Steel
Normal													△	×			△
Fire		△	△	⊙		⊙						⊙	△		△		⊙
Water		⊙	△	△					⊙				⊙		△		
Grass		△	⊙	△				△	⊙	△		△	⊙		△		△
Electric			⊙	△	△				×	⊙					△		
Ice		△	△	⊙		△			⊙	⊙					⊙		△
Fighting	⊙					⊙		△		△	△	△	⊙	×		⊙	⊙
Poison				⊙				△	△				△	△			×
Ground		⊙		△	⊙			⊙		×		△	⊙				⊙
Flying				⊙	△		⊙					⊙	△				△
Psychic							⊙	⊙			△					×	△
Bug		△		⊙			△	△		△	⊙			△		⊙	△
Rock		⊙				⊙	△		△	⊙		⊙					△
Ghost	×										⊙			⊙		△	△
Dragon															⊙		△
Dark							△				⊙			⊙		△	△
Steel		△	△		△	⊙							⊙				△

Legend

⊙	**Very effective** "It's super effective!"	×2
	[No Icon] Normal Damage	×1
△	**Not too effective** "It's not very effective..."	×0.5
×	**No effect** "It doesn't affect..."	×0

● Fire-type Pokémon are immune to the Burned condition.
● Grass-type Pokémon are immune to Leech Seed.
● Ice-type Pokémon are immune to the Frozen condition, and take no damage from the Hail weather condition.
● Poison-type Pokémon are immune to the Poison and Badly Poisoned conditions, even when switching in with Toxic Spikes in play. Poison-type Pokémon nullify Toxic Spikes (unless these Pokémon are also Flying type or have the Levitate ability).
● Ground-type Pokémon are immune to Thunder Wave and take no damage from the Sandstorm weather condition.
● Flying-type Pokémon cannot be damaged by Spikes when switching in, or become afflicted with a Poison or Badly Poisoned condition due to switching in with Toxic Spikes in play.
● Rock-type Pokémon are immune to the Sandstorm weather condition. Their Sp. Def also goes up in the Sandstorm weather condition.
● Steel-type Pokémon are immune to the Sandstorm weather condition. They are also immune to the Poisoned and Badly Poisoned condition. Even if switched in with Toxic Spikes in play, they will not be afflicted by the Poison or Badly Poisoned condition.